Symbol, Sword, and Shield

Defending Washington during the Civil War

A Pensive Lincoln—Worrying About Defending Washington?
(National Archives and Records Administration, Washington, D.C.)

Symbol, Sword, and Shield

Defending Washington during the Civil War

Benjamin Franklin Cooling

 WHITE MANE PUBLISHING COMPANY, INC.

E
470.2
.C74
1991
/ 5 5/72
ma.1992

Second Revised Edition
Copyright © 1991 by Benjamin Franklin Cooling III

first printing 1975
second printing 1991 with supplemental materials

This White Mane Publishing Company, Inc. publication
was printed by
Beidel Printing House
63 West Burd Street
Shippensburg, PA 17257

In respect to the scholarship contained herein, the acid-free
paper used in this book meets the guidelines for permanence and
durability of the Committee on Production Guidelines for Book
Longevity of the Council on Library Resources.

For a complete list of available publications
please write
White Mane Publishing Company, Inc.
P.O. Box 152
Shippensburg, PA 17257

ISBN 0-942597-24-9
(previously ISBN 0-208-01479-9)

Library of Congress Cataloging-in-Publication Data

Cooling, B. Franklin
    Symbol, sword and shield : defending Washington during the Civil
War / Benjamin Franklin Cooling III. -- 2nd rev. ed.
        p.   cm.
    Includes bibliographical references and index.
    ISBN 0-942597-24-9 : $27.95
    1. Washington (D.C.)--History--Civil War, 1861-1865.   I. Title.
E470.2.C74   1991
975.3'02--dc20   91-26949
                                                                           CIP

Contents

Illustrations

MAPS AND DIAGRAMS

Preface to the First Edition

During the hot, dusty July days of 1864 a bedraggled Confederate host besieged Washington D. C. The liberation of a wine cellar in Francis Preston Blair's mansion at Silver Spring supposedly diminished the rebels' ability to punch through the weakly held Union defense line, but meanwhile, for the only time in our history, an American president was under hostile fire while in office. Still, Jubal Early's raid, with its drama and comedy, is hardly the whole story of guarding the national capital in the Civil War. The story assumes additional dimensions when one analyzes it in light of today's concept of "deterrence" and places it in the overall context of strategy and the conduct of the Civil War in the eastern theater.

Among the factors governing the defense of Washington from 1861 to 1865 was the role of the Army of the Potomac as a protective force with a twofold mission. That army was charged both with the defeat of Confederate armies defending the rebel capital at Richmond, and with covering Washington as part of a "team" effort of field fortifications, heavy ordnance, garrisons, and maneuver force. The role of the Army of the Potomac (or equivalent forces in the theater), from First Bull Run through Appomattox, remains best understood in the first context. Still, the army often labored under the second mandate, to the detriment of its primary mission—if indeed capture of Richmond and defeat of Lee was always its primary mission. Similarly, the formal defensive system styled "The Defenses of Washington" has often been treated more from its technical engineering or fortifications aspects than as a vital part of a strategic concept. Washington's defenses can be understood properly by the modern student of the war only by considering both of these two factors, the fixed defenses and the mobile army. Hence, Washington the Symbol was protected by both the Army of the Potomac as Sword, and the massive fortification system as Shield.

It remains dangerous to separate history artificially into distinct phases. A column in the *Washington Post* of July 30, 1972, questioned the capital's need for an antiballistic missile site. An accompanying cartoon showed sibling missiles clustered around Washington's rocket-shaped monument just south of the White House. At the other end of the historical spectrum the Founding Fathers expressed great concern over the location of the nation's capital with reference to matters of naval defense. They constructed a small, inadequate position, variously styled Fort Warburton or Fort Washington, across the river from Mount Vernon. Naturally, the alert British merely circumvented the naval problem of attacking Washington in 1814 by battering down the back door to the city at Bladensburg where they dispersed a rag-tail American army and entered the city by land. The Founding Fathers also feared an attack on the city from the direction of the Blue Ridge, a threat which subsided immediately as the frontier moved westward, only to surface, ironically, once more during the Civil War.

The lessons of the War of 1812 prompted Acting Secretary of War James Monroe and Major Pierre L'Enfant to reconstruct the masonry fort at a cost of $426,000, and it may be viewed today as a relic of a bygone era of brick and stone coastal fortifications. The fort was garrisoned until 1853, and until 1861 Fort Washington provided the sole formal defenses of the Nation's Capital. It still pointed toward a water-borne threat, but as storm clouds gathered over the land in the fifties, the threat was civil not international war. Washington slumbered on, yawning lustily as Congress wrangled over the question of slavery, taking delight in the polite soirees that were the backbone of social life in the capital, while remaining oblivious to the class distinctions which witnessed ordinary citizens braving the mud and dust of Washington streets while the town's elite dined on oysters and red snapper at Willard's and other fancy establishments. An abundance of flora and fauna in the Washington community caused one waggish Englishman to observe that never before had he seen a forest adorned by a city.

That which changed the inner life of Washington also changed the place of the capital in national defense. The Civil War transformed the city from a provincial capital of an emerging country into the veritable nerve center of a major nation. Future generations of politicians and generals would develop an intense concern for the safety of Washington. The massive system of forts and batteries surrounding the city during the Civil War were the physical symbols of this great awakening.

Washington's forts have interested me ever since I played on the eroded outworks of Fort Slocum in the Northwest section of the city. But as a child I knew little about their real meaning in the saga of our nation's epic struggle for unification. My first research came in high school with an English course term paper, based principally upon Barnard's classic *Defenses of Washington*, and from that point forward the dimensions and nuances of defending the capital have never ceased to fascinate me. Generally the topic has been neglected by students of the Civil War, and I hope that this work will lead others to join me on those forgotten ramparts for an appreciation of yet another untapped aspect of Civil War history.

Washington D.C.   B. FRANKLIN COOLING
Summer 1974

Preface to the Second Edition

Fifteen years have passed since original publication of *Symbol, Sword, and Shield*. Continued interest in the Civil War has insured increased attention to interpretation of historic sites from that conflict, including the forts of Washington. Battle reenactments and commemorations, an explosion of publications, and renewed study of the familiar and not so familiar aspects of the epic struggle draw attention to this singularly pivotal moment in American history. While the nation's capital has become an international capital vastly more important than a century ago, millions of citizens can appreciate the role that Mr. Lincoln's City played in the war, and the costly measures undertaken by the Federal government to insure its security as political symbol, as well as military focal point for conducting operations in the conflict.

The abiding question of protecting a capital city cuts across the stream of history. From ancient Troy and Rome to modern Berlin, Moscow, Saigon, and Hanoi, defense of the nerve center of government has always preoccupied rulers and ruled. Today, Washington, D.C., like Moscow, Baghdad, or Tel Aviv remains a target on someone's military map. Symbol of Free World Democracy as well as center of the capitalist west, its sword is now the strategic nuclear forces of the United States, its shield virtually nonexistent. Yet, the city's history suggests that this has always been true in peacetime, and only during the Civil War did a systematic defense blossom on the banks of the Potomac. Over a century ago, Washington was a vast military camp, a strategic center for mobilizing the governmental and military forces of the Union, and its symbolic as well as real value was protected by a vast system of forts, guns, garrisons, and men—designed to function in coordination with the field army, the Army of the Potomac—in time of peril to the capital. For a brief moment in time, Washington was the most heavily guarded and fortified city in the world.

Significant strides have taken place over the past fifteen years to recapture the story of Fortress Washington. City-owned Fort Ward in Alexandria has matured as a center-piece for the study of the ring of earthworks around the city. Its museum and library, as well as the restored bastions of the work itself are a "must" for any serious study of the defenses of Washington. Moreover, documents used not only for *Symbol, Sword, and Shield*, but also the other two works of the trilogy, *Mr. Lincoln's Forts: A Guide to the Civil War Defenses of Washington* (co-authored with Walton Owen and also published by White Mane), as well as *Jubal Early's Raid on Washington, 1864* (published by Nautical and Aviation Publishing Company) have been preserved for public use at Fort Ward.

In addition, the National Park Service which administers the majority of the remaining ruins of Washington's forts, has breathed new life into preservation, interpretation, and maintenance of the parks in which they reside, especially within the boundaries of the District of Columbia. Refurbished ramparts at Fort Stevens where Abraham Lincoln stood under enemy fire in July 1864, remounted heavy seacoast guns downriver at Fort Foote in Maryland, standardized interpretive signs at each fort site in the park system (complimenting historical markers in Arlington and Alexandria for long obliterated Yankee forts in those jurisdictions) all add to the enjoyment and appreciation of the subject. The National Park Service insures proper annual commemoration of the battle at Fort Stevens—the only battle site within the city's limits—and the only battle in which an American president came under enemy fire while in office. Wreaths are laid at the fort, nearby Battleground National Cemetery housing Union dead from the battle, and at the site of seventeen Confederate graves farther out in Silver Spring, Maryland. As this new edition is prepared, the last fort site remaining in private ownership, Fort C. F. Smith in Arlington, shows fresh signs of permanent preservation through enlightened initiative both of its owner and local history enthusiasts.

I have continued to collect materials on defending Washington since first publication of this volume. They have been incorporated where appropriate in this edition. Enhancement and correction, clarification and expansion, not alteration of themes and interpretations have governed such incorporation. Neither the original nor this edition are intended as seminal; new material, new insights will surely flow from its publication for the benefit of future students of the Civil War.

Chevy Chase, Maryland   B. FRANKLIN COOLING
Winter 1990-1991

Acknowledgements
for the First Edition

The author wishes especially to thank Dr. Russell F. Weigley, Temple University, and Dr. Warren G. Hassler, Pennsylvania State University, for their thoughtful reading and comment during the draft stages of this study. Also helpful were Dr. Robert Utley, National Park Service; LTC Joseph P. Mitchell, USA Ret., Curator, Fort Ward Museum, Alexandria Va.; Mr. Elden E. Billings, Mr. Bert Sheldon, Mr. William J. Ellenberger, Mr. Francis Coleman Rosenberger, all of Washington D.C.; Mr. Michael Musick and Mr. Ralph E. Ehrenberg, National Archives and Records Service; Mr. William J. Dickman, Alexandria Va.; Mr. John K. Gott, Librarian, Langley (Va.) High School; Dr. Allan R. Millett, Ohio State University; Mr. John C. Wallace, Batavia, Ohio; Mrs. Carrie Arnold, Fort Morrison, Colorado; Mr. Ralph Donnelly, Marine Corps Historical Office; Colonel William Strowbridge, USA and Colonel Herbert Hart, USMC, of that delightful organization which is doing so much to preserve old forts, the Council on Abandoned Military Posts (CAMP); as well as Mr. Paul Sedgwick, former chairman, District of Columbia Civil War Centennial Commission.

Acknowledgements
for the Second Edition

Since original publication, the following individuals have aided in furthering the study of Washington's defenses. They include Wanda Dowell, Director, and Susan Cumbey, Curator at Fort Ward Museum and Historic Site; Walton H. Owen, colleague and peer authority on the defenses of Alexandria; Robert Ruffner, President of the Friends of Fort Ward; David Smith, Park Ranger at Rock Creek Nature Center and protagonist for perpetuating the memory of Fort Stevens; Ted Alexander, Park Ranger at Antietam National Battlefield and long-time student of the defenses east of the Anacostia; Peter Seaborg, proprietor of the Rock Creek Bookshop in Georgetown whose lay knowledge of Fort Stevens is a delight to any author. Kevin Ruffner of Alexandria, Va., and Lewis Schmidt of Allentown, Pa. added information from their own research. Local historians Nan and Ross Netherton of Falls Church, Va., and Mayo Stuntz of Vienna, Va. have always provided support from their knowledge base of northern Virginia history. Edwin C. Bearss, Chief Historian of the National Park Service has always been equally supportive.

The title of this book owes its inspiration to the work of Paul Sedgwick, Washington lawyer and chairman of the District of Columbia Civil War Centennial Commission with whom I worked during the summers of 1960 and 1961, and in whose memory this new edition is dedicated.

CHAPTER ONE

The First Defenders

Dawn of March, 4 1861 — Inauguration Day — brought cloudy skies and a raw wind which kicked up dust from the unpaved streets of Washington. The weather in the nation's capital was well suited to the temper of the country for South Carolina's secession the previous December and the subsequent departure of the Lower South had introduced a note of foreboding and fear for the future of the United States. Many Americans, northern and southern, looked to Washington that March day for a sign of hope and reassurance. The 75,000 residents of the city had witnessed at first hand the unraveling strands as one by one the ties of unity had snapped and southern politicians and their families had departed in the wake of Republican victory in the 1860 election. Those residents were themselves torn between economic self-interest, transient social contacts, and the vibrant political atmosphere of the capital, all complicated by familial and geographical ties to the southern states. For months a pall of gloom hung over Washington, mixed with the artificially induced excitement accompanying political change, joy entwined with sorrow, and anticipation joined with dread for the future. In this fashion the Symbol of Union profoundly mirrored the national society as a whole. No one was quite sure that there would even be an inaugural ceremony on March 4.

By noon the sharp wind had blown away the clouds and a calm, bright, almost cheerful winter sun stirred the hearts and minds of the host of local citizens and visitors from distant places who had come to witness the installation of Abraham Lincoln as President of the United States. Persistent rumors that the Illinois Republican would never be inaugurated had caused military authorities to take full precautions. Brevet Lieutenant General Winfield Scott, commanding the army of the United States, and his principal assistant, Colonel Charles P. Stone, stationed riflemen along the procession route from Willard's Hotel to Capitol Hill as well as in the windows of the Capitol building. Platoons of cavalry, batteries of artillery, and other military units were stationed just beyond the sight of the citizen spectators to insure against any mob threat. Furthermore, militiamen sealed off the Inaugural platform so that most visitors to the festivities merely saw the fluttering flags and bunting, the sharply dressed guards, the brassy bands, the float of thirty-four young ladies representing as many states, and the tired, retiring president, James Buchanan, at the side of his unprepossessing successor as the reins of power were passed in the early afternoon.[1]

The sun and Lincoln's inaugural call for national unity may have provided the signs many Americans sought that day.

[2]

Certainly the mere fact that the ceremonies took place without incident permitted Washingtonians a measure of relief that their city would not be bathed in a sea of violence. Undoubtedly the precautions taken by the military authorities had much to do with it. But what may have appeared to many people as a well executed ceremony by the national government could not hide the fact that the National Symbol, Washington, was a city in danger; that it had been so for some months, and would continue suspensefully in its precarious frontline position for four years of bloody civil war. The successful inauguration of Lincoln was but one of a series of incidents in the process of defending the nation's capital against capture during the period of disunity and internecine conflict.

Washington, like its eventual Confederate counterpart, Richmond, was a slow-paced, slaveholding community, "a great village" in the eyes of Mrs. Roger A. Pryor, wife of one of the secessionist Virginia congressmen. Stately dwellings mingled with a confusion of squalid outbuildings. Servants idled about the alleys as hucksters offered watermelons and fish from dilapidated carts. The gentry enjoyed silks, velvets, and broadcloth imported from Europe, and their tables sagged under domestic hams, fried chickens, terrapin, oysters, and French wines. The original families from nearby Maryland and Virginia had been joined by a preponderance of nouveau riche from farther south, and the northern and western politicians suffered some discomfort in trying to assert their own prerogatives in the drawing rooms of fashionable Washington.[2]

The Federal City was a unique phenomenon, artificially constructed as the seat of government from a low-lying, malarial wilderness on the banks of the Potomac. Its location was due as much to George Washington's persuasion and considerations of naval defense as it was to Congressional desires to placate sectional factions. Both the Capitol and the

[3]

President's House had been started before there was any urban community, and it required sixty-one years to raise a handful of additional Federal buildings, including the Patent and Post offices, the Treasury, and the smaller State, War, and Navy structures. The red Tudor-style Smithsonian Institution presided over a ragged, open mall, dominated by daisies in summer and scruffy fields in winter. The Navy Yard and Marine Barracks, then as now, gave variety to the southeastern section beyond Capitol Hill, and the Arsenal occupied the tip of the point where the Anacostia river joined the Potomac. City Hall vied with the Patent Office for interest between the Capitol and White House (a sobriquet applied to a restored, white executive mansion after the British had finished burning the nation's capital in 1814). The unfinished Washington Monument and National Observatory supplied the only additional tourist attractions in downtown Washington, discounting, of course, squalid Tiber Creek whose odor and eyesore added a disconcerting touch south of the White House.

The streets of Washington were dustbowls in summer and quagmires in winter, with Pennsylvania Avenue, "the Avenue," as the sole exception. It was paved with cobblestones, and horsedrawn omnibuses plied its length, operating between the Navy Yard and Georgetown, across Rock Creek to the west. Most of the other streets were mere pencil scratches on surveyor's maps, and while sometimes leading to isolated hamlets or estates outside the District of Columbia, more often they simply meandered into the trackless forests, over hillocks, and through marshes, before emerging farther out in Maryland among tobacco and corn fields. Only five of these arteries extended beyond "Boundary Street" (modern Florida Avenue). The main roads leading out of town connected Maryland Avenue with the Alexandria road via Long Bridge (modern Fourteenth Street bridge), and the pike to Leesburg was gained by the Chain Bridge upriver. In between,

[4]

an innocuous ferry connected Georgetown with the Virginia shore. Northward, roads crossed Benning's bridge and the Eleventh Street bridge en route to southern Maryland. Bladensburg road led past the scene of the disastrous defeat in 1814, and the Rockville pike led through Georgetown and Tennallytown, D.C., toward western Maryland. The Baltimore and Ohio Railroad terminated at a frame depot near the Capitol, whence travelers going south might then take a carriage or steamer to Alexandria or Aquia landing to make rail connections. Coastal steamers and sailing vessels deposited freight and passengers at wharves in Washington, and the Chesapeake and Ohio canal (one of George Washington's projects), conveyed fuel, lime, and other goods to the District from Cumberland on the upper Potomac.

Fluctuations of a largely transient population, varying in political hue with changes of administration, sharply emphasized the nature of Washington life. Laborers, tradesmen, government servants, boardinghouse keepers, as well as other "professionals" like their wealthier and more distinguished neighbors, had to contend with difficulties in everyday living. Wells and springs provided most of the water supply, although an aqueduct was under construction to bring the Potomac water from Great Falls. In warm weather flies swarmed in to blanket the city, as mirrors, picture frames, clocks and ornaments were covered with netting to protect them from the bugs. Sunday afternoons were a time for family gatherings and promenades, perhaps even more the hallmark of antebellum Washington than the countless soirees and other events at the homes of leaders of Washington society. Among those who conspicuously participated in the Sunday festivities was a sizeable delegation from the Negro population, dressed in multicolored garments and rustling crinolines of the latest popular fashion. This element of the Washington community might well have been considered the most likely target for revolutionary groups seeking to disrupt the functions of government. But in reality, officials perceived little danger from this quarter.

General Scott frankly failed to see any possible threat to Washington when queried in October 1860 about possible rupture of the Federal Union. Yet, within two months, rumors of conspiracies to capture Washington, to effect a coup d'etat, and to destroy the national government began to surface in numerous places. The seriousness of these rumors caused Scott to move his headquarters from New York to Washington. No sooner had South Carolina left the Union than such worthies as Senator Alfred Iverson of Georgia pronounced on the floor of the United States Senate that he could see no reason "why Washington City should not be continued as the capital of the Southern confederacy." One well-meaning army officer, Major David Hunter, stationed at Fort Leavenworth, Kansas, wrote to President-elect Lincoln recalling the earlier disclosure that prior to Buchanan's election, Governor Henry A. Wise of Virginia had openly announced himself ready to lead 20,000 men on Washington should the Republican candidate, John C. Fremont, have won the election. When Buchanan had rebuffed the South Carolina commissioners, certain politicians, such as Lewis T. Wigfall and John B. Floyd, hinted at possible "kidnapping" of the president so that Vice President John C. Breckinridge of Kentucky would then become acting president. Even the Richmond *Examiner* boldly asked on Christmas Day of 1860: "Can there not be found men bold and brave enough in Maryland to unite with Virginians in seizing the Capital in Washington?"[3]

Much of this was little more than wild talk of angry and disorganized men. Some people probably wondered whether the capital was worth seizing anyway; after all, it still labored under the sarcastic title of the "city of magnificent distances." Certainly several things emerge clearly, if not the existence

[6]

"Washington: Why Don't You Take It?"

(Alfred S. Roe, *The Fifth Regiment Massachusetts Volunteer Infantry*)

of an actual conspiracy or plot. The nation's capital during the secession winter was not only an inelegant, overblown southern town with a few stark public buildings spread across boggy flatlands and linked by bottomless roadway. It was also a festering seedbed of treason, and secession, rumor mongering, and panicky planning. For every wild comment in a southern newspaper there were numerous public officials and civil servants in Washington who openly plumbed for the breakup of the Union. For every Wigfall and Floyd there were northern spokesmen such as Hunter, or Lyman Trumbull, Horace Greeley, and E. B. Washburne who tended to fan the flames of alarm by their letters to Lincoln and the Buchanan administration carefully outlining threats to the capital.[4] The wild rumors did lead Washington officials to finally analyze the state of their defenses, and what they discovered was not overly encouraging.

At the time of southern secession the duties of the United States Army were varied, and they were mainly focused upon the land west of the Mississippi river, although eighteen companies of artillery and one of engineers were serving in the east. Before the fall of Fort Sumter, Washington's military defense was more an illusion than a reality. Unlike other national capitals, the city never contained large complements of garrison or parade forces. As a military post the city had no natural strength, and despite the presence of the stone ramparts of Fort Washington downriver on the Maryland shore, most astute observers thought the city was accessible to an enemy from any side. In fact, Washington could boast of little more than the usual number of dottery old bureau chiefs and a sprinkling of gold-laced officers from the Navy Yard. Colonel Stone, describing the situation that prevailed when he was appointed Inspector General of the District of Columbia by Scott, observed bleakly:

The only regular troops near the capital of the country were three or four hundred marines at the Marine barracks, and three officers and fifty-three men of ordnance at the Washington Arsenal. The old militia system had been abandoned (without being legally abolished), and Congress had passed no law establishing a new one.[5]

Unionists naturally believed that the southern members of Buchanan's administration had purposely positioned the regulars far from the capital. It is difficult today to see how it might have been otherwise, given the needs of coastal defense, pacification duties against the Indians and Mormons in Utah, and general peacetime operations of any military institution, especially one containing only 16,367 officers and men. Furthermore, if Buchanan had wanted to concentrate regular troops in great numbers at Washington, he might have precipitated the very conflict he assiduously sought to avoid, given the unsettled state of the public mind. Thus, while Scott and other regulars fretted about the lack of forces available for the defense of the national capital, this inadequacy was simply another manifestation of the traditional pattern whereby military preparedness remains wedded to political reality. The answer to the problem seemed to lie in making do with whatever force was at hand or could be moved quickly and quietly to the banks of the Potomac.

The sole regular troops near Washington were those mentioned earlier by Stone, which could be reinforced only by militia. The armed militia-volunteer organizations in the city were the Potomac Light Infantry, the Washington Light Infantry, the National Guard Battalion, and the National Rifles, all well armed and schooled in fundamental drill. Only the National Rifles openly displayed disloyalty, as their captain announced the unit's purpose "to guard the frontier of Maryland and help to keep the Yankees from coming down

to coerce the South!'' Overall command of these militia-
volunteers was exercised by seventy-four-year-old Major
General Roger C. Weightman, a Virginian, a veteran of the
War of 1812, former mayor of Washington, and long-time
Patent librarian. His principal subordinates were Brigadier
General Peter Force (a distinguished historian and writer),
Robert Ould, (the city's District Attorney and an ardent seces-
sionist), and two additional younger general officers. They
were all nonregulars by experience and background, but when
Scott and Stone renewed their own Mexican War acquaintance
on New Year's eve, the senior commander sensed the dire
necessity of relying initially on the District's militia-volunteers.
He told Stone bluntly: ''These people have no rallying-point.
Make yourself that rallying point!''[6]

Stone became Inspector General of the District of Columbia early in January. He set to work to reform the
volunteers and purge secessionist elements from their ranks.
He ordered that all commissions of new officers in the militia,
as well as any draft for additional arms and ammunition for
any local unit, bear his countersignature. When he asked forty prominent ''gentlemen'' in the city to raise defense companies, some replied sarcastically, some courteously declined,
while some simply ignored Stone's letter altogether, but a few
willingly agreed.

Meanwhile, other administration officials were moving
independently toward the same goal, insurance of the safety
of Washington. On January 5, Secretary of the Navy Isaac
Toucey ordered Marines to garrison Fort Washington. Forty
''Leathernecks'' under Captain A. S. Taylor with fifteen days'
rations embarked for the fort. They soon found themselves
to be a rather isolated guard for the long neglected fortress.
Lieutenant George Washington Custis Lee of the Engineers
labored to strengthen the work but it was not long before
Taylor was asking for reinforcements. U.S. Marines were also

dispatched to Fort McHenry in Baltimore until army troops could relieve them.[7]

Additional Federal troops were now moving to Washington from far distant posts in Kansas, upstate New York, and Louisiana. Scott, too good a soldier to trust raw militia "under a shower of brickbats and stones," desired to stiffen the backbone of Stone's D.C. volunteers with more regulars. Still, he was hamstrung by Buchanan's vacillatory policy and fear of driving more southern states from the Union. The president even directed that the D.C. militia-volunteers not be issued arms and ammunition for fear that old feuds might break out among rival fire companies comprising some of the units. Stone forced this issue stating that the executive directive was either nonsense or treason, for weapons could be purchased in many Washington stores. His command received the required weapons.

Finally, even "Old Fuss and Feathers" himself had had enough. Moving with alacrity, Scott directed eight companies of regulars, infantry, artillery, and the Sappers and Miners company, to concentrate at Washington. The army commander pointedly told a caller who voiced fear for the meeting of the electoral college at the Capitol in February:

> I have said that any man who attempted by force or unparliamentary disorder to obstruct or interfere with the lawful count of the electoral vote . . . should be lashed to the muzzle of a twelvepounder gun and fired out of a window of the Capitol. I would manure the hills of Arlington with fragments of his body, were he a senator or chief magistrate of my native state! It is my duty to suppress insurrection —*my duty!*[8]

The chilly winds of January were accompanied by steadily heightening tensions. Military units in Massachusetts, New York, and even distant Iowa, were beginning to form for possible use by the national government in an emergency. By

[11]

January 13, Captain William F. Barry's Battery A, Second U.S. Artillery rumbled into town from Fort Leavenworth, giving a measure of confidence to Unionists in the city. Eight days later the Sappers and Miners from West Point joined them. Congressmen and other public officials noted the presence of the regulars as well as several hundred of Stone's colorfully clad D.C. militia-volunteers under Major Irvin McDowell, who garrisoned the Capitol each night. Other forces guarded the City Hall, Patent, and Post offices. Commissary stores were stockpiled at all locations. As Stone reported to Scott, the Executive Square provided an additional stronghold with the White House, War, Navy, State, and Treasury departments, as well as Winder's building, Army headquarters opposite the brick War Department. Stone suggested some defensive moves for the city whereby his outposts at Benning's bridge and the northeast arteries to the city were to retire to the Capitol and City Hall hill, with similar bodies from the north and west regrouping at the Treasury. The city's broad avenues would permit concentration of military forces at all three locations and in any event, a stout resistance might gain time until the Northern states could marshal relief columns. Scott was skeptical; he urged concentration at only one citadel, the Treasury, with even the president and his cabinet quartered there, for "they shall not be permitted to desert the Capital!"[9]

Other officials were also making plans for defense although apparently without coordination of ideas, actions, and resources. Naval authorities such as Captain Franklin Buchanan and Commander John A. Dahlgren developed plans for guarding the Navy Yard. On January 23, Dahlgren reported that he had placed eight howitzers, 800 muskets and rifles, and the yard's supply of ammunition in the attic of the main building, thus forming a fortress of some strength. He believed that he could defend the place with 100 good men.

Three days later certain members of Congress, pushed relentlessly by the new attorney general, Edwin M. Stanton, and spurred by Buchanan's vacillation in the face of apparent danger, decided to investigate formally the seriousness of the rumors that underground plots existed for attacking and capturing Washington.[10]

Congressman William A. Howard's committee of the House of Representatives was charged with investigating subversion in the city and among Federal employees. By early February not only were Secretary of War Joseph Holt, Scott, and Stanton sure that subversive activity was taking place, but they had alarmed others, including prominent Republicans and members of the cabinet-elect, such as Salmon P. Chase and William Seward.[11] Perhaps the apprehension and preparedness measures had a deterrent effect. Arrival of the West Point battery under Lieutenant Charles Griffin, Captain Harvey A. Allen's Company K, Captain Arnold Elzey's Company E, and Brevet Lieutenant Colonel Horace Brooks' Company H of the Second Artillery, as well as Brevet Major J. A. Haskin's Company D of the First Artillery raised the total number of regular units to six in addition to the Marines. On February 5, Stone reported that he had fourteen volunteer companies of 925 men to reinforce the 480 regulars and 300 to 400 Marines. A week later Congress literally found itself imprisoned by blue-coated soldiers at every door when it met to count the electoral votes.

Great fears were expressed by President-elect Lincoln and others that the greatest test might come on February 13 during the meeting of the Electoral College. By February 12, the defense of the capital had been as well arranged as could be. Special orders were dispatched to all officers on that day. Every man was to report to his station upon the sounding of the alarm. Two companies of the First Artillery were to guard the White House and Executive Square buildings, with Elzey's company of the Second Artillery in position at the Treasury. Griffin was to cover the General Post Office and Patent Office along with Allen's company. Haskin and Barry were to be stationed with their guns in the vicinity of the Capitol. All dragoons were to be held at their stables ready to mount; the Sappers and Miners were to take a position at the First Unitarian Church, and Colonel John Harris, Marine Corps commandant, was to lead his Leathernecks to the Capitol Square to await further orders in the event of "alarm, outrage or mob violence." D.C. volunteer infantry were to cover all bridges, including those at Georgetown, and officers of the staff of the General-in-Chief were directed to wear a blue scarf running over the right shoulder to the left hip in addition to the regular uniform to assist in identification.[12]

Scott thus countered the action of an unruly mob which gathered on February 13 from Virginia, Maryland, and the District. Under the frowning gaze of artillery, Vice President John C. Breckinridge was thus able to announce without incident that Abraham Lincoln had been duly elected President of the United States. The next day Howard's congressional committee reported that it had been unable to find direct evidence of any secret organization planning to overthrow the government although it did note the abundance of wild talk and hostile factions, hardly secret since everyone knew of them. Therefore the events of early February had a twofold effect. They quieted somewhat the alarm of the timid and at the same time offered a warning to subversive elements that the Federal government was alert and prepared to cope with insurrectionist activity in Washington. Lincoln was relieved to learn that the formal legality of his election had passed without trouble.

Late in February another display of strength by the Federal government accompanied the celebration of George Washington's birthday. Certain congressmen such as Daniel

Sickles of New York felt that the time was propitious for a celebration calculated to inspire national unity. Holt and Scott naturally wanted to take advantage of the situation in the nation's capital to make a military exhibition and overawe plotting secessionists. A grand parade of artillery, infantry, and the Marines, indeed, every scrap and detachment of men in the city, was arranged. Then, at the very last moment, ex-president John Tyler of Virginia pressured Buchanan to revoke the parade order. But when the chief executive ordered Holt to keep the regulars in their barracks on the morning of the 22d, the situation in the streets of the city moved beyond the government's control.

Thousands of citizens had not received news of the revocation of the parade order and they were out early to see the spectacle. The militia-volunteers were in ranks with their splendid regalia, and when Sickles confronted Buchanan about the situation, the president backed down. A diminished parade took place, the column marching past the White House where Buchanan, Holt, Scott, and various cabinet members received the salute. Buchanan later apologized to Tyler for revoking the order and in the process appeared to be expressing regret at having allowed the military forces of the nation to carry the flag of the Union through the streets of the national capital on the birthday of the first president. It was a strange act for a public official charged with defending and upholding the honor of his country.[13]

Meanwhile, Lincoln had left Springfield, Illinois, on February 11, and was expected to arrive in Washington on the 23d after a leisurely, speech-filled journey eastward. Once more ugly rumors held that he would never reach the capital alive; investigations by officials of the Philadelphia, Wilmington and Baltimore Railroad uncovered evidence of plots to destroy track and bridges as Lincoln's party traveled over the line; even Scott discovered independently (thanks to Stone and some undercover agents), that secessionist elements in Baltimore planned to prevent Lincoln's open passage through that city. The situation was generally getting out of hand in Maryland anyway, with Governor Thomas Hicks unable, or at least reluctant, to show requisite force in the face of firebrands among the populace. In any event, Seward, Scott, Stanton, and Senator Charles Sumner were firmly wedded to the proper installation of the incoming administration. They persuaded Lincoln to change his itinerary, passing secretly through Baltimore (much to the derision of an unfriendly press), arriving safely in Washington on schedule.[14] But the quiet situation in that metropolis was deceiving. The continued trouble in Maryland left the capital isolated from the north and, of course, Lincoln had not yet been inaugurated, a fact which continued to alarm Scott, Seward, and the rest.

Top military planners had been carefully preparing for the Inauguration. Stone had removed dissident elements from the D.C. militia-volunteers. He surmounted Buchanan's ignorant uncertainty about issuing arms to those units and ascertained the difficulties of protecting the president-elect all the way from Willard's Hotel through the actual ceremonies on the east steps of the Capitol. Every morning and evening Stone reported the activities of the day and received instructions from Scott, directed the operations of undercover agents such as Leonard Swett, and on the afternoon of March 3, met in final conference with Scott, Colonel E. V. Sumner, and key staff members. Elaborate preparations were developed whereby the carriage conveying Lincoln and Buchanan was to be escorted by D.C. cavalry and infantry while the Sappers and Miners company of the regulars was to march in front. Squads of riflemen were to take stations atop houses along the parade route to insure against snipers, while cavalry squadrons of regulars were to guard the side-crossings of Pennsylvania

Avenue and District of Columbia riflemen covered the east side of the Capitol. Agents warned Stone later that evening that there would be an attempt to blow up the inaugural platform at the time Lincoln took the oath, and authorities quickly moved to place the National Guard Battalion commanded by Lieutenant Colonel James A. Tate as a guard for the structure. Police in plain clothes were directed to move freely throughout the anticipated crowd. Scott also ordered a battery of horse artillery to take position on the brow of the hill commanding the entire east front of the Capitol.

The inaugural festivities passed without incident as Scott watched carefully from his carriage just beyond the solemn assemblage on March 4. The regulars and militia-volunteers saluted smartly, a new administration received the sceptre of power and its accompanying worries, and Unionists breathed a sigh of relief. The firm grasp of the situation as evidenced by the stringent precautions of Scott, Stone, and civilian officials had brought results. Of course, it was never apparent that the various seceding states possessed sufficient organization to launch what was tantamount to offensive warfare— seizure of the capital by crossing the territorial domain of states of the Upper South. Perhaps only well organized local secessionist groups in Maryland and Virginia could have succeeded at the time. There were several months when capture of Washington by surprise would have been perfectly feasible. As the actions of Federal authorities indicated, it was never certain until some time after Lincoln's inauguration that such an attack would not be made and the city captured. But the alertness and superior organization of the armed forces, as well as decisive action by certain prominent Unionist leaders, rendered a coup by mob action impossible. The first crisis of defending the symbol of the nation passed into history.

[17]

CHAPTER TWO

The Isolated Capital

Confederate batteries in Charleston harbor opened fire on Fort
Sumter on April 12, 1861. Two days later at noon the Stars
and Stripes dipped to the ground in surrender. Official
Washington was shocked, although the issue in South Carolina
had been in doubt for months. On April 15, Lincoln called
for 75,000 volunteers to suppress the rebellion; other slave
states pondered secession; and eventually four, including
Virginia joined the Confederacy. Yet for Washington the
crucial event was an ordinance of secession passed by the
Virginia convention on April 17. Its popular ratification appeared to be merely a matter of time, placing unfortified
Washington on a military frontier.

Actually the period between Lincoln's inauguration and the fall of Fort Sumter was quiet on the banks of the Potomac. Popular opinion in the capital held that neither Fort Sumter nor Fort Pickens (in Florida) threatened to embroil the feuding sides in a war, and it was not until early April that the situation seemed to change when it appeared that the Lincoln administration had decided to resupply the two posts and hold them. Once again Washington became uneasy; many of the troops brought to the city for the electoral vote counting and inauguration had been shifted elsewhere, and rumors abounded that the fiery Texas Ranger Ben McCulloch and five hundred men were about to stage a lightning raid upon Washington from Richmond. As one senior naval officer, Commodore Hiram Paulding, told Secretary of the Navy Gideon Welles: "If in conspiracy against the Government with an able leader at their head, they can move secretly and with great celerity what, with this view, will prevent the army of the cotton States from coming to Washington when they are ready?"[1]

Events moved rapidly after the first of April. On that day Lincoln asked Scott to provide daily reports on the military situation across the nation. The following day he conferred with Commander Dahlgren at the navy yard concerning the state of defenses there as well as the river approaches to the city. By the end of the week troops in and about Washington passed from overall command of the southern-born Brevet Lieutenant Colonel John B. Magruder, to the aging but more reliable Brevet Colonel Charles F. Smith, and the impact of Scott's latest report on troop strength hit home. Scott noted that except for eighty cavalry recruits from the depot at Carlisle, Pennsylvania, Magruder's and Griffin's horse batteries, Elzey's and Haskin's foot artillery acting as infantry, and approximately 200 Marines, "there is not another company of regulars within reach of Washington," except 50 recruits at

Fort Washington, 100 recruits at Fort McHenry, and seven companies at Fort Monroe, all desperately required for protection of those posts.[2]

Lincoln and his advisers grew steadily more concerned with the unfolding crisis. By April 5, the chief executive queried the commanding general as to the legality of calling for volunteer units from the states. Scott still doubted the advisability of mustering the District of Columbia militia to defend the city, but admitted "the necessity of such call . . . may not be very distant [since] . . . machinations against the Government & this Capital, are secretly going on, all around us—in Virginia, in Maryland & here, as well as farther South. . . ." Admitting a lack of intelligence information, Scott requested authority to employ agents in Baltimore, Annapolis, Washington, Alexandria, Richmond, and Norfolk. Three days later he cited the movement of reinforcements of cavalry and artillery, including Brevet Major Thomas W. Sherman's battery of the Third Artillery, from Texas and Minnesota to aid Washington, and reported that "all these reinforcements, excepting Sherman's may be too late for this place." Therefore, he ordered Smith to ascertain the numbers of reliable D.C. volunteers which could be secured from the militia. Finally, he suggested to the president "that a small War Steamer, to cruise between Alexandria & the Long Bridge, over the Potomac, would be of great importance to the system of defense that we are planning."[3]

Secretary of War Simon Cameron met with Scott, Smith, and Stone on April 9 concerning the calling of D.C. militia to protect public property. Stone was proud of the D.C. units, which had been reorganized under his careful supervision, and he thought that twice the ten suggested companies would volunteer to serve the Federal government. Scott cited an 1803 act as authority for such a call, (the act provided for organizing the D.C. militia more efficiently), and Lincoln soon ordered their muster.

At first there was the predictable breakdown in communications as the government failed to inform the militiamen of the nature and duration of their required service. Thus, when the first day of muster arrived many units proved reluctant to report, and it was not until Major Irvin McDowell, an Assistant Adjutant General, explained that they would not have to serve beyond the boundaries of the District that six rifle companies swore allegiance. The movement seemed timely, for on April 11, Scott learned that heavy snows had delayed the departure of the regular contingents from Minnesota, although the next day brought more reassuring information that six companies of dismounted cavalry and one of infantry had landed at New York from Texas. By April 13, Scott could tell Lincoln that a total of fifteen D.C. militia companies of approximately 600 men, besides six companies of regulars and about 200 Marines stood ready to guard the capital.[4]

The presence of militia guarding public buildings while regular cavalry and artillery maintained positions at the bridge approaches to the city did not allay all the fears in Washington. John G. Nicolay thought the militia were unpredictable and suggested that they might turn against the Federal government when put to the test. "We were not only surrounded by the enemy, but in the midst of traitors," he wrote his wife. Even Scott suspected that old Fort Washington might be taken simply by a small quantity of whiskey. While the D.C. militia were the first volunteers to respond to the rebellion, an air of unreality continued to hang over the city. Lincoln's formal request for troops from the remaining loyal states of the Union sparked yet another crisis by mid-April.[5]

Many states reacted to Lincoln's proclamation with offers of men, money, and arms, but the two key states of Virginia and Maryland were not among them. Within days pressure from the Lincoln government caused the Old Dominion to join the Southern Confederacy with merely the thin ribbon of the Potomac thus separating Washington from rebellious territory. Marylanders were slightly more hesitant. Still, secessionist sentiment ran strong in the Free State, and even Washington, which depended upon both Virginia and Maryland for its communications with the rest of the country, was the scene of only lukewarm patriotic fervor in support of war. Scott continued to tell visiting politicians like Governor Andrew Curtin and A. K. McClure from Pennsylvania that Washington was not endangered, but they could see themselves just how weakly defended was the city. Even the presence of Scott's requested gunboat in the Potomac provided meager solace for the president.[6]

Yet, Washington to all appearances was the scene of great activity with militiamen and regulars rushing to their posts, construction of barricades moving apace, and volunteer vigilante groups such as the Clay Battalion and the Frontier Guards adding to the confusion by drilling in the Capitol and White House. But if men like Cassius Clay, James Lane, Senator Samuel C. Pomeroy, and Adam Gurowski represented citizen response to danger, one prominent Virginian moved in quite the opposite direction. Colonel Robert E. Lee declined command of the Federal army on April 18, at about the very moment when a company of regulars from Minnesota and 475 Pennsylvania volunteers were being stoned and harassed by a mob in secessionist Baltimore.[7]

Relief for the beleaguered capital was on its way from the north. By land came a motley attired and equipped array of Pennsylvania militiamen — the so-called "First Defenders." The ninety-two men of the Logan Guards from Lewistown in the central part of the state under thirty-four year old Captain John B. Selheimer were joined at Harrisburg by the Ringgold Light Artillery of Reading (105 men, Captain James McKnight); the Allen Infantry from Allentown (49 men, Captain Thomas Yager); the Washington Artillerists of

Pottsville (131 men, Captain James Wren); and the National Light Infantry also from Pottsville (105 men, Captain Edmund McDonald). Traveling south on the Northern Central Railroad, these half-trained, partially uniformed and armed volunteers looked forward to receiving promised government equipment when they got to Washington. But, at Baltimore, they encountered the full fury of a secessionist mob when they transferred from one railroad depot to another. The Pennsylvanians, led by regular artillerymen of the 4th U.S. Artillery under Lieutenant (later Confederate Lieutenant General) John C. Pemberton, himself a Philadelphia native, braved the bickbats of the mob. Pemberton soon took his troops off to relieve the Marines at Fort McHenry. The Pennsylvanians continued on under the fusillade of insults, hurled paving stones, and other violence from the Baltimoreans (totally unprotected by Marshall Kane's local police force). The illusion of fully capped and loaded Logan Guards muskets apparently awed the crowd sufficiently to get the northerners through the city streets from Bolton Station to Camden Station and aboard the Washington bound train of boxcars. But, there were injured soldiers — the first casualties in the subsequent mission of defending Washington.[8]

Reaching the Baltimore and Ohio depot at Washington about dusk of April 18, 1861, the "First Defenders" marched to the Capitol, tired and hungry but still resolute enough to set about barricading that building against insurrectionist intruders. "In a short time," recorded Private William F. McKay of the Logan Guards, "every gas jet was lighted" so that the secessionists down in the city heard that "ten thousand Yankee volunteers" had just marched into the capital. About 9:00 P.M., they descended to the basement. In the presence of President Lincoln, Secretary of State William Henry Seward, and Secretary of War Simon Cameron, the young volunteers finally received new Springfield muskets, accoutrements, and

[23]

ammunition. Now they could defend themselves and the city, and the next morning found them commencing guard mounts, close-order drill, and further barricading of the building. Flour barrels and iron plating intended for the unfinished capitol dome were pressed into service. They anxiously awaited further reinforcement from other northern volunteer groups running the secessionist gauntlet in Maryland.[9]

Baltimore, in fact, proved to be the greatest bottleneck in the movement of troops to protect Washington. As Brevet Captain Fitz John Porter, another assistant adjutant general posted in Washington, noted later in an extensive report for Scott, troop concentrations at Harrisburg and York on the Northern Central Railroad, and at Philadelphia and points to the east, were ready to move to relieve Washington. But all land lines of communication converged at Baltimore. Calm disintegrated in that city on April 19, the day that Lincoln announced a blockade of southern ports. The Sixth Massachusetts, which had mustered and departed Boston the day after Lincoln's proclamation asking for troops, met the same unfavorable reception from a Baltimore mob as the Pennsylvanians and regulars. It extricated itself at a cost of 4 dead and 31 wounded.

Twelve companies of the unarmed Washington Brigade from Philadelphia met a similar fate later in the day. At least one fatality, many injuries and disintegration of the brigade as an organized force came at the hands of the mob. Many in the ranks dispersed into the city to make their way independently back to the Keystone state while the remnants of the brigade, which hung together through it all, subsequently retired ignominiously by train to Philadelphia. Other volunteers from northeastern Pennsylvania seeking to converge on the Baltimore chokepoint via Harrisburg and the Northern Central railroad were turned back before ever reaching the Monument City's outskirts.[10]

[24]

Now Washington seemed ringed by rebellion as Baltimore authorities actually burned bridges and destroyed communications in order to prevent more northern volunteers from moving through the city to Washington, all in the name of maintaining public order. Maryland state officials appeared to look on idly; many citizens began to panic; and the weekend of April 20-21 witnessed a mass exodus of women and children via the erratic trains and overcrowded roads from the capital. Militiamen and regulars shifted uneasily at their posts. By Monday, April 22, Quartermaster General Joseph E. Johnston, Captain John B. Magruder, and Commodore Franklin Buchanan had resigned their commissions and departed to serve the Confederacy. Even government clerks began to refuse to perform their duties for fear reprisal awaited them when Confederate forces captured Washington.

Scott, a Virginian who declined to command Virginia troops against the United States just as Lee, a Federal officer, had refused to lead Union forces against his native state, now took a stiffer position. Rebuffing wild firebrands such as "Kansas" Jim Lane and Major David Hunter who wanted to burn Baltimore to the ground, the senior military professional decided to circumvent that troublesome city. He endorsed an alternate route, proposed by railroad officials, for moving reinforcements by water from Perryville on the northern shore of the Susquehanna river to Annapolis, thence overland via the railroad to the nation's capital. Lincoln and his advisers approved, and, in essence, abandoned all overland routes including the Northern Central and Philadelphia, Wilmington, and Baltimore railroads which passed through Baltimore. Officials in New York and Philadelphia were directed to utilize the maritime strength of the nation in order to save its capital city. Navy Captain Samuel Francis Du Pont had organized a seaborne rescue operation from his Philadelphia Navy Yard headquarters. He planned to employ

[25]

the steamer *Boston* and a railroad ferryboat, *Maryland* to convey troops by water to Maryland's state capital at Annapolis, near Washington. The troops could then advance along a railroad line to reach the city safely. Such use of seapower proved fortuitous when on Sunday, April 21, Lincoln and his anxious advisors learned that Major General Benjamin F. Butler had his Massachusetts contingent as well as the Seventh New York and First Rhode Island standing offshore at Annapolis. Disembarking at the U.S. Naval Academy, the soldiers took possession of that abandoned government facility and began rebuilding the rail line towards Washington. Maryland governor Thomas H. Hicks and other timid state politicians protested briefly, but the northern were ashore and bivouacked in the state house grounds and there was little that the Marylanders could do about it. Soon, the blueclad volunteers began their march through hostile countryside towards Annapolis Junction on the main rail line to Washington.[11]

Meanwhile, news of the loss of the Norfolk navy yard and the Harpers Ferry arsenal plagued Federal officials, as did the chore of establishing communications with Butler's column. Washington stood almost deserted with docks, offices, groceries, and amusement parlors vacant. Prospect of famine threatened as the stock of provisions ceased to flow into the city from Maryland and Virginia. Inflation hit Washington food markets, but the government had confiscated large amounts of salted meats, flour, and other stores, and an announcement that the city was provisioned for a siege dropped prices back toward normal. Still, apathetic, discouraged, or anxious faces appeared each day at the depot seeking solace from any approaching train.

While Washington waited, its citizens contented themselves with three-day old newspapers which told of flag raisings, organization of volunteers, and ceaseless activity to preserve the Union elsewhere in the North. Washington newspapers, however, lacked telegraph connections with the outside, and while patching together bits and pieces of news, their columns could not match the startling stories that were flying about the streets. Rebel flags could be seen fluttering in the wind at Alexandria; rebel scouts were purportedly at the Virginia bridge approaches to Washington; and other tales held that mobs were marching to sack the capital from Richmond, Baltimore, and even Harpers Ferry. The number of enrolled militia companies in the district now totalled thirty-three, but even Lincoln began to wonder if the capital could survive much longer. He told some of the soldiers of the Sixth Massachusetts: "I don't believe there is any North. The Seventh Regiment is a myth. Rhode Island is not known in our geography any longer. *You* are the only Northern realities." Over in Georgetown the Potomac Light Infantry went out of existence for the duration with the toast: "The P.L.I., invincible in peace; invisible in war." The same slogan seemed applicable to the rest of the country also.[12]

The pressure upon Lincoln was great. He fretted about unusual sounds of gunfire — the militia were training — or the sighting of unidentified craft on the Potomac. His testy letters to Marylanders such as Reverdy Johnson, Governor Hicks, and Mayor George Brown of Baltimore displayed little patience with state obstruction to protection of Washington. He snapped at the Baltimore committee: "The rebels attack Fort Sumter, and your citizens attack troops sent to the defense of the Government, and the lives and property in Washington, and yet you would have me break my oath and surrender the Government without a blow. . . . I have no desire to invade the South; but I must have troops to defend this Capital." He also observed that since troops could neither burrow under or fly over Maryland, then they had to march across the state. He demanded that Baltimore officials control the mobs since "if they will not attack us, we will not attack them; but if they do attack us, we will return it, and that severely."[13]

Even Scott was not too reassuring when he reported to the president on April 22. Intelligence reports indicated that 1,500 to 2,000 Confederates were supposedly erecting a battery below Mount Vernon; a similar force was reportedly gathering to attack Fort Washington; and transportation ostensibly had been provided for gathering contingents from Harpers Ferry to threaten the Virginia approaches to Washington. Scott thought his forces could hold the public buildings if the enemy were no better than the D.C. volunteers. Against such an ominous background, Lincoln turned to other pressing matters relating to the war. Backed by his cabinet on April 21, the president signed emergency war measures for purchase of ships as well as transportation of munitions and troops.[14]

The tension finally broke on April 25. Only two days before, the powerful warship USS *Pawnee*, under Commander Stephen C. Rowan had arrived from Norfolk, adding its firepower to Washington's defense. Now as the sounds of whistles and cheering at the railroad depot brought citizens scurrying to see what was transpiring, the dashing Seventh New York (albeit the worse for wear from several days in the field), accompanied by the National Rifles of the District as escort, detrained to the applause of the assembled multitude. The dandy New Yorkers were always good for a show, and so with flags fluttering in the soft spring breeze, the regiment precision-marched past an ecstatic Lincoln, washed the Maryland grime from their grey uniforms at Willard's, and by evening were comfortably ensconced with the Sixth Massachusetts at the Capitol. As their spokesman Theodore Winthrop observed, bayonets now replaced buncombe in those hallowed halls. He might have added that it did not take long for the gentlemen of the Seventh to mount the Speaker's rostrum and deliver some buncombe of their own. The young lions from Gotham would soon prove as incorrigible as the elder statesmen of the nation.[15]

The next morning the Eighth Massachusetts and portions of the First Rhode Island arrived, followed within days by the Twelfth, Twenty-fifth, and Seventy-first New York as well as the Fifth Pennsylvania and Fifth Massachusetts. Most of these units followed the same hostile route from Annapolis, to be met at the Junction by D.C. volunteers, greeted warmly, and then conducted by train to Washington. Others in the procession included Thomas A. Scott, vice president of the Pennsylvania Railroad, and Andrew Carnegie, youthful and ubiquitous telegraph operator—all comprising a vanguard of countless thousands who were to funnel through the Baltimore-Washington corridor for the next four years en route to the war zone farther south.

The U.S. Navy had likewise been active during that week of crisis, trying both to save the Norfolk Navy Yard but at the same time insure the defense of the capital. Rowan and the *Pawnee* added firepower to the meager naval strength on the Potomac. The U.S.S. *Anacostia* under Lieutenant Thomas S. Fillebrown was ordered to prevent emplacement of obstructions in the river at Kettle Bottom Shoals, and the army cooperated by seizing the Potomac river steamers *Baltimore, Mount Vernon, Philadelphia,* and *Powhatan* (much to the discomfort of travelers fleeing south and Virginia authorities who wanted them as gunboats). Manned by D.C. militiamen, they were taken to the Washington Navy Yard and reoutfitted by Commander Dahlgren's workmen for service on the Potomac. Forerunners of a "flying flotilla" proposed by Commander James Ward on April 22, these ships began reconnoitering the Virginia shoreline for enemy batteries and replacing navigational buoys in the river. On April 27, the

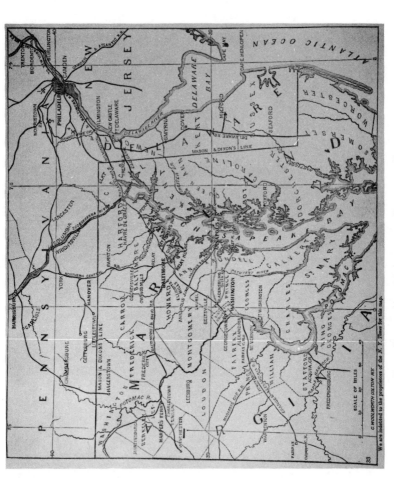

The Sensitive National Capital Region
(undated New York Times Map)

We are indebted to the proprietors of the *N.Y. Times* for this map.

U.S.S. *Pocahontas* under Commander J. P. Gillis convoyed the transport *Bienville* with the rest of the First Rhode Island up the Potomac to the Washington wharves, thereby illustrating the fallacy of reports reaching Scott about enemy batteries on the Virginia shore. As Gideon Welles reported later: "For several months . . . the navy, without aid, succeeded, more effectively than could have been expected, in keeping open for commercial purposes, and restricting, to a great extent, communication between the opposite shores [of the Potomac]."[16]

Nearly 11,000 troops were in Washington by the end of April. Lincoln instructed Scott on April 27 to suspend the writ of habeas corpus in Maryland if any additional trouble were experienced regarding movement of troops across that state. But communication with the north was now open, Lincoln was the happiest man in the capital, and the colorful uniforms of volunteer units mingled with the faded blue of the regulars. The city became a vast military camp, a sea of white canvas tentage, a massive mixture of military plumage and spring flowers. The regulars—infantry, cavalry, artillery—were everywhere, but the volunteers kept to specific campsites. Colonel Edward Jones's Sixth Massachusetts, Colonel Marshall Lefferts's Seventh New York, and Colonel Timothy Munroe's Eighth Massachusetts as well as five miscellaneous Pennsylvania companies were quartered at the Capitol. The Seventy-first New York under Colonel Abram S. Vosburgh was positioned at the Navy Yard, while Colonel Robert P. McDowell's Fifth Pennsylvania manned the Inauguration Hall. Colonel Samuel C. Lawrence's Fifth Massachusetts encamped at the Treasury; Colonel Ambrose Burnside's First Rhode Island held the Patent Office; and Colonel Michael K. Bryan's Twenty-fifth New York bivouacked at Caspari's House on Capitol Hill. Stone's D.C. volunteers, like the regulars, were posted in numerous places. The "First Defenders," organized finally as part of the Twenty-Fifth Pennsylvania, went downriver with the navy to garrison archaic Fort Washington where they helped tidy up that long-neglected river defense post. Later they would form the vanguard of a "Corps of Observation" above Washington in Montgomery County, Maryland. The clouds of dust raised by the troops gave to Washington a dash and comfort, as well as a sense of things to come. Still, as Secretary of State William Seward confided to his wife: "Preparations in Virginia and Maryland indicate a conflict here, or in the vicinity, in which the forces will be counted by the hundred thousand on a side." His prediction was to prove quite near the mark.[17]

Indeed, the central concern of the Federal government by late April moved from events in Maryland—where the insatiable Ben Butler was utilizing Lincoln's authorization to suspend the writ of habeas corpus with a heavy hand (or as the compilers of the *Officials Records* of the war later termed it ironically, "the Union policy of repression in Maryland"—to the situation across the Potomac. Lincoln's comments to Reverdy Johnson on April 24 illustrated such a shift in policy. He told the ex-senator from Maryland and sometime member of the 1861 Peace Conference: "I *do* say that I have no purpose to *invade* Virginia, with them or any other troops, as I understand the word *invasion*. But suppose Virginia sends her troops, or admits others through her borders, to assail this capital, am I not to repel them, even to the crossing of the Potomac if I can?" More importantly, asked Lincoln, suppose Virginia were to erect, or permit erection by Confederate authorities, batteries to bombard the city. "In a word," asked the President, "are we not to strike back, and as effectively as we can?" By early May such fears were becoming fully justified as Virginia positioned men close to her northern frontier—across the river from Washington.[18]

Despite subsequent intelligence reports that enemy batteries on the Potomac were myths, Scott and Colonel J. F. K. Mansfield, new commander of the Washington department, estimated that 17,000 to 20,000 troops were now necessary "to give security to this Capital against the forces of the enemy known to be within 24 hours of us." Even one energetic major general in the Ohio department, George B. McClellan, proposed offensive action against Richmond from the Ohio valley to relieve pressure upon Washington, although Scott had little regard for that scheme. The old general was more conservative. He realized that the western part of Washington (including Georgetown and Executive Square), lay within range of possible enemy guns on Arlington Heights, yet he also knew of the inexperience of the troops at his command. He debunked McClellan's plan as folly and piecemeal subjugation of the seceded states (as opposed to his own vaunted cordon or anaconda strategy). As he told Lincoln on May 4: "Besides the forces designed to occupy Arlington Heights, to retake Harpers Ferry, & to threaten from Fort Monroe the Gosport Navy Yard, & other important points on the navigable waters falling into the Chesapeake, I deem it inexpedient to make other aggressive movements with three months' levies." As early as May 3, he directed Mansfield "not to lose a moment in anticipating the enemy" by occupying Arlington Heights with redoubts sufficient to hold them.[19]

Actually neither Scott nor his principal subordinates had much time in early May to undertake an immediate offensive, even across the river into Virginia. The initial stages of marshalling large forces to suppress the rebellion involved questions of organization, subsistence, procurement, and training. Scott had to deal with events elsewhere, in the departments of the Ohio and the Missouri, where blue-clad volunteers were streaming into Federal camps and rendezvous. The initial rush to the colors on both sides necessitated long hours, patience, endless correspondence, and sound administration by staff and

[33]

field officers. Only when such problems had been solved could suppression of the insurrection begin—whether south of the Ohio or south of the Potomac.

Meanwhile the volunteers in the District of Columbia were on a lark, experiencing new sights and sounds, seeing new faces and scenery, and thoroughly fatiguing local inhabitants with their antics. The First Rhode Island had a large number of college students in its ranks, whose songs and pranks cut a new figure for Washington. Their sister regiment, the Second Rhode Island, soon joined them, arriving complete with their own artillery, and both regiments moved to the northeastern limits of the city and encamped in a grove called Gale's Woods, constructing tents on frames with wooden sides and floors. The dandy Seventh New York moved from the Capitol to Meridian Hill; Colonel Michael Corcoran's Irish Sixty-Ninth New York encamped at Roman Catholic Georgetown College; Daniel Butterfield's Twelfth New York arrived without uniforms, quickly acquired Union blue, and settled at Franklin Square—and all of these units perfected their close order drill and manual of arms in the warm May sunlight.

Much of the service proved monotonous, a goodly number of young sentinels fell asleep at their posts, and altogether, the youthful recruits waited anxiously for weekend passes. Only then could they really get to see Washington, the public buildings, spark with whatever local belles remained in the city, or be led astray among the fleshpots south of Pennsylvania Avenue. These men represented a microcosm of the northern states ranging from Colonel Elmer Ellsworth's Eleventh New York Zouaves, filled with riff-raff full of play and fun to the swains of Gramercy Square in the Seventh New York. Millhands from Massachusetts vied with Ohio farmboys— they were all out to save the Union and the national capital in a day. Their dress parades, band concerts, and universal promenading gave Washington a livelier air than ever before, but most of the local citizenry grew quickly blasé about them and wished that they would move across the river and away from town.[20]

Notwithstanding the advisability of securing all the high ground around the city, Lincoln and his advisers dared not move onto Virginia soil until after May 23 when the ordinance of secession (passed by the Virginia convention in April) was due for popular referendum. When the voters approved the document, the stage was set for a Federal "invasion" of the Old Dominion. Of course, state authorities had been using Alexandria as a rallying point for some time. Many D.C. secessionists (including firebrands of the National Rifles) joined Virginia units at the seaport town. Lieutenant Colonel A. S. Taylor had orders from Richmond to hold the town "unless pressed by overwhelming and irresistible numbers," and on May 5, he interpreted those orders to permit evacuation of his 481 untrained, mostly unarmed, and completely unorganized recruits. Alexandria remained unocccupied for awhile until the Confederates sent in some better troops as a garrison. But even then Major General Robert E. Lee, now commanding the state forces, told local commanders at Alexandria and Manassas Junction (the main rebel staging area in Northern Virginia): "It is not expected possible with the troops presently under your command, that you will be able to resist successfully an attempt to occupy Alexandria, but you may prevent extension of marauders into the country & the advance of troops on the railroad."[21]

On May 21, Confederate authorities decided to make Richmond their capital. They erected a battery at Aquia Creek landing, covering the northern terminus of the railroad to Richmond, as Commander Ward's "flying flotilla" of Union naval craft discovered about midway through the month. Thus the Confederate high command began its adherence to a defensive strategy which remained virtually unchanged for the lifespan of the Confederacy. Yet, the Lincoln government remained unsure of initial Confederate intentions. The unfriendly hills and shoreline across the Potomac from Washington seemed too threatening. By May 23, Lincoln, Scott, and the Federal planners decided to seize the initiative.[22]

At 2:00 A.M. the next morning, a three-pronged Federal drive under the command of Major General Charles W. Sanford of the New York militia moved onto Virginia soil. The dramatic crossing was billed by one *Harper's Weekly* artist as "Advance Guard of the Grand Army of the United States," and the muffled tramp of feet and wagons mingled with low commands as the expedition was carried out in greatest secrecy. Of course the town had been filled with rumors the day before, and even Lincoln asked Scott whether it was not about time to move across the Potomac? But to the war correspondents and the youthful soldiers here was all the high drama of the first of the campaigns in the Old Dominion—campaigns which would drag on until that fateful day at Appomattox four years later.

Staff, engineers, pioneer troops, cavalry, and artillery mingled with the infantry volunteers which crossed by the Aqueduct and Long bridges under the command of Majors W. H. Wood and Samuel P. Heintzelman, and by steamer from across the Anacostia in charge of Ellsworth. Stone's D.C. volunteers gained the Virginia approach to Long Bridge before the rebel pickets could give the alarm, and the U.S.S. *Pawnee* covered the Alexandria landing. Sanford was under strict orders to assure local Virginia citizens of the peaceful intentions of government forces, and scouting parties moved quickly from the initial bridgeheads toward Falls Church and Ball's Cross Roads.

The only serious trouble developed at Alexandria. First, Commander S. C. Rowan of the *Pawnee* acted without orders in sending ashore a subordinate to demand the town's surrender before the foot soldiers even entered their boats. He subsequently received a rebuke from Secretary Welles for actions ". . . so manifestly inconsistent with correct discipline and the obligations due to the army which was making a secret movement. . . ." But the land forces were equally anxious to gain glory, and they quickly lost the services of the impetuous Ellsworth. It was not a matter of determined Confederate resistence. Colonel George H. Terrett, the local rebel commander, lost little time in getting his token forces aboard an Orange and Alexandria train for Manassas. Yet, in the process one local hothead, Captain Delany Ball, and thirty-five of his comrades resisted and were captured. More important, the hyperactive Ellsworth decided upon a grandstand play by removing a secessionist banner from the Marshall House, a hotel in the center of town. Naturally, the proprietor of the establishment took offense. He cut down the flashy Zouave officer with a blast of his shotgun and, in turn, was dispatched by the bayonet of one of the enlisted men of the Eleventh New York. When the news trickled back across the river all Washington was dumbstruck; Lincoln was especially bereaved, and the city went into official mourning. Ellsworth was the only casualty of the invading force and the Union had its first martyr in putting down the rebellion.[23]

The morning of May 24 dawned mild and sunny. Young blue-coated soldiers lounged in bivouacs under shade trees near Robert E. Lee's abandoned Arlington House. Engineer officers such as Captains D. P. Woodbury, B. S. Alexander, and Horatio G. Wright, assisted by Lieutenants O. E. Cross and F. E. Prime, hastily laid out field fortifications nearby under the close supervision of the departmental engineer, Major John G. Barnard. As the Washington *Evening Star* observed: "At 4 o'clock this morning a large number of government wagons went across the Long Bridge loaded with picks, and shovels, and all manner of tools . . . and accompanied with a full corps of carpenters and workmen. The United States forces are now busily throwing up fortifications on the heights of the Virginia shore, commencing at daybreak. Theodore Winthrop of the Seventh New York was somewhat more whimsical—"Nothing men can do—except picnics, with ladies in straw flats with flowers—is so picturesque as soldiering."[24]

The first fortifications which emerged from this activity bore little resemblance to any defense system. They did provide a foundation for future development, however. Situated for the most part on low ground, they were intended only as tetes-de-pont or points d'appui (ie., support bases), for defending the bridge crossings. Among the earliest works were Fort Corcoran, with a perimeter of 576 yards and emplacements for eleven cannon; Fort Haggerty, having a 128-yard perimeter and but four gun emplacements; and Fort Bennett, 146 yards in perimeter and mounting five cannon. Along with block houses and eventually rifle trenches, these three forts guarded the Aqueduct. Forts Runyon (1,484 yards, two gun emplacements), and Albany (429 yards, eleven gun positions), were constructed to cover the Long Bridge, while Fort Ellsworth (618 yards, twenty-seven gun emplacements), was located on Shuter's Hill just to the west of Alexandria. Of course, the various regiments which crossed the Potomac quickly established camps and training areas nearby, and the entire Virginia countryside seemed alive with white tents and raw red clay fortifications, as viewed from the windows of official Washington.

During the next seven weeks all efforts were devoted to completing this first formal defense of the southern approach to the capital. Little thought or attention was given to more general studies or reconnaissance necessary for planning a circumferential defense system. Even Mansfield evidenced complacency as he announced that northern approaches to Washington could be "readily fortified at any time by a system of redoubts encircling the city." Perhaps the judgement was sound at the time, for the Confederates were hardly bestirring themselves to mount any major offensive. Nonetheless, almost daily alarms sent the green Federal units to seize arms and stand formation, and the feelings of professional engineer officers about Washington's defenses as a whole were best represented by Barnard's comments concerning Fort Ellsworth: "It might exert an influence over the inimical population of the city of Alexandria; it might help defend the place against small expeditions; but in its relation to the operations of armies it could neither offer much aid to the defense nor materially deter the attack."[25]

Part of the problem was a general lack of planning and coordination on the part of the Union high command. In turn, a nasty political intrigue soon surfaced whereby newly promoted Brigadier General Irvin B. McDowell assumed command of the "Department of Northeastern Virginia" on May 27 only to discover his appointment by Secretary of War Cameron was not to Scott's liking. McDowell was a protege of Secretary of the Treasury Chase and others while Scott was partial to Sanford, or even more noticeably, to Mansfield, his departmental commander in the District of Columbia. The result was tantamount to a vote of no confidence from Scott. Mansfield displayed a marked petulance toward helping McDowell get organized in Virginia, and McDowell himself remained insecure for his whole period as commander of the field force in front of Washington. By the end of May he was complaining loudly about lack of food and fodder for his men and animals, absence of proper tools and equipment, poor communications, and the absence of guidance about reimbursement of local citizens for destruction of property and occupation of land. At least the last problem found solution in a general order directing commanders of volunteer regiments to keep careful records so that the Federal government might reimburse local landowners for losses or damage. Still, the blundering and confusion tended to hide the fundamental achievement of Scott's invasion of Virginia. The pressure upon Washington had been relieved at least temporarily, and footholds had been secured on Confederate soil.[26]

Meanwhile, Washingtonians were becoming increasingly complacent as the tension eased slightly. No longer did the daily arrivals of new units at the depot evoke large crowds of onlookers. The clutter and clatter of wagons and carts at the wharves and in the streets attracted few bystanders, and the District began to assume the ramshackle air of a wartime capital and sometime supply depot. The Washington *Star* noted early in May that Ned Buntline (E. Z. C. Judson) was cavorting with Virginia pickets and intimidating government clerks on political grounds around the unfinished Washington monument. White tents continued to spread out beyond Boundary Street as the Kalorama estate, Meridian Hill, even places far out the Seventh Street Road, became inundated with training and bivouac areas for the defenders of Washington. One young Maine soldier waxed: "We are about two miles from the Capitol. Going a little [to] one side of our grounds I can see the whole city and over into Virginia where for seven miles there is one continuous encampment, a line of sentinels reaching the whole extent, guarding the Potomac so that it is impossible to get into Virginia without a pass." Hoosiers, New Yorkers, New Englanders, and young men from the Middle Atlantic states—all surged into Washington, always with the wide eyes of youth. Going to the front became a major event in the lives of nearly 30,000 volunteers who passed through the Washington area by early June of 1861. Their campsites hovered on the outskirts of the city on the north and on Arlington Heights and behind Alexandria to the south. Their uniforms cast a circus hue with as many units clad in gray as in blue and other colors also abounded. Cumbersome havelocks to protect necks from sunburn, useless leggins and heavy overcoats, with uniform trimmings of every describable color betrayed their militia origins. Indeed, what it all symbolized was a militia army, not yet molded into a proficient national fighting force.[27]

Yet, the colorfully clad vivandieres of the Zouaves, and the Bersaglieri of the Thirty-ninth New York (Garibaldi Guard), as well as tarten-clad Seventy-ninth New York "Highlanders" became strangely tiresome to the gaze by early summer. Perhaps local citizens were simply disgusted with the pay day antics of the volunteers. McDowell had to issue strict orders against "trespass, depredations, and attempts at burglary" among his troops (especially the D.C. volunteers), perpetrated on local citizenry in Virginia. More realistically, many people simply thought that it was time that the army on the Potomac took a more active role in suppressing the rebellion. By early June Confederate officials had moved into the Virginia state capitol building and a Confederate main force stretched from Aquia Creek, through Manassas Junction, to Leesburg, at a distance of only about thirty miles from Washington. Sergeant Chauncey M. Shull of the "First Defenders" down at Fort Washington, declared in his diary on June 6: "We are in no danger here now. We are just as safe as if we were at home. The very devil himself could not take our fort now." The northern press chorused the need for an advance; McDowell's protests about lack of training and experience were beginning to sound shrill; and people began to forget that the panic of the previous month was about defensive, not offensive, operations. It mattered little that Maryland remained shaky despite Butler's "occupation" of Baltimore on May 13. Quickly forgotten were the facts that Lincoln and his policymakers initially had to utilize their meager forces throughout the upper Potomac and upper Chesapeake regions to protect Washington. A quick dis-

[41]

persion of the rebel army at Manassas, prompt capture of Richmond—these were the thoughts uppermost in the minds of the majority of Northerners by summer. Cautionary injunctions against premature advance were drowned out by cries of "on to Richmond." Only a Union disaster at Manassas in July cultivated an awareness that the nation's capital remained quite inadequately protected against a far from somnolent enemy.[28]

CHAPTER THREE

Changes in the Wake of Bull Run

June opened with a series of clashes between Federal and Confederate forces in northeastern Virginia. In fact, the month turned essentially on a succession of skirmishes and picket fights—minor affairs—as Federal commanders on land and river sought to test the Confederate buildup in the area. None of the engagements proved decisive; each was an extension of the campaign to defend Washington as Federal columns fanned out into the Virginia countryside. Then too, the Federal command constantly feared a Confederate counterthrust upon Alexandria via the line of the Orange and Alexandria.[1]

The U.S. Navy's Potomac Flotilla precipitated the first action when the ever alert Commander James Ward sought to keep the river open to Union traffic to Washington and, at the same time, to interdict a lucrative, troublesome, and illegal transriver trade between southern Maryland and Virginia. In 1861 only the Baltimore and Ohio railroad entered Washington directly, thus making the waterborne commerce on the Potomac very important to the city. Not unlike other rivers in the antebellum south, the Potomac teemed with shipping. Steamers from the north and from Europe, coasting freighters, military and naval vessels, fishing and oyster boats, and smaller craft plied these waters. It was in the Confederacy's best interest to blockade this artery to the nation's capital.

It was hardly surprising that as early as May 8, Massachusetts born Brigadier General Daniel Ruggles of the Virginia state forces received directions from Brigadier General Philip St. G. Cocke, commanding the "Potomac Line," to establish a battery of thirteen heavy guns at Aquia Landing, located twelve miles north of Fredericksburg at the mouth of Aquia creek. The southerners worked methodically and it wasn't until May 14th that Union naval forces detected the new Aquia creek battery mounting four heavy guns. As Confederate authorities worried that the Union Navy might try to land and capture both the battery and the railroad leading to Fredericksburg and Richmond, naval authorities in Washington contemplated how best to overcome this threatened interdiction point on the Potomac. By the end of the month, Ward was able to mount a punitive expedition against the Aquia battery with the steam side-wheel ferryboat, *Thomas Freeborn* (two 32-pounder guns); the screw steamer *Resolute* (one 24-pounder and one 12-pounder howitzer); and the *Anacostia*, a twin-screw sloop—carrying two 9-inch Dahlgren smoothbores. The redoubtable regular sloop-of-war *Pawnee* later joined the expedition, adding firepower with her eight 9-inch guns mounted in broadside and two 12-pounders.[2]

Actually, the Confederate battery, commanded by Captain William F. Lynch of the Virginia navy, was not intimidated at all as heavy artillery fire echoed up and down the Potomac valley on May 31 and June 1. The Federal ships poured over 600 projectiles onto the Confederate position. This fire demolished Lynch's headquarters, tore up the earthworks and railroad track, and killed a stray chicken and a horse. The Federals did not force the Confederates to surrender; in fact, Lynch's accurate return fire damaged the *Freeborn's* port wheel and hull and hit the *Pawnee* nine times, splintering mizzen and top masts, puncturing her smokestack, and shattering parts of the bulwarks and deck. Losses were only one man wounded on each side, and the action could hardly be called decisive.

If the shelling of Aquia Landing proved inconclusive, a similar fight late in June at Mathias Point, eighteen miles farther downriver, brought worse results for the Union. Here the river turned sharply toward the Chesapeake, the channel swept close to the Virginia shoreline, and General Ruggles decided that it was another opportune place to erect a battery. But Ward and his flotilla had the same idea, and on the morning of June 27 he landed two cutters containing thirty-five seamen with the intention of erecting a sandbag breastwork as a base for operations. Late that afternoon a Confederate unit under Major R. M. Mayo attacked the sailors; Ward was killed, four seamen were wounded, and the landing party departed swiftly for the safety of the ships. Ward was the first Union naval officer killed in the war, and he quickly joined the pantheon of Union heroes. Like Ellsworth, his name was subsequently memorialized by one of the forts in Washington's defense line. Commander Thomas T. Craven succeeded Ward in command and continued the Potomac Flotilla patrols out of the chief rendezvous at Nanjemoy Creek, Maryland. His vigorous patrolling netted many dissident citizens plying contraband goods along the sixty miles of channel below Alexandria.

Meanwhile, the Confederates found that battery sites at Mathias Point and Aquia were relatively ineffective because of the breadth of the river at these points. But they could not profit from locales where the river narrowed until they had consolidated their control over northeastern Virginia. Federal land forces had no intention of permitting that to happen and, like the navy, began active patrolling. As Washington newspapers vied with Confederate authorities at Fredericksburg in reports about who was winning control of the river, they also noted the rush of a small U.S. regular cavalry unit into Fairfax Courthouse on June 1 to the embarrassment of Confederates posted there.

The incident was minor but typical. Lieutenant Charles H. Tompkins led a company of the Second Cavalry on a reconnaissance of the area around the drowsy county seat. Discovery of a rebel garrison prompted a display of mounted skill by the regulars, with the net result that Captain Quincy Marr of the Warrenton Rifles was killed thereby becoming a popular hero to local Confederates, and Colonel R. S. Ewell was wounded and embarrassed by being caught offguard. Several enlisted Confederates were captured, and Tompkins was awarded a Medal of Honor —thirty-two years after the action.[3]

Slightly more significant was the action of June 17, near Vienna, when a railroad-borne reconnaissance by units of Brigadier General Robert G. Schenck's Ohio brigade ran into an ambush by South Carolina troops under Colonel Maxey Gregg. Other Federal movements during this period included Stone's expedition of D.C. and Pennsylvania volunteers into the Poolesville and Darnestown areas on the Maryland side of the river. All of these early episodes near Washington were disjointed, poorly coordinated affairs, with fuzzy orders emanating from Scott's headquarters. Few people on the Federal side really knew what to do with the great concentration of Federal volunteers in the staging area near the capital. The minor clashes were bungled by inexperienced commanders and ill-trained men on both sides. Yet, all these operations gave a certain grim reality to soldiering for the green troops.[4]

Federal power was clumsily flexing its muscles all across the strategic front, from an innocuous little place called Big Bethel near Fort Monroe on the Virginia peninsula to the mountainous sections of western Virginia. Federal strategists were not at all certain of the direction to be taken in suppressing the rebellion. Some of the trouble lay at the top where the magnitude of the effort and the mere transition from a peacetime army to a striking force for war traditionally caused American army leaders much trepidation. Scott was caught offguard in late April and early May when the youthful and exuberant McClellan stole a march on the old general by suggesting a transmontane campaign from the Ohio directed at Richmond. Scott replied ponderously with his famous "Anaconda" scheme—strangle the confederacy via a blockade and launch a joint army-navy expedition down the Mississippi to liberate New Orleans and open the great river trade route. The only problem lay in securing the troops and building the gunboats.[5]

Meanwhile, closer to Army headquarters, the Confederates held Harpers Ferry—a strategic point at the confluence of the Shenandoah and Potomac rivers where railroad lines joined and the remains of a former government armory could be seen amongst the weeds. Major General Robert Patterson's force of 14,000 men was apparently well contained by Brigadier General Joseph E. Johnston's equal number of Confederates in this sector. At first, Union strategists indicated that Patterson's area was to be the main arena in the East, with everything subordinated to clearing the Confederates out of the lower Shenandoah valley and Harpers Ferry. Throughout June, Patterson dallied along the Potomac, Stone moved to link up the Union forces before Washington with those in the Hagerstown area, and the main thrust in the eastern theater quietly and subtly slipped downriver closer to the nation's capital.[6]

Within a week of McDowell's assumption of command at Arlington, he received orders from Scott to develop a plan for a secondary attack on Manassas as a diversion to Patterson's main thrust at Harpers Ferry. McDowell's resultant plan was modest. A 12,000-man column was to advance upon Manassas with 5,000 left in reserve at Alexandria. But the Confederate force opposite Patterson shifted from Harpers Ferry in order to counter what Johnston took to be the advance guard of a massive Federal thrust from Ohio through Romney. Scott's continual cautionary injunction to Patterson only compounded the latter's inertia, and by mid-June, Scott once more panicked at the thought that the Confederates might be advancing directly upon Washington from Manassas.[7]

The panic may have been touched off by the bombastic tones of General P. G. T. Beauregard's letter to local northern Virginians upon taking command at Manassas on June 1, or merely by the implied threat posed by the presence of the successful "hero of Sumter." Perhaps the cause was Scott's hypersensitivity after months of serving on the front line in an embattled Washington, or perhaps intelligence reports that the Confederate command was planning an offensive had an effect. In any event, by the time that McDowell presented his superiors with a plan for a movement on Manassas late in the month, the "on to Richmond" cries of the Union populace had worked their wiles upon the Lincoln government. Scott quietly retracted his opposition to piecemeal suppression of the rebellion, and official Washington somehow decided that the best way to protect Washington and suppress resistance in the Old Dominion was a quick, cheap victory over Beauregard at Manassas by McDowell and his ill-organized and undertrained soldiers. By early July McDowell received marching orders which placed his operation at the forefront of the Federal drive southward.[8]

Scott's fears were not unfounded, especially after Confederate spies in Washington carried word of McDowell's planned movement to the Confederate higher command. One Washington spy, D. L. Dalton reported to President Jefferson Davis in a letter dated June 29, 1861 that the northern volunteers "are the very dregs of creation collected from cities—can't stand the sun, a brisk march of a mile would leave very many by the wayside, and the officers are generally 'Sunday Militia' ala Col./Benjamin F./Butler." Most of them had "volunteered to defend the Capital," he noted, but he found the plethora of free "Negroes" with each Yankee regiment seemed to be "all the forces of Republican abolitionism at work for "they were brought along for the purpose of *operating* with the Negroes of the South." Such reports may have led the ever impetuous Beauregard at Manassas to send his trusted aide, Colonel James R. Chesnut, to Richmond to place an offensive scheme before the Davis administration. Chesnut met with the president and his principal advisers, Robert E. Lee and Samuel Cooper, the adjutant and inspector general. He divulged a plan whereby the forces of Johnston and Beauregard would unite, quickly attack the divided army of McDowell (which was thought to be advancing on the axes of the Alexandria, Loundon, and Hampshire railroad as well as the Orange and Alexandria), and defeat him in a pitched battle in vicinity of Fairfax Court House. Johnston would then return with the bulk of rebel forces to defeat Patterson at Winchester while Beauregard laid siege to Washington. Brigadier General Richard Garnett would move from western Virginia (defeating Union forces under McClellan), unite with Johnston, "and the two cross the Potomac at the nearest point for Maryland, and, arousing the people as they proceeded, march to the rear of Washington, while [Beauregard] would attack it in front." Needless to say, the Richmond authorities were more inclined toward defensive than offensive ideas of this sort. They rejected Beauregard's scheme as lacking man-power and overlooking McDowell's ease of retreat back to the protection of the Washington position. Davis, Lee, and Cooper all overestimated the strength of this position, especial-ly the defenses at the time, but they probably realized cor-rectly that McDowell could rely upon a greater reserve at the capital than Beauregard possessed for operations at a distance from his base. Certainly, Dalton for one had told Richmond authorities that Union fortifications defending the city on the southern side "are quite formidable and extend from about the 'Three Sisters' /islands/ above Georgetown to Alexandria, having been constructed under the direction of skillful engineers." So Richmond authorities, at least, labored under few illusions about any successful offensive to the gates of the Federal capital.[9]

Miscalculation and paralyzing fear governed the high commands on both sides early in the summer of 1861. Beauregard's offensive plan would appear later to sour rela-tions between Richmond and its premier general at Manassas. But north of the Potomac, the threat of Beauregard's army mesmerized Scott, and contributed to rather ill-defined orders to the already hesitant and bemuddled Patterson. Moreover, Federal perception of the threat led most senior professional soldiers (excepting McDowell perhaps), to minimize the danger that Union forces were insufficiently trained for a standup fight. Many units were due for dismissal from service at the end of three months. Others were hardly more than mobs in uniform, and altogether, the dust clouds of review and drill in the Potomac valley that June indicated little beyond confusion—at regimental, army, and senior staff levels.[10]

Meanwhile, more young soldiers arrived in the Washington area. They spent their initial days in the war zone learning pioneer chores such as digging entrenchments and setting up permanent camps, while writing home of the picturesque side of war near the capital. They guffawed when they read Beauregard's colorful words to the citizens of Loudon, Fairfax, and Prince William counties, about how a tyrannical Lincoln had thrown abolitionist forces ". . . among you, who are murdering and imprisoning your citizens, confiscating and destroying your property, and committing other acts of violence and outrage too shocking and revolting to humanity to be enumerated." On July 4, twenty-three New York regiments marched past the reviewing party of President Lincoln, his cabinet, General Scott, and aides, while the Garibaldi Guard contributed to the festivities by tossing flowers (liberated from neighborhood gardens), before the feet of the reviewing party. It was all heady stuff, little wonder that many northerners thought their soldiery invincible.[11]

The sad truth became evident late in the afternoon of July 21 on the sunny, heat-drenched plateau at Manassas. McDowell's army had finally gone forward on the 16th, directed to brush away the Confederate force at Manassas Junction and capture the rail route to Richmond. The details of berry picking on the approach march, the pre-battle skirmishing at Blackburn's and Mitchell's fords on the 18th, and the successful Union flank attack on the morning of the 21st are well known. But the initial victory disintegrated into defeat as McDowell's bluecoated host simply melted before the sustained pounding of the combined strength of Beauregard and Johnston (who had quietly eluded Patterson and joined the Manassas force by rail). By nightfall Lincoln and Scott received the unwelcome news that the Federal army in northern

Virginia no longer comprised an organized fighting force. Washington was once again in serious danger of capture, and Lincoln and Scott wondered why Beauregard did not follow up his victory. The cycle of events returned the condition of the unprotected capital to the days prior to the inauguration— or so it must have seemed to many Washington observers.[12]

Whether or not Washington could have been captured by the Confederates on July 22 or 23 has produced much speculation over the years. Stonewall Jackson purportedly claimed after the battle that he could have taken the northern capital with 10,000 fresh troops. Even a recent biographer of Jefferson Davis suggests:

> By approaching Washington via White's Ford, the Southern troops could have avoided Federal gunboats down the Potomac. There were indications that the Government would have fled at the Confederates' approach. If Washington had been occupied, pro-South Maryland would doubtless have been liberated from the Federal domain and seceded; in which case both Kentucky and Missouri would have joined the Confederacy. With Southern forces holding Washington, recognition in Europe would most likely have been forthcoming. And with the strong antiwar element in the North daring to make itself voluble, a peace giving the South independence might have been made.[13]

Still, Beauregard, Johnson, and even Davis who arrived immediately after the battle from Richmond, concluded at the time that the Confederate army was too demoralized by victory to mount a rapid pursuit in the gloom and rain which swept the area the night after the battle. By morning the rising streams and bottomless roads impeded rapid movement even though the steady stream of fugitives—the remnants of McDowell's army—posed little threat. Modern analysts point further to the reserves of the Union army such as the troops of Colonel Dixon Miles at Centreville, those of Colonel Theodore Runyon at Arlington, plus additional fortress and camp troops totalling in excess of 13,000 fresh soldiers, plus the gunboats on the river, and the broad Potomac itself—all as deterrents to Confederate capture of the city immediately after Bull Run.[14] What most observers overlook is the fact that the Confederates did not actually have to march into Washington. They could have pushed McDowell's rear guard back against the Potomac, perhaps across the river, and simply occupied the heights of Arlington.[15] Spread along the river from Alexandria to Chain Bridge, they could have effected a siege—just as Lincoln, Scott, and Mansfield had feared Confederate authorities might do before May 24. Then, with well entrenched artillery and infantry, a grayclad army might well have held the Federal capital hostage with irreparable harm to the political, if not the military, efficacy of the Lincoln administration.

The Civil War provides a story of missed opportunities, of laggardly pursuit, of uninspired leadership incapable of quick thought amidst the fatigue of battle. Perhaps the whole question of Confederate pursuit after First Bull Run was best summarized by one contemporary Union officer, who, citing Johnston's claim that Confederate demoralization had prevented capture of Washington, simply observed: "To *that* disorganization and *that* demoralization the safety of Washington was due; for though it is quite true that there remained (numerically) strong bodies of [Federal] troops that had not shared in the battle, they were *all* much demoralized by its final results. The *intrenchments* would have offered little *aid* [in resisting] an organized army advancing with the flush of recent, and confidence of renewed victory."[16]

But the fact remains that the Confederates did not push forward any organized force in the wake of McDowell's rout. Davis, Beauregard, and even Johnston were to agonize long and exhaust much ink in quibbling about the lost opportunity. The Confederate chief executive supposedly penned a letter to pro-Confederate sympathizers in Maryland urging them to hold fast, suppress rioting in Baltimore until his army could cross the lower Potomac and advance through southern Maryland to Annapolis. Then, having two approaches to the Yankee capital closed, Baltimoreans might rise up and burn the bridges and completely surround Washington. But nothing came of the scheme, and there is question as to even the missive's authorship. More directly to capturing Washington after First Manassas, the southern military leadership remained obdurate. Beauregard was particularly petulant about lack of support for his notions of an offensive. But the Manassas army regrouped, licked its battle wounds, and celebrated its victory. Meanwhile, the flotsam of the Union army straggled back into the Washington area, pelted by a pouring rain, undaunted by possibility of mob takeover of the capital, conscious only of a desire for rest and relief. Slowly, as no horsemen in gray appeared before the approaches to Long Bridge or the Aqueduct, order began to return to the streets of Washington and the heights at Arlington. Regiments like the First and Second New Jersey and George Sykes's regulars manned the ramparts on the Potomac, while Scott's orderlies sought to institute rendezvous where disintegrated regiments might rally, be fed, and reassemble. The scene just across the Potomac at Fort Runyon, through which all traffic passed across Long Bridge, was captured by a young New Yorker:

Morning dawned on the scene. We should hardly have known our usually quiet little fort, for everywhere within and without were grouped around their colors the broken cohorts of the Union. All the tents were full of sleeping men, not of the Twenty-First, for no one of them slept. All were busy in various ways, some caring for the wounded, details were preparing the heavy guns for action, carrying shot and shell from the magazines, and in sailor phrase, "clearing for action," for all expected that the rebel army would soon knock at the portals of Washington, and we were determined that they should not want a welcome.[17]

[54]

Lincoln, at the Executive Mansion, had commenced, meanwhile, to grapple with rebuilding the shattered hopes of victory. But no higher than seventh on a rating of nine was the priority given to reorganizing "the forces late before Manassas" as the Chief Executive's list of July 23 pointedly termed them. Lincoln cited the needs of other theaters, and of maintaining the blockade, and he mentioned the need to rush forward new volunteer units as well as to dismiss the inept and inadequate three-months forces. Four days later he declared: "When the foregoing shall have been substantially attended too—let Manassas junction (or some point on one or other of the railroads near it); and Strasburg, be seized, and permanently held, with an open line from Washington to Manassas; and an [sic] open line from Harpers Ferry to Strasburg—the military men to find the way of doing these." The last phrase was crucial; the Union star in western Virginia, Major General George B. McClellan, was called to Washington to accomplish the task.[18]

When McClellan assumed command of forces around Washington on July 27, the situation on the Potomac was quite uncertain. The thirty-four year old Ohioan later recalled: "I found no army to command—a mere collection of regiments cowering on the banks of the Potomac, some perfectly raw, others dispirited by the recent defeat. . . . The city was almost in condition to have been taken by a dash of a regiment of cavalry." He reported finding 50,000 infantry, less than 1,000 cavalry, and 650 artillerymen organized into nine imperfect batteries of thirty pieces. McDowell's brigade organization still prevailed among the units in Virginia, with troops positioned near Forts Corcoran, Runyon, and Ellsworth, as well as at Arlington, Roach's and Cole's mills, and a detachment at the Episcopal Theological Seminary. But there were no troops south of Hunting Creek, and many regiments were encamped on low bottom land near the river—scarcely the best positions

[55]

for defending the long line from Fort Corcoran to Alexandria. On the Maryland side of the Potomac, two regiments stood guard on the heights above Chain Bridge—but they were not under unified command. The important Tennallytown road (among others), was not picketed; camps were not located with regard to defense or instruction; and there was no brigade organization in this sector. In McClellan's view:

> There was nothing to prevent the enemy shelling the city from heights, within easy range, which could be occupied by a hostile column almost without resistence. Many soldiers had deserted and the streets of Washington were crowded with straggling officers and men, absent from their stations without authority, whose behavior indicated the general want of discipline and organization.[19]

Such sentiments were also echoed by former Attorney General Edwin M. Stanton, William ("Bull Run") Russell of the London *Times,* Walt Whitman, and army spokesmen such as Colonel William T. Sherman. But dispatches in the *Official Records* showed staff officers dampening the news of disaster for a barometric public, rushing about in an effort to reconstitute McDowell's forces, and preparing to resist any threat mounted by the Confederates. Meanwhile Congress met complacently enough on July 22; the Senate entertained measures concerning the tariff, while the House of Representatives addressed itself to payment of recently deceased Senator Stephen A. Douglas's salary to his widow as well as to the first and second readings of a bill about a Pacific railroad. The only official mention of Bull Run at the Capitol was a resolution calling on the people for their support in the wake of the disaster although, of course, Congress promptly voted for additional troops.[20]

Actually, what McClellan found at Washington in late July were the disassembled bricks with which to forge a structure—the men, rudiments of organization, and the shame of defeat. It was his job to transform these ingredients into a sword and shield for the capital. Among the bricks wanting only mortar and design were the nascent outlines of a system of fortifications for Washington. The works constructed south of the Potomac in the spring and early summer "were far from constituting a defensive system which would enable an inferior force to hold the long line from Alexandria to Georgetown or even to secure the heights of Arlington." McClellan termed them mere ". . . tetes-de-pont," and said, "it is probable that we owe our exemption from real disaster which might have flowed from the defeat of Bull Run—the loss to the enemy of the real fruits of his victory—to the works previously built . . . and an exaggerated idea on his part of their efficiency as a defensive line."[21] Perhaps too much credit has been accorded McClellan for fortifying Washington. McDowell's contribution should not be minimized—isolated posts they might have been, those forts named Corcoran, Runyon, Albany, Ellsworth, Bennett, and Haggerty, but they were also rallying points after Bull Run. It was to McClellan's credit that they were transformed into a truly defensive system, from which a field army could maneuver in the traditional European manner.

The House of Representatives had resolved early in July that the secretary of war should furnish plans and estimates for the completion of a chain of defenses to guard Washington from attack from the south and also report on the expediency of constructing fortifications north of the Potomac. Undismayed by the large circumference of the city, McClellan blithely endorsed proposals for a system of forty-eight forts, lunettes, redoubts, and batteries, mounting three hundred guns.[22] In August, he ordered Major John G. Barnard, a quiet, middle-aged regular engineer officer, and quite deaf, to construct the system. Thus, to this efficient officer—the true

BARNARD—FATHER OF THE DEFENSES OF WASHINGTON
(National Archives and Records Administration, Washington, D.C.)

"father" of the defenses of Washington—passed a duty which over the next four years of war became increasingly frustrating, expensive, and to a large extent unappreciated, either then or now.

Barnard felt that there was no time to prepare "elaborate plans or detailed estimates," but he and his engineer staff began to improvise defensive arrangements and construct them as rapidly as possible using the pool of available manpower in the area—soldiers and hired civilian laborers. Attention was at once given to completion and perfection of the position on the heights at Arlington. Initial redoubts and forts were placed to protect sensitive points, especially roads. Then, as the industrious engineers found time, additional works were built to fill weak, unguarded spaces.

The stern law of military necessity governed possession of the land for the fort sites. Lines of rifle trenches, massive earthworks and military roads were eventually located with scant regard to cultivated fields, orchards, dwellings, or even churches. Local property owners howled in protest, but military authorities felt the interests of "national security" dictated such action. With sites properly selected, the fort construction was then begun in earnest. The process of construction must have been a fascinating spectacle. One observer from the Seventy-ninth New York "Highlanders" described the process of felling trees for the forts:

It was an interesting sight to witness the simultaneous falling of a whole hill-side of timber; the choppers would begin at the foot of the hill, the line extending for perhaps a mile, and cut only part way through the tree, and in this way work up to the crest, leaving the top row so that a single blow would bring down the tree— then, when all was ready, the bugle would sound as a signal, and the last stroke of the axe be given, which brought down the top row; these falling on those below would bring them down, and like the billow on the surface of the ocean, the forest would fall with a crash like mighty thunder.[23]

The descriptive New Yorker quickly added that work on the defenses "was the hardest kind of manual labor; spades were trumps and every man held a full hand." Indeed it was hard work, for the main forts, placed nearly one-half mile apart, were constructed with parapets twelve to eighteen feet thick on exposed fronts. Surrounding each work was an abatis of cut trees, entwined and placed with branches pointed away from the line of defenses. Barnard's people meticulously based their work on D. H. Mahan's *Treatise on Field Fortification.*[24]

Alexandria's defenses, as well as those of Arlington, also concerned military authorities. This Virginia town had now become a valuable supply base, and the defense line south of the river was extended to cover it. At the time, however, no continuous line of rifle trenches connected the separate posts. There were many open intervals in the line, which stretched from Fort Corcoran near the Potomac through a chain of lunettes (Forts DeKalb, Woodbury, Cass, Tillinghast, and Craig) to Fort Albany, one mile beyond Fort Runyon. Forts Blenker and Richardson extended the line beyond Albany (with Fort Scott as a reserve position on the heights near the mouth of Four Mile Run) and linked with Forts Worth and Ward on the ridge occupied by the seminary behind Alexandria. Late in the summer a force occupied the high ground south of Hunting Creek and built Fort Lyon in this area. To the northwest, near Chain Bridge, an isolated defense position covering the District side of the bridge, Batteries Martin Scott and Vermont were erected in addition to bridge barricades.

Engineers had also surveyed the topography of the northern approaches to Washington in May and June but had not considered the construction of actual works. Now, with low water in the Potomac, there was insufficient time for study, for "there was apprehension that the enemy might cross the Potomac and attack on this side." The first step lay in securing the roads leading into the city. In August, Penn-

CAMP OF THIRTY-FOURTH MASSACHUSETTS NEAR FORT LYON
(Loyal Legion Collection, US Army Military History Institute, Carlisle Barracks)

sylvania troops began a work which was to bear that state's name. It was located atop the heights at Tennallytown, whence its guns could sweep the intersection of River road, Rockville pike, and a connecting road to Brookville road. Lieutenant Colonel William Dixon of the Sixth Pennsylvania Reserves (Thirty-Fifth Pennsylvania) wrote his wife on September 6, 1861 that the fort of eleven guns was about finished and regarded as one "of the strongest works about Washington City." A. S. Brey of Company H, Third Pennsylvania Reserves (Thirty-Second Pennsylvania) noted a few days before that the troops thought nothing of devastating the locale to build this fort; "we cut down orchards with fine apple and peach trees with fine peaches and also some large corn fields," he recounted to his brother, and "we have destroyed two houses that were in our way to build the battery." At the same time, Massachusetts units began a fort named for their home state as well as adjacent works Fort Slocum and Totten, all of which were designed to block hostile passage in the general vicinity of the Seventh Street road. Farther to the east, Fort Lincoln was built to guard the turnpike and railroad to Baltimore. Before the end of the year, work was well along on Forts Saratoga, Bunker Hill, Gaines, De Russy, Slemmer, and Thayer—all designed to fill the gaps and constitute a chain of defense across the northern boundary of the District of Columbia.[25]

Barnard and his small coterie of engineers also built massive field works and auxiliary batteries on the high ridge east of the Anacostia or Eastern Branch of the Potomac. The first idea for fortifications on that side included only the protection of debouches from the Navy Yard Bridge and Benning's Bridge, and the occupation of the high ground overlooking the first structure. But, from Fort Stanton, begun during August, the system expanded to pass from Fort Mahan at the northern end successively through Meigs, Dupont, Davis, Baker, Wagner to Stanton, and thence through Battery Ricketts, Forts Snyder and Carroll, ending at Fort Greble nearly opposite Alexandria. Stuart O. Lincoln wrote a friend in December that his unit, encamped "one square above the Navy Yard" provided details of one hundred men day and night to complete a nearby fort just across the Anacostia. The thirty-two forts in the defenses of Washington officially received names at the end of September. By winter, with the inclusion of additional works, such as several unconnected redoubts covering the "receiving reservoir" of the Aqueduct—the city's water supply—the engineers could point with some pride to an array of forty-eight works encircling the city. They cost $344,053.46, or over $7,000 per work. Still, the engineer officers, seldom more than a dozen at any given time, had defied terrain, weather, temperamental volunteer officers, and soldier laborers. Thirty-seven miles of fortifications had been built in eight months—over half of the forts during the last six months of 1861. But in the period after Bull Run Union officials were probably too busy to worry about statistics in the face of repeated threats from the Confederates.[26]

While the engineers and laborers worked on forts, McClellan's principal commanders reorganized and trained the fighting forces. Provost Marshal Colonel A. J. Porter and his small guard of regulars swept Washington bars and streets free of stragglers. Newly arriving units of volunteers were formed into provisional brigades and placed in suburban camps of instruction. Artillerymen went under the control and direction of Brigadier General W. F. Barry, chief of artillery, while the chief of cavalry, Brigadier General George Stoneman, took charge of the mounted units. When regiments were in proper condition for transfer to the commands across the Potomac, they were then assigned to brigades serving there. McClellan set up brigades of four regiments each and later grouped these into divisions. He recognized that there were few officers in the army who knew how to command any more than three brigades; as yet he created no corps organization. Only following such basic reorganization could the Union high command again confront the strategic issue.[27]

McClellan had submitted a plan within a week of assuming command. It was offered in response to Lincoln's request. It was hastily prepared but "carefully considered," and, while quite similar in essence, it nevertheless contradicted the basic assumptions of Scott's so-called "Anaconda" scheme. McClellan wanted to subordinate everything to operations in the Virginia sector, while seaborne expeditions were to seize Confederate sea coast fortifications and capture southern ports. Although Washington would require only 20,000 men for a garrison, the young general estimated that 273,000 men would be needed in Virginia alone, for "shall we crush the rebellion at one blow, terminate the war in one campaign, or shall we leave it as a legacy for our descendants?"[28]

Lincoln's reaction remains unknown; much less so that of Scott. By early August the two generals were at loggerheads; Lincoln having intervened to prevent Scott's resignation. Still, in the end, McClellan gained more control. On August 20, his command was enlarged, contrary to Scott's wishes, to include the Shenandoah valley, Maryland, and Delaware, and its name was changed to the Army of the Potomac. Underlying the continued bickering between Scott and McClellan was the central issue of Washington's protection. Scott simply discounted the young warrior's quickly formed conviction that the capital was in imminent danger of attack and capture by the Confederates. "If Beauregard does not attack tonight," McClellan wrote to his wife on August 8, "I shall look upon it as a dispensation of Providence. He ought to do it." Scott was somewhat less feverish; after all, troops were pouring into the staging area, training was proceeding nicely, and the sagacious Scott was probably much less willing to believe rebel

FORT ETHAN ALLEN AND CAMP OF FOURTH NEW YORK HEAVY ARTILLERY
(soldier stationery, Defending Washington files, Fort Ward Park, Alexandria)

troop strength figures than McClellan. On the other hand, much of Scott's stance was simple petulance brought on in the wake of Bull Run and the advent of a young Caesar from the West to whom all, from the President to ordinary people, continually bowed and scraped.[29]

Indeed, the Confederates under Johnston had shown some offensive spirit as they moved closer to Washington in the late summer and fall, concentrating mainly in the neighborhood of Fairfax. Two corps now comprised the Confederate "Army of the Potomac," although supplies were short, sickness was rife among the uninitiated men, and the Confederate command settled into senseless bickering with Richmond over rank and supply questions. In addition, there was a general sense of frustration that the Confederate forces really had not pushed the routed Yankees and marched into Washington on the heels of McDowell's army.[30]

Confederate outposts dotted Munson's and Miner's hills, from which might be seen the spires of the capital. Such phenomena intimidated McClellan despite random efforts to disperse the Confederates. Johnston finally withdrew his exposed forward observers toward the end of September. Then came the revelation disclosed by the New York *Tribune* on the 29th:

> Munson's Hill will hereafter be the expression and measure of military false pretensions. There were no intrenchments there; there had been no cannon there. In the terrible batteries behind the hill there is but a derisive log, painted black, frowning upon the Federal army.[31]

McClellan's credibility immediately came into question. Why was he taking so long to redeem the loss at Bull Run? But as the summer breezes gave way to dusky browns and golds of a Virginia autumn, all the Union commander appeared capable of accomplishing was to quibble further

[66]

with Scott and to engage in a numbers game as to Confederate strength and his own requirements. He told his superiors: "As you are aware, all the information we have from spies, prisoners, etc., agrees in showing that the enemy have a force on the Potomac not less than 150,000 strong, well drilled and equipped, ably commanded, and strongly intrenched." Much of this was pure fantasy, as shown by modern scholars such as K.P. Williams who has contended "McClellan [had] 85,000 effectives for a march column, as contrasted with the 30,000 effective infantry, artillery, and cavalry that Johnston stated he had at that time [October 27] at Centreville." But "Little Mac" may have been more interested in political intrigue than in an offensive, waiving any chance to advance late in the year because plans could not be coordinated for a united Federal push both in the east and beyond the Appalachans, and because he was psychologically unprepared to effect the best defense for Washington by pursuing a vigorous offense. Then too, the Confederates did not cooperate by remaining inert.[32]

Johnston and Beauregard both hoped to take the offensive in the early autumn. But strategic reserves were lacking, and all Johnston could do was to placate his restless troops and plead with Davis to visit Army headquarters at Fairfax and consult with his principal military commanders in northern Virginia about the situation. Davis did so on October 1. Johnston, Beauregard, and G. W. Smith urged a concentration of forces in front of Washington, for they thought that there lay the main chance of victory for the Confederacy. To wait until spring would bring disaster, for the army was in its finest fighting order, and the enemy would only build up strength during the winter while sickness and desertion would reduce Confederate ranks. They estimated that 50,000 or 60,000 men would be required for their offensive.[33]

Davis quickly pointed out the lack of "seasoned" reinforcements available for any offensive. Foreign aid had not been forthcoming; "the whole country was demanding protection at his hands, and praying for arms and troops for defense." Davis essentially vetoed the concentration scheme, urging instead "certain partial operations" such as raids on outlying positions in order to encourage the people of the Confederacy. The Confederate president had the unenviable task of trying to bend states rights politicians, locally oriented citizenry, and inadequate and dispersed resources for the benefit of the whole nation. In the autumn of 1861 he was simply incapable of doing so. Thus, the result of the Fairfax conference caused the army to remain stalemated along its Potomac line.

Johnston and McClellan each remained afraid of his adversary's potential moves rather than his real moves. The Confederate position was not strong; it commanded no palisades along the river across from Washington; its outposts were in daily contact with a superior enemy. In fact, skirmishes occurred at Pohick Church, Potomac Creek, Bailey's Crossroads, Lewinsville, Seneca Creek, Point of Rocks, Freestone Point, Springfield Station, Ball's Bluff, Budd's Ferry, and Dranesville between August and the end of 1861. All such clashes were natural outgrowths of hesitant Federal probing operations. The Confederates occasionally struck back hard, as at Ball's Bluff on October 21 and Dranesville on December 20. Neither of these battles redounded to the credit of the Federal army—Ball's Bluff in fact spawned the notorious Congressional Committee on the Conduct of the War. But, in retrospect, those bloodlettings tested portions of the army being reconstructed by McClellan and partially offset the appearance that the young general was reluctant to conduct any active campaigning.[34]

Even more troublesome were the events of mid-October lower down on the Potomac. The Confederates had constructed river batteries along the Potomac below the Occoquon beginning in September. Freestone Point, Cockpit Point, Shipping Point, and Evansport (site of the modern Marine Corps base at Quantico), all became locations of powerful earthworks and heavy ordnance. Each position dominated a wide sweep of river, and each had backup positions on the hills rising 60 to 100 feet above the shoreline where more artillery could be positioned. Working secretly behind a screen of trees along the banks of the river, the Confederates mounted 32- and 42-pdr. guns, a 9-in. Dahlgren, and an English fabricated Armstrong cannon firing a 135-pound projectile. At least seven such batteries, each mounting four or more guns, with more battery positions to their rear, dotted the landscape. The works were redans, or V-shaped works of crenelated trace to accommodate guns in embrasure, with one face of the V bearing upriver, the other downstream. As early as September 25, the Federal gunboats *Jacob Bell, Seminole,* and *Valley City* spotted and engaged several of the batteries, but to no conclusion.[35]

In essence, the Potomac was closed to normal traffic and Washington had become "the only city in the country really blockaded."[36] The issue came to a peak in mid-October when several large warships, having been outfitted at Washington Navy Yard, attempted to run downriver en route to Flag Officer S. F. Dupont's expedition to Port Royal, South Carolina. The passage of the *Pocahontas, Seminole,* and *Pawnee* on October 15 and 16 received vigorous protest from the Confederate shore batteries. Each ship succeeded in passing the batteries, but the heavy fire convinced Commander Thomas T. Craven of the Potomac Flotilla that his small riverine craft had lost effective control of the stream. He told Secretary of the Navy Welles on October 25: "The Potomac is now so far obstructed that it is no longer used by the army for the transportation of supplies, and the sole dependence for that purpose and for the supplies of this city is limited to the railroad alone. . . ." Moreover, even Dahlgren at the navy yard felt constrained to reinforce Craven's opinion, going so far as to state that twenty-five to thirty miles of the Potomac lay open to Confederate exploitation, both for trade and blockade purposes. Union authorities reacted quickly. The army command feared that the presence of large numbers of Confederate infantry near the river batteries betokened an attempted invasion of southern Maryland. Therefore, McClellan sent the division of Brigadier General Joseph Hooker with three batteries of field artillery to occupy Prince Georges and Charles counties as far as Port Tobacco. Hooker sent detachments to the landings such as Budd's Ferry and positioned field guns opposite the Confederate batteries. But the Federals attempted neither to cross the river and capture those batteries nor to suppress them by artillery barrage from the Maryland shore.

Frankly, Washington would remain a blockaded city from October 1861 until the following spring, as far as the Potomac river access route was concerned. Higher prices for food and fuel for the civilian populace, short forage supplies for the army's animals and a complete shutdown of any offensive plans for McClellan's army. Moreover, it was humiliating that the capital of the Union was beleaguered. Only the Baltimore and Ohio railroad would provide a precarious lifeline from the north that winter. Here then would have been the auspicious time for some rising in Baltimore to shut down the rail link. But, the moment had passed, the Monument City lay under tight Federal rule, and the Confederacy missed a golden opportunity to capture Washington, not by military attack, but by starvation.[37]

Nevertheless, by this time Johnston had become worried about Federal intentions. He decided to pull his dispersed land forces into a more compact defensive position, and on October 19, the Confederates slipped back to a triangular enclave with its apex resting on the heights at Centreville. Below Alexandria the Confederate position on the river was shielded from

Union forces by the Occoquon, while northward near Leesburg, Brigadier General Nathan Evans' contingent guarded the other flank. As winter approached, the war in northern Virginia appeared to be a standoff.

On the Federal side, seven divisions of 70,000 men paraded before Lincoln, McClellan, and prominent politicians on November 20 at Bailey's crossroads. J. E. Morgan of Company B, Fifth Pennsylvania Reserves (Thirty-fourth Pennsylvania), wrote a friend back home in Northumberland, Pennsylvania that "the rebels had a view as well as we had" of the proceedings and "many of our men thought that we were going to fight that day as every man was prepared with 40 rounds of cartridges with a sufficient number of caps." But, nothing untoward occurred; both armies were content to "observe one another." Winfield Scott was gone, having been forced into retirement on November 1, and somehow Washington no longer seemed to be in quite the danger of July 22. But, as one student of the war has aptly observed: "Everywhere, except about Washington, Northern armies were on the stir with a measure of success. But nothing had been done to atone for Bull Run; nothing had even been done to make up for the humiliation of Munson's Hill."[38]

The worst suspicions of citizens North and South were confirmed as the first touch of winter came in December. North of the Potomac, Washington lounged despondent and indifferent as confidence in the Lincoln administration wavered under continued inaction. The threat of war with Great Britain was in the air in the wake of U.S. naval seizure of Confederate commissioners to Great Britain and France aboard the British mail steamer *Trent*. Then too, the President had asked McClellan on the first of the month ". . . how long it would require to actually get in motion?" The general replied dutifully on December 10 that by mid-month, or Christmas at the very latest, he could send 106,000 men of the Army of the Potomac against the enemy. But Lincoln's

[71]

strategic plan—included with the questions—received no answer or comment from McClellan. The President proposed a two-pronged movement with one attack concentrated against Centreville and the second as a flank assault via land and water across the Occoquon to catch Johnston's forces in a pincer and break the Confederate stranglehold on the control of the river. Apparently the military chieftain did not think well of the Chief Executive's amateurish attempts to devise strategy. In any event, by December 11, communiques were going out from army headquarters directing the Federal forces into winter quarters.[39]

Similarly Johnston's forces were also preparing their winter encampments. Richmond authorities had been slow to supply the forces in northern Virginia with portable sawmills and other equipment even though Johnston requested support as early as October. Still concerned with McClellan's overwhelming buildup, the Confederate command at Centreville hoped for one more victory in the wake of Bull Run and Balls Bluff but hesitated to undertake an offensive against the Union behemoth. The boredom of a winter encampment soon descended on the raw red earthworks stretching from Manassas to Centreville. Drill in the snow, guard mounts, letter writing, cards, and checkers became the lot of Johnny Reb—along with the deadly measles and mumps which ravaged an army unused to war in the winter. As 1861 closed, both sides in northern Virginia had gained victory; both had suffered a setback.

McClellan had certainly not redeemed the disaster at Bull Run. Still, his reorganization of the defeated eastern field army, the construction of the earthen forts and the mounting of their heavy ordnance; the restitution of morale and fighting spirit in the Sword of the Union—all might be counted as a victory of sorts by the Lincoln government. Senator Preston King reflected the thoughts of many of his Congressional colleagues when Chief Engineer Bernard asked for an additional

$150,000 for "completing the defenses of Washington" on December 7. To King, ". . . I would not expend an additional cent on the fortifications of Washington. In my opinion, the best defense for Washington is the destruction of our enemies where they can be found—at a distance from Washington."[40] Obviously, what most of the north wanted was an unsheathing of the Sword as well as a burnishing of the Shield.

Meanwhile, at Centreville, the brilliant victory by arms on the Manassas plains in July had not been followed up by ultimate capture of Washington and dispersion of the hated Lincoln regime. Still, Confederate arms had been sustained, the thought of Southern independence nurtured, and the Confederate army in the Old Dominion remained a sword in being, sharply honed, and pointed directly at the heart of Federal power. The issue in the Potomac region was left unresolved as the divided nation faced its first wartime Christmas and New Year. In Washington City, moreover, festal boards were decidedly sparse that holiday season thanks to the Confederate blockade of the river.

CHAPTER FOUR

Watchfires of a
Hundred Circling Camps

Crossing the Long Bridge over the Potomac was a crossing of the Rubicon for many young soldiers in blue. Some would live to recross the river and return to their homes in the north; others would end in graves beneath southern soil. But for all it was a transition, between boy and manhood, between home and the world writ large, between the flush of first enlistment and the realities of the battlefield. Countless thousands matured on the banks of the Potomac as they trained and guarded Washington during the autumn and winter after Bull Run.

Arrival in the theater of war was usually accompanied by confusion, lost baggage, and endless countermarching, until at last a regimental commander located some knowledgeable staff officer who could direct his unit to its proper position within the great encampment encircling Washington. Regimental histories abound with glowing tales of sore backs but happy hearts as the young volunteers received their baptism to camp life. Mosquitoes, ubiquitous "graybacks" or lice, throat-choking dust and monotonous drill, as well as the hard pioneer work of constructing camp and fort, symbolized this crucial phase in the buildup of an army. It was much the same for the Confederates on the Centerville line. Taken together, the objective for both armies was Washington—either its protection or capture. But to the young soldiers in training, the immediate issue was more one of transition and hardening, a process of education in the art of war.

One of the first sights for the young Federals when alighting from the Long Bridge was the abandoned Arlington house looming from the hill above them like some aging strumpet, since ". . . everything fades where armies camp, and the old mansion was looking somewhat soiled."[1] The grounds of Lee's plantation were soon converted to campsites, and later arrivals had to search farther out in neighboring Virginia for suitable locations. The experience of the Twenty-second Massachusetts may have been typical, when it encamped on Hall's Hill northwest of Ball's Crossroads. The unit historian recalled:

It was a round top, sloping in all directions from the flagstaff which was planted in front of the centre of the line. The camp faced the west, the 'line' running north and south, with three Sibley tents on each side of the company streets for the men, with two wall-tents for the company officers, facing down the company streets, a line of cook-houses behind the officers' tents, and the staff and other tents disposed in proper position at the rear. An ample parade-ground for company and battalion drills was afforded inside the regimental guard-line. A fine stream of water ran along the base of the hill, affording water for cooking and bathing. The supply was re-enforced by wells, dug by the soldiers, and carefully guarded to secure purity.[2]

Such scenes were repeated throughout the Washington area. New Yorkers near Fort Lyon, south of Alexandria, cut down the magnificent oaks on Spring Bank, George Mason's estate located one mile beyond Hunting Creek, in order to give firing space for the artillery. The Fourth Michigan on Meridian Hill, the Twelfth Pennsylvania at Tennallytown, the Tenth Massachusetts at Brightwood, as well as the Eleventh Massachusetts near Bladensburg—all north of the river— reenacted the scene on other fronts. The campsites were literally carved out of the timberclad countryside. Several commentators deplored such "ecological" destruction and graphically described the ten-man details which went out daily from each company, equipped with axes "to level the old monarchs of the hills, in order to make room for the new reign of the 'grim-visaged.' " A New Yorker from the Twenty-First Regiment noted: "It was a sad necessity that thus compelled the spoiling of nature's fairest handiwork and stripped the beautiful hills of their green robes,—but so it must be." Still another son of the Empire State summarized the situation: "I remember to have watched from our encampment, the disappearance of these forests, and as giant after giant was seen to fall along the edge of the woods, the forest seemed to melt away and disappear as snow gradually dissolves from the hillsides in the springtime."[3]

Most of the duty at this stage was routine drill and training in order to mold fighting units from motley contingents. Close-order manual, regimental and brigade exercises, manual of arms, assignment to picket posts and guard mounts in the fortifications, exacting inspections of equipment and persons, as well as intermittent target practice filled the lives of New England and Mid-Atlantic units. One Confederate drily observed: "The enemy wasted numberless charges of powder and ball at target practice near Arlington Heights, while we were in the vicinity, until their noise became annoying."[4] Evening schools were established in some regiments; two a week under the supervision of the regimental commander, for the instruction of commissioned officers in battalion and brigade drill, in the making of returns and in comprehension of Army rules and regulations. Similarly, noncommissioned officers received nightly instruction from officers in company and battalion drill and guard duty. Hardee's or Casey's *Tactics* and the *Army Regulations* were the textbooks.[5]

Lighter moments intermingled with the sober ones— receipt of state flags, "guard running" when many men managed to escape to the city under cover of night and return without detection before reveille, and upset stomachs caused by supplemental diets of sutler's lemonade, beer, or cider, pie, watermelon, strawberries, and cucumbers. Sudden catastrophes to well-pitched tents battered by thunderstorms mixed with executions of comrades for desertion and branding or flogging for lesser crimes. The schedule of the First Connecticut Heavy Artillery may have closely approximated the norm for most of McClellan's regiments. Their hours of duty were noted in regimental orders Number 4, September 29, 1861:[6]

Reveille at sunrise	First Sergeant's call, 12
Breakfast immediately after	Dinner at 12:30
Police Call at 6:45	Drill from 3:30
Surgeon's call at 7	Dress parade half an hour
Drill from 7:45-8 to 9:30	before sundown
Guard Mounting, 10	Tatoo, 9
	Taps, 9:30

Smallpox, measles, or some other epidemic disease occasionally ravaged the ranks. Vaccination was primitive and hygiene depended upon the sophistication and enlightenment of a particular regimental surgeon. As the unit historian of the Sixteenth New York recalled about the campsite near Fort Lyon: "The long hours of work, the constant vigil, and the low grounds on Hunting Creek produced much sickness, and numerous fatal cases of typhoid fever and long suffering occurred during the Fall and Winter." But the presence of two women nurses, Mrs. Solyman Merrick and Miss Helen Wolcott, apparently helped to improve conditions of Massachusetts troops on the Seventh Street road near Fort Massachusetts.[7]

One device which armies have employed since time immemorial to deter disease was good hard work. Certainly the necessity of constructing encampments, fortifications, and roads around Washington provided ample opportunity for developing physical fitness in the post-Bull Run army. Almost all of the regimental accounts of service on the Potomac in this period mention the pick and shovel details which alternately fatigued and exhilarated the young soldiers in blue. Details were ordered daily for building earthworks, digging trenches, and felling trees that might interfere with the line of fire of the fortress guns. The Pennsylvania Reserves completely built the square fort at Tenallytown, and the historian of the Sixteenth New York reported from Fort Lyon that: "The entire camp was surrounded with breastworks, and daily rumors of 'the enemy are advancing in large numbers,' compelled them to go to their daily work, rifle in hand, and to sleep at night upon their arms, ready to repel an attack at a moment's notice." Even sailors found useful employment at Fort Ellsworth, "in fact a complete frigate's crew—and they have been spending the past two months in putting the fort in complete order, just as sailors do, sodding, and whitewashing everything and planting evergreens, until the inside of the works is the very picture of neatness. . . ."[8]

A spokesman for the First Connecticut Heavy Artillery observed after that unit crossed to Virginia:

WASHINGTON'S DEFENDERS—BATTERY KEMBLE
(Charles J. House, *The First Maine Heavy Artillery, 1862-1865*)

The next morning found us drilling with pick and shovel, grubbing up the stumps at Fort Richardson where the engineers were at work; while a regiment of Michiganers, together with companies from several other camps in the locality, were employed in clearing the grounds here and at Fort Scott. But we soon relieved the other companies and had things all to ourselves. The work of clearing the grounds around Fort Richardson continued until we had been over fully ten acres of what had been Virginia forest, but when our work was completed the ground was as smooth as a hall floor, and then the company streets were laid out and arranged very much after the manner of a well laid out flower garden.[9]

One Bay State soldier concisely reported that "the trees were cut about three feet from the ground, and all made to fall with their branches toward the enemy." Such abatis surrounded the forts and lay across roadways. Since the work occupied many days and provided a great change from incessant drilling, "our men took to it as to a pastime." Still, "the appearance of thousands of dead trees all lying in the same direction added greatly to the desolate looks of this war afflicted vicinity."[10] Added to the devastation of the land were various demoralizing effects upon the local populace. Construction of winter camps consumed more timber (for tent bases, floors, and cabins), and orchards, dwellings, and even churches often fell before the cause of military necessity. In one perhaps apocryphal story the house of a free Negro, Elizabeth Thomas, was torn down when Fort Massachusetts was built and the cellar enlarged for the western magazine. Aunt Betty (as she was called) remembered later:

The soldiers camped here at this time were mostly German. I could not understand them, not even the officers, but when they began taking out my furniture and tearing down our house, I understood. In the evening I was sitting under the sycamore tree—my only house—with what furniture I had left around me. I was crying, as was my six-months old child, which I had in my arms, when a tall slender man, dressed in black, came up and said to me: 'It is hard, but you shall reap a great reward.' It was President Lincoln.[11]

[80]

Apparently the Union soldiers received more work than many had bargained for at the time of enlistment. It may have been only later that regimental chroniclers such as those of the First Connecticut Heavy Artillery could wax poetic about the final product of their exertions: 'On this side are Fort Albany . . . and Scott. As we turn toward the sunset, others rise on every side. Every hill is covered with an earthwork or crested with a camp. The plains in all directions are snowed on with tents. The hills beyond Fort Blenker and about the Fairfax Seminary are occupied by Franklin's troops. Seldom does it fall to one to see so vast a military spectacle as Washington and the adjacent country presented last winter.''

Most of this "military spectacle" came together magnificently during the mass parades and reviews which symbolized so much of McClellan's effort to instill pride and élan in the body of troops under his command. Various regimental and brigade parades were held, especially on holidays. "Sometimes a review takes place & then there is a full turnout of soldiers who represent the Penna. Reserve Corps commanded by Gen. McCall," wrote J. E. Morgan of the Fifth Pennsylvania Reserves to a friend at home in late November. "This is a fine spectacle, first the Artillery of Col. Campbell, 6 cannon, & then the Bucktail regiment after which the 5th is found &c. for 15 regiments, which would do considerable execution at the work of death," declared Morgan. After a line of battle was formed, he continued, and the General and his staff approached, "several volleys are fired with blank cartridges by the artillery after that the General and his Staff rides up and the proper salutation is given & returned while the band greets them with its flourishes as they pass down the line and soon we march off from the field to our homes." Just eight days before, Eben H. Gilley of Company F, First Massachusetts Heavy Artillery, wrote from Fort Runyon at the Virginia edge of the Long Bridge across the Potomac:

[81]

"Major General Blenker's division passed through the fort last night on their way to Washington to have a torchlight procession in honor of McClellan. We could see the fire works from the fort and hear the guns. It looked splendid. They returned about three oclock this morning. They had a great time as there was between two or three thousand in all and each one had a torch it was a splended night, the moon shone." Periodically, President Lincoln himself appeared at such reviews as in September when he had helped Governor Andrew Curtin present colors to his Pennsylvania troops at Tennallytown, north of Georgetown on the Washington City side of the river. These same troops were busily constructing Fort Pennsylvania (later re-named Reno) atop the highest hill in the District.[13]

McClellan as General-in-Chief often visited the various camps, accompanied on occasion by the President and cabinet officials. But at least one impromptu visit by the "high brass" proved embarrassing. One night a heavy carriage went across the Aqueduct bridge only to be stopped by alert pickets of the Third New York Artillery near Fort Corcoran. The whole party was sent under guard to Lieutenant Colonel Charles H. Stewart, whom they found diligently studying tactics in his tent. Stewart looked up to a testy comment: "Well, Colonel, you've captured the administration." Indeed, General McClellan, President Lincoln, and Secretary of State Seward all filed into Stewart's quarters. The New Yorker recovered quickly, stammered out something about strictness of orders, and sent the official party on to General Porter's headquarters which was their original destination.[14]

Perhaps the grand review of November 20 left the most indelible impression upon the memories of the Union soldiers in northern Virginia that fall. Taking place in the open fields between Munson's Hill and Bailey's Crossroads, the review included the units of McCall, McDowell, Heintzelman, Porter, Franklin, Smith and Blenker—ninety infantry regiments, twenty batteries numbering 100 pieces of field artillery, and nine cavalry regiments—approximately 100,000 men. McClellan appeared towards noon, accompanied by Lincoln and other distinguished personalities, and cheer after cheer rent the air as they rode down the line. The weather was mild, the roads in good condition, and the men evidenced excellent spirits. J. E. Morgan noted that "the rebels had a view as well as we had and since that they advanced their pickets who have since held their position," he heard that everybody in "the grand army" was prepared for a battle, but the flurry of activity passed without incident. The festivities completely fatigued the troops, but one enlisted man in the Twenty-Second Massachusetts recalled: "This is a day long to be remembered by thousands of people as one of the most eventful of their lives. Never before in this country has there been assembled together such an immense body of armed men as were reviewed to-day on the 'sacred soil' of Virginia."[15]

The repetitious quality of reviews naturally led some tongues to wag, and one Pennsylvanian complained: "When the Major or Brigadier General are favored with the visits of some particular friends, of course, a big review must be had. This is as necessary as dessert to a dinner. 'It is fine fun to the boys, but death to the frogs' as Mr. Aesop would say."[16] Still, the parades, as well as other training exercises and inspections, gave the soldiers a chance to see and assess their commanders—from noncoms and lieutenants to the general-in-chief. Allowing for the naivete of the times, the men in the ranks and junior officers whose impressions have survived expressed great confidence and respect for their superiors. No doubt the reviews contributed much to development of such feeling.

One Massachusetts soldier observed of his regimental commander: "A thorough tactician, with the bearing of a courageous soldier, he impressed the men with the idea that

[83]

he was a leader it was an honor to follow. No order of his was ever questioned, much less disobeyed, because every man in his command believed that the colonel would not make a mistake and always meant what he said.'' One of the "Mozarters" of the Fortieth New York noted: "Although we had a surfeit of reviews, inspections, drills and reconnoissances [sic], our indomitable Colonel was constantly studying some new method to increase our proficiency. He did not regard our education as completed, and was one of those who believed that a soldier's education could never be finished, hence his fertile brain was forever exercised, and who but he could have conjured up the novel idea of a sham battle."[17]

The long training period on the Potomac in late 1861 actually gave McClellan's men a superb opportunity to study and understand the frauds and charlatans masquerading as leaders. They admired fairness, concern for the men in the ranks, and realistic exercises, designed to mold an organized fighting machine. The historian of the Ninth Massachusetts appropriately described the difficulties in that regiment when its leadership proved unequal to the task. He wrote:

By judicious management one detail for fatigue duty under charge of an officer or two would have answered all purposes and relieved the regiment of much annoyance and friction, besides giving every one else a chance to attend to their personal and company affairs. This easy and proper method, however, would not suit our active sergeant-major at all. It would not impress the colonel and others with his untiring activity in pushing things around headquarters or show his subordinate non-commissioned officers his authority over them. The inoffensive man of fifty years who was adjutant at that time, moved about apparently paralyzed at the way his sergeant-major was rushing everything, and seemed satisfied that he was relieved of all care while he occasionally hobnobbed with other forces who were taking things easy.[18]

[84]

Of course, none of the soldiers could actually know how well either he or his unit might perform in combat until he actually witnessed the ardors of maneuvers and battle. Numerous reconnaissance operations and skirmishes took place during the winter of 1861-1862 and some units received their baptism in this type of experience at that time. From Budd's Ferry, opposite Quantico, upriver past Great Falls, Federal units conducted maneuvers designed to probe Confederate strength, to provide officers and men with the feel of campaigning, and, if nothing more, to decipher the terrain and road patterns. There were periodic upheavals in Alexandria, such as the February burning of the office of the pro-Confederate Alexandria *Gazette*, which necessitated the use of Federal troops in suppressing domestic riot. But the general bloodletting at this time came from the numerous skirmishes and picket fights which made a quasi-mockery of the slogan "All Quiet Along the Potomac."[19]

Two levels of combat activity took place along the Potomac during the fall and winter. The major actions such as Ball's Bluff and Dranesville hardly equaled the larger and better known battles of Manassas, Fredericksburg, or Gettysburg. Still, they were a cut above the more general picket skirmishes and minor, small-unit actions forming a second level of activity for blue and gray in this theater.

Most of the soldiers who recorded anything about the "battles" spent more time on the gory details of the dead and wounded (new to most of the volunteers), and less on the tactical maneuvers. Mention of prisoners, and captured equipment ("several of the Artillery-men are running around with secessh hats, over coats, pistols, belts, etc.") obviously made more of an impression on the men in the ranks than the fact that objectives went unachieved or general officers' reputations were ruined. The battle at Dranesville in December was dismissed briefly by a Pennsylvanian writing home:

[85]

Last Friday morning, the third Brigade under General Ord was sent out to Drainsville [sic] which is about fourteen miles from camp to capture a lot of forage in possession of some rebels. They had got to the town when they found some regiments of rebels laying in the woods with a masked battery in front of them. They left the buck-tail Regiment pass and when the ninth regiment got opposite they fired on them and then the fight began. They fought very desperate for an hour and by the time the first and our Brigade got up the fight was all over. We passed three rebels prisoners that our fellows took and they were mighty looking soldiers.[20]

This same observer had commented at even greater length several months before when his regiment had been exposed to a brisk artillery duel at Great Falls on the river. Perhaps the battles were becoming standard fare by the time winter snows supplanted fall colors in northern Virginia.

Sniping at one another by opposing pickets also became standard procedure at this stage. Nevertheless, some observers claimed that "soldiers on picket duty are not expected to fight." Indeed, much cordiality developed between the soldiers on both sides assigned to such duty as the war progressed. But early in the conflict the combination of cow bells and strange animal noises in the night, rainy or stormy weather, and loneliness engendered by the fear of sudden death away from comrades led to restless fingers on musket triggers as accompaniment to sentinel duty. A soldier of the Twenty-first New York appropriately summarized this type of fighting as it extended across the entire front of the Army of the Potomac whether at Pohick Church or Ball's Cross Roads. He observed that many young volunteers were "rash and venturesome," and exposed themselves so as to provoke a shot just for the fun of returning it. "Picket shooting is quite an ordinary occurrence," he said, "and so it must be until both armies are disciplined into a realization of the fact that merely *killing men* in this way, is *murder*, simply, and has no bearing on

[86]

the main result.'' He concluded ''the killing of one man, in cold blood, where the only object is the gratification of the destructive propensities of the assassin, or his desire to stain his hands with the blood of a fellow being that he may boast of the deed, is a miserable achievement.''[21]

While the battles and skirmishes enabled men and officers to train realistically, the campaigning such as it was also permitted Yankees from afar to gain impressions of the locale and its inhabitants. Regimental accounts tell of the slave cabins and mansions of the genteel. But they also say much about the northerners' fascination with new sights and experiences— the unsung ramifications of the Civil War. Among those sights, Washington City ranked high on the list of soldier impressions. The euphoric tones of Edward A. Walker of the First Connecticut Heavy Artillery more than amply praised the capital as it appeared in the eyes of its defenders:

> I remember it as we saw it first in the purple hues of autumn, — the deep red light of the setting sun glowing over the city, bringing out in bold relief the vast proportions of the Capitol, whose windows sparkled like gems, lighting up the majestic facade of the Treasury building, the unfinished shaft of the Washington monument, and the deep red feudal turrets of the Smithsonian Institute. Rising above a pile of buildings are the gables of the Post-office and Patent-office buildings. Down there on the right are the buildings of the navy-yard. Across that branch of the river, in deep light and shade, reminding one at this distance of some old medieval castle on the Danube, stands the Retreat.[22]

Only slightly less intriguing to the men in blue were Alexandria and Robert E. Lee's abandoned mansion at Arlington. One Pennsylvanian dismissed the old port town with the thought: ''Alexandria at this time was an old-fashioned city of several thousand inhabitants, most of whom were rank secessionists with decided aristocratic and old English tendencies, the very streets resounding with such royal names as

[87]

King, Prince, Princess, Queen, Duke, St. Asaph, Royal . . . indicating the antiquity of the town as well as the Tory sentiment which prompted such names." Nevertheless, W. H. Peckham of the Thirteenth New Hampshire thought ". . . of all the nasty looking holes that I ever saw Alexandria is the worst. I don't know a place in the North that begins to be so nasty & filthy." Similarly, one son of the Granite State reflected his abolitionist leanings after visiting Lee's mansion: "A visit to Arlington House, very fine, and to the mud-chinked, and mud-floored, mud-and-sticks huts of the slaves belonging to the estate, reveals at a glance both sides of the picture of slavery's curse, while the whipping-post nearby adds a bold stroke of color to the dark side."[23]

Some of the soldiers met local scions of old families in northern Virginia. Newton M. Curtis of the Sixteenth New York recalled that George Mason of Spring Bank (just south of Hunting Creek) "was of the old school, a man of culture and extensive reading, and of frigid dignity; he had been for many years the Chief Justice of the Court of Fairfax County, and the solemnity of his bearing comported with the dignity of judicial procedure in open court." Mason particularly disliked incursions from the Union soldiers, and he "was reduced to the greatest destitution in his later years, and lived to taste the bitterness of defeat which he bore as became a Mason, without asking for sympathy or yielding aught of his belief in the sovereignty of Virginia."[24]

Other representatives of "first families" such as Basil Hall (who owned the 327-acre farm and promontory known as "Halls Hill"), told Union soldiers: "I go in for the Union but I ain't no abolitionist, and any man of common sense will say that slavery is the very best thing for the South." The men in blue particularly enjoyed association with a large Quaker community and with other northerners who had been wooed to the area before the war by the promise of good farmland.

[88]

E. C. Gibbs (one of Mason's lesser neighbors whom the judge had told: "Never fear, when Virginia bonds are sold at a discount, all securities will be depreciated, and Federal securities will be the lowest of any") represented the Quaker meeting— "an industrious Union-loving people who abhored war, but were ever ready to care for our sick, supply us with fruits and vegetables and do all that was possible to promote our well-being."[25]

If most of official Washington was pleased to have the soldiery about the city, many of the local citizenry were not. Farmers on both sides of the river were hard hit, and at least one "Subscriber" to the Washington *Star* complained about the "undisciplined mob" which "take what they please and destroy what they do not want." He observed: "Our fruit trees have been stripped, our cornfields have been overrun and plucked, our cows milked, our fences torn down. Our potatoes are pulled up half-grown and useless, celery plants plucked up and strewn about the ground, young cabbages uselessly destroyed, and turnips carried off by the bushel." The writer cited the frustration of complaining to the officers who while civil did not think it was their own men. He wondered: "Are we to be abandoned to this lawless mob, or must we attempt to defend our lives and property with force of arms? The *Star's* editor pontificated that "The Government will pay when the legal proof of the injury, and that it was done by Government troops, may be made."[26]

Observations of local color formed but one facet of soldier entertainment in the camps around Washington after Bull Run. Diversion took various forms—enthusiastic receipt of jam, cookies, and socks from home, writing letters to loved ones, reading, and frequenting of sutlers' stores. For a time there was that crazy balloon of Professor Thaddeus Lowe to watch soaring over Fort Corcoran and drawing Confederate fire when on September 24 he directed Federal counterbattery fire in the vicinity of Falls Church.[27]

Games and recreation of a physical nature were not lacking either. One officer in the Twenty-second Massachusetts provided his regiment with a football and placed a checkerboard in every tent. As the unit historian recounted: "After dress parade, every pleasant day, the football would make its appearance on the parade-ground, and a lively game would be had, which had a good effect on the health and spirits of the men. After 'retreat', the candles would be lighted and the men would busy themselves with cards or checkers, telling stories, or singing." A spokesman in a sister regiment, the Seventh Massachusetts, observed that the evenings of early fall were spent playing checkers or chess, "some playing bluff straight, five-cent chips, or ten-cent straddle," and as much higher as the skill and wishes of the players required; while others studied tactics and army regulations, endeavoring to perfect themselves for the duties of higher positions in the service."[28]

Actually, the singing blended nicely with the religious fervor of the era, and just about every regiment erected a chapel tent (the Thirty-third New York collected $400 for such a purpose), agonized over temperance issues, or sang choruses of "Old Hundred." A schedule of divine services and activities of the First Connecticut Heavy Artillery best represented the scope of religious interest. "Some idea of the uses to which the chapel tent was put," claimed the unit historian, "may be obtained from the notices read at our first meeting in it on Sunday afternoon: Sunday evening, divine service; Tuesday evening, prayer and conferences meeting; Wednesday evening, singing-school and glee-club; Thursday evening, class-meeting; Friday evening, Bible-class lecture; Saturday evening, rehearsal of sacred music." In addition, the chapel tent was always open " . . . affording to such as cared to avail themselves of it an attractive place of resort from the crowded company tents."[29]

The Fortieth New York even found time to develop the "Mozart Drum Corps," and provided the basic support for a theatrical association. To the dismay of not a few ranking officers, the "Sedgwick's Brigade Lyceum" provided entertainments until the onset of the spring campaign. A typical program included ballads, minstrels, and "an amusing farce," "Number One Round the Corner." Stamping, smoking, and other sundry disturbances were prohibited, and "military men" were ordered to appear in full dress without side arms! Unfortunately, the enterprise did not prove financially profitable, and those who purchased stock ended up losing their entire investment.[30]

Holidays such as Thanksgiving, Christmas, and New Year's Day were particularly memorable occasions, with German regiments the merriest over lager beer; treats from home delighting all the soldiers; and on the first day of the new year, "according to a time-honored custom, the officers of the army, in full uniform, paid their respects to the President; and afterward the foreign ministers and their wives made their accustomed visit of ceremony to the Executive." Actually, according to the former commanding officer of the 104th Pennsylvania, war was not allowed to infringe on the gaieties of Washington—the White House levees were held as usual. He attended the first of the season on December 19, with Mrs. Lincoln doing the honors of the evening. He decided " . . . if to achieve success it requires a great crowd, squeezing and pushing, smashing of hoops and treading on tender dresses, all sorts of people in all sorts of costumes, and homely women with sharp shoulder-blades and low-necked dresses." Colonel W. H. H. Davis further noted the absence of form and ceremony as the Marine Band played delightful music from a vestibule. In the opinion of that representative American of his era, "It was made very apparent to my mind, that the President is the servant of the people, and that the house he lives in belongs to them."[31]

The first war winter on the Potomac, although generally mild and rainy, did produce the first snowball fighting between units as well as increased fraternization between pickets of the opposing armies. Moreover, the soldiers became increasingly opinionated concerning national events. Union victories at Roanoke Island, Mill Spring, and Forts Henry and Donelson caused massive celebration in the camps along the Potomac, and even a whiskey ration was passed around the ranks of the Twenty-second Massachusetts. Men like Colonel Davis expressed displeasure at the imprisonment of Brigadier General Charles P. Stone in the wake of the Ball's Bluff disaster. The Mason-Slidell incident was thoroughly discussed in the army, and "it was generally the opinion that England very wisely refrained from assuming a threatening attitude." Private Leo W. Faller of the Seventh Pennsylvania was less diplomatic when he wrote home:

> You want to know what we think of Jonny Bull coming over to fight us. Well I will tell you. If he come over here you need not look for me untill every Englishman is driven out of America for I would want nothing better than to fight John Bull for I never saw but one Englishman that I liked and that is Banes. But I do not want him to come untill we have settled the Rebels. Then let him come and then we will give hime what we gave him in 1776 and 1812 with a little extra.[32]

President Lincoln and his family tried to boost the spirits of the soldiers encamped around Washington. On January 9, 1862, he and Mrs. Lincoln attended a celebration with Regis De Tobriand's Fifty-Fifth New York—"the French regiment" at Fort Gaines near Tennallytown and delighted in that unit's regimental mess. Apparently the French cooks in the unit were noted around town for their cuisinary delights. Lincoln complimented the officers on the best meal that he had in Washington and told them that if their men could fight as well as they cooked, then the regiment might do very well in battle. Still, the nuances of camp life began to pall upon officers and men alike in time. One soldier of the Twenty-first New York commented in the autumn: " 'All quiet on the Potomac,' is still the gist of the daily telegraph reports, and we of the rank and file hardly know whether to laugh with the stay-at-homes, who always mock at what they do not understand, or to take dignified refuge in the belief that we *do* understand the delay, and that it is a necessary one."[33] Eben H. Gilley complained in early January from Fort Albany on the Arlington line about moving so frequently from fort to fort: "we cut a flag staff and had to move to Fort Runyon then we cut a one for that fort we had to move up here, I suppose when we get our barracks finished we shall have to move. . . ." But as the winter shadows lengthened more reflective soldiers took the stance of Chaplain Edward A. Walker of the First Connecticut Heavy Artillery about experiences on the Potomac:

> Looking back over the five months spent at Fort Richardson, the mind is confused with details that struggle for expression. We see them as in kaleidoscopic vision. Long lines of snow-white gloves, of glistening bayonets, of polished brass, and spotless uniforms, mixed up with carriage-loads of ladies, officers on horseback, flags and cannon-smoke; and with these, soberer bits of glass in the shape of sling-carts, statuary, and spread eagles; and again, stumps, picks, shovels, and the like, set off by mud and cold and wind; and these again relieved by gorgeous sunrises and sunsets, lovely days and nights, and the ever changing, ever charming views from the summit of the hill. Turn the glass, and again we have the same things in different combinations. But in every scene may be detected the vigilant eye of our commander scrutinizing everything, approving every soldierly act or trait, and punishing with rigor each minute offense against perfect military discipline.[34]

Perhaps these kind of thoughts led a poet to set down the words of "The Picket Guard," the second stanza of which particularly fit McClellan's army as it girded itself for the campaigns of 1862:

All quiet along the Potomac to-night
  Where the soldiers lie peacefully dreaming,
Their tents in the rays of the clear autumn moon,
  Or the light of the watch-fires are gleaming.
A tremulous sigh, as the gentle night wind
  Through the forest-leaves softly is creeping.
While stars up above with their glittering eyes
  Keep guard—for the army is sleeping.[35]

Just how effective was this army in the eyes of its commander? McClellan told the secretary of war on February 3, 1862:

> The capital is secure against attack; the extensive fortifications erected by the labor of our troops enable a small a garrison to hold it against a numerous army; the enemy have been held in check; the State of Maryland is securely in our possession; the detached counties of Virginia are again within the pale of our laws—and all apprehension of trouble in Delaware is at an end; the enemy are confined to the positions they occupied before the disaster of the 21st of July: more than all this, I have now under my command, a well drilled and reliable army, to which the destinies of the country may be confidently committed; this army is young and untried in battle—but it is animated by the highest spirit, and is capable of great deeds.[36]

Nevertheless, a few small clouds had already begun to appear on the horizon by early 1862. McClellan's euphoria was shared by neither his chief of artillery nor chief of engineers. Both brigadiers, W. F. Barry and J. G. Barnard, repeatedly enjoined the army commander to investigate the dilapidated fortifications north of the Potomac. Twenty-eight works were without garrisons beyond small guard units which changed daily. "Of course they have no idea of what is required to keep the armament or earthwork in condition . . . and . . . perform even their duties as guard very inefficiently," complained Barnard.

The engineer explained further that the ungarrisoned works mounted 200 guns but lacked ammunition in the absence of regularly assigned ordnance sergeants. Then too, local troops constantly pillaged the works for timber with which to floor tents and use as firewood. Only the Fourteenth Massachusetts and Fourth Connecticut seemed to be taking care of the fortifications in their charge. Writing on January 13, Barnard pointed out that: "I look upon the garrisoning of these works—that is, with artillerymen—as under all circumstances indispensable, and an absolutely necessary preliminary to any offensive operations of the Army."[37] Such a philosophy very quickly became the main tenet in the agreement by the Lincoln administration for sending McClellan on his waterborne attempt to take Richmond via the Peninsula.

Was McClellan simply overconfident? Apparently not, as he concluded: "That so much has been accomplished and such an army created, in so short a time, from nothing will hereafter be regarded as one of the highest glories of the administration and the nation." The winds of change began to stir as winter turned to spring in the country surrounding Washington.[38]

ARTILLERY PARK, WASHINGTON ARSENAL

The Civil War changed Washington from a sleepy southern city into a major command center and military supply depot for the Union armies as illustrated by this artillery park for Wiard guns.

(US Army Military History Institute)

CHAPTER FIVE

McClellan

Shield of the Union

The spring campaign of 1862 began as early as November of
the preceding year—at least in terms of planning and resulting
controversies which engrossed key military and civilian officials of the Lincoln administration. An autumn of fair skies,
dry roads, and procrastination by the general-in-chief did
little to quiet the ever-present voices of dissent. Even Joe
Johnston and the Confederate host at Centreville marvelled
at the Federal inaction. Historians have pointed to faulty intelligence reports, McClellan's search for perfectionism, and
various behind-the-scenes political intrigue as causes for the
delay. One eminent scholar simply concluded that Little Mac
"should have marched to Manassas, should have cleared

the Potomac, and should have forced the enemy out of Nor-folk."[1] Yet the inescapable fact remains that he did not do so, for whatever reasons, not the least of which may have been simply that subconsciously neither McClellan nor his inex-perienced officers felt prepared to cope with the immense machine which they had constructed in the suburbs of Washington, given the poor state of command and control, unsophisticated communications, and poorly understood con-cepts of logistics at this stage of the war. Over all hung the fear of another Bull Run and the real threat that this time the Confederates might march directly to Washington.

McClellan envisioned a bold, waterborne movement outflanking the Confederate position in northern Virginia. It would land at Urbana, a tiny hamlet near the mouth of the Rappahannock river, some fifty miles east of Richmond. This plan solved rather quickly the problem of bypassing the ma-jor Confederate forces astride the railroad at Manassas and occupying the water batteries blocking the Potomac. It would force evacuation of those positions without a fight. Advanced by the general-in-chief in conversations with Secretary of the Treasury Salmon Chase in November, and further refined following a reconnaissance by his chief engineer, McClellan's plan experienced predictable difficulties when confronted with Lincoln's abiding concern for the safety of the nation's capital. McClellan and J. G. Barnard calculated the need for 100,000 men as a covering force to protect Washington, but Lincoln advanced his own notion for dealing with rebel forces in nor-thern Virginia. He wanted a more direct approach to Johnston's Leesburg-Aquia line which might keep the main Federal force between the enemy and Washington. McClellan's sudden illness in December only prolonged the agony of indecision and impasse.[2]

Lincoln's dabblings with military planning came at a time when the *Trent* affair, political and financial problems of

[98]

the administration, and a stalemate across the war front from Virginia to Missouri all plagued the chief executive. Actually, his plan, as explained to McClellan in early December, interspersed boldness with naivete, Lincoln sought to use the Federal forces in Virginia in a two-pronged drive "to menace the enemy at Centreville" and strike directly down the road from Alexandria to Richmond across the Occoquan. The latter drive would be coordinated with a cross-Potomac landing of Federal forces from the Maryland and D.C. side of the river.

The objective of the Occoquan operation would be to move rapidly inland by road to Brentsville, thence to the Orange and Alexandria just south of its crossing over Broad Run. A strong cavalry force would strike ahead to "destroy the railroad bridges south and north of that point." In the president's view: "if the crossing of the Occoquan by those from above be resisted, those landing from the Potomac below to take the resisting force of the enemy in rear, or, if the landing from the Potomac be resisted, those crossing the Occoquan from above to take the resisting force in the rear." He concluded that both points could not be successfully defended at the same time by the Confederates. Still, if the Union force advancing on Centreville were to run into trouble, it should be prepared to retire slowly back to the fortifications before Washington. Similarly, the U.S. Navy was to be prepared to evacuate the survivors if the expedition failed in the Occoquan sector. McClellan apparently pigeonholed the president's memorandum, returning it on December 10 with slight pencil notations as to forces available for the scheme. It was at this point that he fell ill.

The month of January was filled with profitless meetings between Lincoln, radical congressmen, and various military officials—all in search of a policy. The mood of the country at this point regarding McClellan may have been summarized best (if rather indelicately), by his own engineer officer, Barnard, who wrote Senator John Sherman on January 6:

> If you were to 'count noses' among the officers of the A.P. [Army of the Potomac] whose opinions are worth anything, I believe you would find [many] who think and express the opinion that he must be a most stupendous failure. He showed himself incapable in the outset of appreciating & grasping his position by utterly failing to do anything—permitting the Potomac to be blockaded in face of his 250,000 men—Norfolk to be kept—until he lost the essential requisites to success—the confidence of the Administration and of the country. Who was George B. McClellan—a young man unknown to fame—that this whole country should wait for 2/3'd of a year for some stupendous thing which he would *ultimately do,* while the enemy in numbers vastly inferior was shutting us up in our very Capital! Bah! History records [few] such opportunities of *greatness offered*—and so stupendously (if I may use such a word) *lost;* and the country brought to the very verge of ruin by the failure.[3]

Still, McClellan refused to lift his veil of silence concerning his plans; Lincoln directed a general movement of all Union forces for February 22; both secretaries of war and navy plumbed for dispersal of the Confederates from the "blockade" of the Potomac; Radicals in Congress were unhappy, and the president finally yielded to the pressure. He promulgated Special Order Number 1 on January 31, which directed: "That all the disposable force of the Army of the Potomac, after providing safely for the defense of Washington, be formed into an expedition for the immediate object of seizing and occupying a point upon the railroad southwestward of what is known as Manassas Junction. . . ."[4]

An unhappy army commander immediately penned a lengthy explanation of why the president's plan was unfeasible and explained why his Urbanna idea made better sense, pointedly reminding Lincoln that his plan also guaranteed the safety of the capital. But, since the Confederate batteries ostensibly had closed the Potomac to large-scale Federal movements, McClellan's amphibious operation would have to be mounted from Annapolis. Lincoln correctly mirrored northern opinion in rejecting what might be construed as a retrograde movement—Federal troops would have to recross the Potomac—and the councils of war continued. Meanwhile, McClellan was alerted to the need for some show of activity. An abortive attempt to free the upper Potomac and end the threat to the Baltimore and Ohio railroad foundered on inept management—a simple thing, really, but someone miscalculated the size of canal boats which were supposed to pass from the Chesapeake and Ohio canal into the main river and form a pontoon bridge, but could not pass the locks.[5] Lincoln became thoroughly exasperated by the whole situation. February 22 passed without a major forward movement in Virginia and by early March the president was again drafting orders.

Lincoln warned McClellan of the political dangers attending further delay. Yet the army commander was facing other dangers, within his top command. Several of his senior division commanders thought little of the Urbana scheme, and they proceeded to tell him so in a meeting on March 7. Brushing aside pleadings from McClellan's chief of staff that the general faced ruin unless his subordinates stood unanimously in favor the plan, three of the division commanders—Sumner, McDowell, and Heintzelman as well as the chief engineer, Barnard, advocated a cross-Occoquan attack which could cut the rail communications behind Johnston's forces, while a second column struck straight for the Centreville-Manassas line. They refused to make the decision unanimous when the other seven division commanders voted to accept McClellan's scheme.

The minority group was unable to advance their plan when they met later with Lincoln, McClellan, and the secretary of war. Nonetheless, the chief executive remained vitally concerned for the capital's safety so long as Confederate guns commanded the Potomac channel. The next day Lincoln told the top army leaders that he had decided to send 50,000 men on to the Chesapeake as soon as possible to be followed by an additional 50,000 men if the Potomac batteries were reduced or the enemy began to withdraw his main force from Centreville. The minority dissent was not quieted and Heintzelman submitted a brief of the group's views to the president, yet, as he recalled: "The minority had no opportunity to explain their reasons for their vote. We were also asked our opinion of the propriety of leaving the batteries behind, on going South. No one considered it a military necessity to destroy them, but many thought it advisable. For the prestige of the thing we ought not to change our base of operations. There is no where we can gain what we lost at Bull run [sic], but here & I so said in the paper I handed the President."[6]

Meanwhile, Lincoln ordered a reorganization of the Army of the Potomac into four army corps (plus a fifth to be organized later), and he named as commanders certain generals more or less politically tied to the administration—McDowell, Sumner, Heintzelman, Erasmus D. Keyes, and Nathaniel P. Banks. In addition, the troops to be retained at Washington to defend that city were placed in charge of Brigadier General James Wadsworth, a wealthy Republican and sometime enemy of McClellan, who was designated "Military Governor of the District of Columbia."[7]

Perhaps more striking was Lincoln's General War Order Number 3 of March 8, for it related directly to the safety of Washington and affected McClellan's Peninsula campaign to no little degree. The chief executive stated bluntly that the army was to make no change in its base of operations "without leaving in and about Washington such a force as, in the opinion of the General-in-Chief and the commanders of army corps, shall leave said city entirely secure." Furthermore, no more than two corps or fifty thousand men were to be moved en route to a new base of operations until the navigation of the Potomac was opened from Washington to the Chesapeake, and the army and navy were directed to "cooperate in an immediate effort to capture the enemy's batteries" in that regard. Finally, all of these events were to transpire not later than March 18—ten days hence.[8]

McClellan's dismay at these orders was further compounded by his opponent's rapid evacuation of Manassas-Centreville on the following day. Johnston's army withdrew from the strong position on March 9 and took up a new line behind the protection of the Rappahannock. The Confederate commander had long anticipated the inherent danger of being outflanked by a rapid trans-Potomac attack by the Federals from lower Maryland or a direct assault via the Telegraph road in the Occoquan sector. The first days of March produced increased skirmishing by Heintzelman's division along the latter stream as well as heavier artillery bombardment from Hooker's men across the Potomac. There were additional indications that both Federal contingents were ready to cross the two streams in force. Johnston had discussed the matter with Davis and his cabinet in February, and all agreed to the planned withdrawal. While vast quantities of invaluable supplies and heavy ordnance were lost in the withdrawal, the Federals were completely baffled by the secrecy of the move, and at one sweep both Washington and the Potomac were freed from any direct Confederate threat. Then too, the Urbana plan was rendered irrelevant.[9]

Reaction in Washington was predictable. Where inactivity had formerly prevailed, now all was haste. Union contingents rushed from muddy camps via quagmire roads to view empty trenches, Quaker guns, and piles of smouldering bacon and other stores at Centreville and Manassas. Additional contingents rapidly crossed the Potomac and Occoquan to see what the Confederates had left behind at Evansport and Cockpit Point. One soldier described how "we was much gratified by seeing the proud old flag waving triumphantly over Cock Pit Battery where no more than an hour before Seseha reigned in all his boasted pride," and pointed out that five large cannon had been taken off that battery while "the Gun Boats then proceeded on down the river taking one battery after another untill they have cleared the Potomac entirely of the Rebble Blockade." But other sentiments attended McClellan's march to Centreville and Manassas. Dismay in Washington was reflected in the comments of Wadsworth's eldest daughter:

> A great slaughter, a great victory, we all surely expected and how did it all end? These magnificent columns, which have been waiting so impatiently all winter, this splendid corps d'armee marched to Manassas to find the enemy had quietly given them the slip, to find only empty fortifications with stove-pipes representing cannon, and so they were ordered back to Washington. For one thing we certainly have to thank him [McClellan]—by his inactivity he has gained for us the contempt of Europe.[10]

McClellan tried to save face by claiming a bloodless victory, but even he realized that aside from a training exercise in toning leg muscles for the long marches which lay ahead, little could be gained by trekking about in the red Virginia mud. So, leaving a token guard at Centreville, he ordered the Army of the Potomac back to Washington.

Despite the greater publicity attending the Centreville-Manassas operation, more was probably gained by developments in the Occoquan-Evansport sector. Lieutenant Commander R. H. Wyman, commanding the navy's Potomac flotilla agreed with Hooker that the works along the Potomac

were stronger than anticipated. Several good heavy guns—
one or two of British manufacture—were saved from the ordnance which the Confederates had attempted to spike in the
batteries. A large amount of tentage, ammunition, clothing
and other stores were captured; the *George Page* had been
burned in Quantico Creek, and all things considered it had
been a bad time for Confederate hopes along the river shore.
In any event, the major accomplishment of restoration of free
navigation on the river was a much more glamorous achievement than occupation of empty redoubts at Manassas.[11]

Events were quickly passing beyond McClellan's control.
Lincoln and his cabinet had grown quite tired of procrastination—Seward for one spoke openly of the ''imbecili-
ty'' of McClellan's recent operations.[12] March 8 and 9 proved
to be momentous days indeed for the young commander. In
one stroke of the pen, his army was reorganized, its movements
vastly constricted and he himself reduced from the lofty realm
of supreme command to control only of the forces on the
Potomac. Moreover, the appearance of the Confederate warship *Virginia* and the resulting disaster to part of the Union
fleet at Hampton Roads nearly wrecked the army's strategic
plans and once more threw fright into the politicians concerning the safety of the capital. The absence of effective naval
strength and Federal shore batteries on the Potomac pointed
to a weak chink in the armor of Washington's defenses. While
Secretary of the Navy Gideon Welles maintained his com-
posure, Stanton panicked, fearing that the *Virginia's* next
move would be to steam up the Potomac, disperse Congress,
and destroy the Capitol and public buildings. Stanton even
intruded upon the naval sphere by directing Dahlgren at the
Navy Yard to scuttle sixteen gravel-laden boats in the Potomac
where hastily gathered shore batteries might then pound the
Confederate ironclad to pieces. Hooker, downriver, also

planned to use his Whitworth gun to batter the *Virginia* but neither the army nor the navy had a chance to put such emergency schemes into practice. Neutralization of the Confederate ironclad by the *Monitor* obviated such precautions. Still, naval defense of the capital assumed new importance, and the whole issue kept tempers frayed concerning Washington's vulnerability.[13]

A council of corps commanders met at Fairfax Courthouse on March 13 and placed their imprimatur upon McClellan's scheme of operations for the spring. They approved the idea of a waterborne movement to the vicinity of Hampton Roads; vetoed the Urbana scheme in favor of a move via the peninsula between the James and York rivers (provided the navy continued to neutralize the *Virginia* and offered fire support against enemy shore batteries on the York river); and specifically addressed the weighty issue of what force should be left to cover the capital. In the council's words, "the force to be left to cover Washington shall be such as to give an entire feeling of security for its safety from menace." Corps commanders Keyes, Heintzelman, and McDowell interpreted this force to comprise full garrisons plus a maneuver element of 25,000 men on the Virginia side of the river and "occupying" units in the northern defense line. Sumner flatly estimated the total manpower need at 40,000.[14] Thus was inaugurated the statistical game which so befuddled strategic planning during much of the subsequent Peninsula campaign. Stanton told McClellan that same day that Lincoln had assented to his plan.

As the picturesque embarkation of the Army of the Potomac took place with its 130,000 men, 15,000 horses and mules, 1,100 wagons, and 44 batteries, official Washington continued to ponder the thorny issue of the city's safety. Actually, it was not as if McClellan had failed to consider the problem. As early as October 18, 1861, he directed Barnard and Barry, his chiefs of engineers and artillery, to "determine the minimum strength of garrisons—artillery and infantry— required for the various works in and about Washington to satisfy the conditions of a good defense." Within a week they reported a need for a total force of 33,795 men (both garrison and reserve) for the defense of Washington. These senior officers based their estimates on the lines of Torres Vedras, where the Duke of Wellington had held off a French force more than twice his size from eighty-seven connected redoubts in the winter of 1810. Allowing for variation in circumference between the two systems (but not the intervening half century's progress in weapons technology), both U.S. officers in 1861 thought that as few men as possible should be actually shut up in the forts themselves unless under direct attack. Rather, they estimated that total garrisons of 11,045 were needed, with 22,750 men in reserve. They assumed "that the army moves from here in force, fully occupying the bulk of the enemy's forces by its own movement, leaving the capital so strengthened by its defensive lines as to prevent danger of sudden seizure by a strategical movement of the enemy, and enable it to be held a reasonable time in case of serious reverses to our own arms in the field."[15] Here then was the concept of sword (field army) and shield (fortification system), advanced by professionals who knew what they were doing.

Barnard and Barry enclosed actual strength figures for October with their recommendations. They showed only 19,789 officers and men in garrison. Such statistics neglected to note the overwhelming and decisive presence of the Army of the Potomac in the area at that time. Barnard continued to press the matter of garrison strength although he doubled his earlier figure of necessary troop strength to 22,674 in his December report to the Chief of Engineers, Brigadier General Joseph Totten. Moreover, he urged the general-in-chief to fully garrison the works "up to the standard fixed upon," with troops "who have some familiarity with their positions and duties," lest the forts imperfectly serve their purpose. Actually, even at that early date, the various definitions of the term "fully garrisoned" provided a microcosm of the problems which clouded relations between McClellan and the Commander-in-Chief later in the campaign. Nonetheless, Barnard had gone on record on several occasions as advising his superior "if the army moves, particularly if it makes a flank movement, leaving the enemy in front, the measures for the defense of the city cannot be too carefully taken."[16]

Orders were issued on March 16 to Banks and Wadsworth as to their assignments while the main army moved to besiege Richmond. Banks's orders included the phrase tucked away at the end: "The general object is to cover the line of the Potomac and Washington." But the details stood in more prominent relief, for Banks was to leave a division covering the Shenandoah Valley at Winchester and to concentrate the effort at Manassas, where the remainder of his V Corps might guard the Orange and Alexandria and Manassas Gap railroads. The railroad would provide the linchpin for widely dispersed units of this command and Union forces watched the line of communications closely all that spring and summer. J. E. Morgan and the Fifth Pennsylvania Reserves numbered among the rail guards and on May 5, he wrote home: "I have heard it said several times that our services were prefered by the managers of the road and threatened through a petition to the Secretary of War to resign if we were removed," adding that no accident had happened while his unit was on duty.[17]

Wadsworth's direction of the close-in district and defenses of Washington was equally important. Despite Banks's presence, McClellan wanted the New Yorker (a politician-general whom he distrusted), to "exercise vigilance in your front, carefully guard the approaches in that quarter, and maintain the duties of advance guards." All troops not required for policing duties in Washington and Georgetown or for garrisons north of the Potomac were to be moved south of the river. The major concentration was to occur "in the center of your front" with energetic patrolling, intensive exercising of guns and troops in the forts, and heightened security of railroads, canals, depots, bridges, and ferries. Of course, Wadsworth received other chores such as forwarding new contingents to the main army. Wishing to leave nothing to chance, McClellan also ordered that in addition to the regular reports to the Adjutant General, Wadsworth should provide consolidated reports to army headquarters both weekly and monthly.[18]

The problem of assuring Washington's safety while McClellan's army went to the Peninsula came to a head in late March, when Confederate forces under Major General Thomas Jonathan Jackson used the transfer of major components of Banks's command as an opportunity to attempt a recapture of Winchester. Brigadier General James Shields's division proved stiffer opposition than expected at the battle of Kernstown on March 23, but Jackson's activities in the Shenandoah sent a ripple of fear through official Washington. Jackson might be planning to disrupt the Baltimore and Ohio railroad again—Washington's direct route to the west. Or he might even be on the verge of marching across the mountains toward Washington itself. In any event, Brigadier General Louis Blenker's division was pulled back from McClellan's forces with orders to reinforce those units charged with the defense of the railroad. This move upset McClellan's intricate timetable on the Peninsula. In readjusting it, a fatal miscalculation of troop strength (based on juggled statistics), was introduced into the picture.

Before departing for the Peninsula, McClellan had sent a tabulation of his strength to the Secretary of War with the notation that defensive forces for Washington included 35,467 under Banks in the Shenandoah, 10,859 at Manassas, 7,780 at Warrenton, and 1,350 on the lower Potomac, as well as Wadsworth's 18,000 in the defenses of the capital. This force seemed adequate to McClellan, depending upon how one interpreted statistics and locations of various units. The total force approximated the needs as expressed in the Barnard-Barry report and the response of the corps commanders. However, Stanton and Lincoln took a more rigid view of Washington's needs. At the time, Jackson was ranging widely in the valley. Johnston was still somewhere below the Rappahannock, but poised astride the railroad to Manassas and Alexandria for all the administration knew. The Orange and Alexandria had been the axis of Confederate movements in the past. Might it not be used by Johnston for a lightning thrust back toward the Federal capital while McClellan's huge force was in waterborne transit and Banks's thousands were pinioned in the valley? Lincoln and Stanton were so sensitive to Washington's safety that they remained quite skeptical of the second-line troops in both Banks's and Wadsworth's commands.

McClellan's case was not helped much when Wadsworth complained on April 1 that his resources were entirely inadequate to the task. The Committee on the Conduct of the War caught the scent of scandal, and Lincoln and Stanton quickly realized the seriousness of the situation. It should not have surprised anyone that the New York politician-general had only 19,022 effectives in his command. But when he said that McClellan had called on him for reinforcements from those men, that "nearly all the force is new and imperfectly disciplined" and that he had no mounted light artillery, then other people began to take notice. He might have added that he had been so unsure of exactly what units he did command that newspaper advertisements were necessary in order to have his subordinates report to him immediately. Perhaps the really decisive point came when Wadsworth observed: "I am not informed of the position which Major-General Banks is directed to take, but at this time he is, as I understand, on the other side of the Bull Run Mountains, leaving my command to cover the front from Manassas Gap [about 20 miles beyond Manassas] to Aquia Creek."[19]

Lincoln, prodded by Stanton, the radicals, and Wadsworth, studied McClellan's statistics. He asked Lorenzo Thomas, the adjutant general, and Ethan Allen Hitchcock, his venerable military adviser (who only shortly before had declared McClellan to be a better judge than he of the necessary means for defending the capital), to check the arithmetic. Together with other staff officers like Totten, Joseph P. Taylor, Montgomery C. Meigs, and James W. Ripley, they all declared that the army commander had not adhered to Lincoln's earlier order for leaving Washington absolutely secure. Admittedly, they failed to go on record as actually stating that it was insecure. The President, however, issued orders on April 3 detaining one of the corps of the Army of the Potomac—McDowell's corps—in front of Washington. The next day a Department of the Rappahannock was created encompassing the District of Columbia within its confines.[20]

McClellan had now closed with the enemy on the Peninsula, and he complained bitterly about the denial of McDowell's corps to the army. Lincoln was favorably disposed to forwarding these troops once Jackson had been cleared from the Valley, but he stated to McClellan on April 9: " 'Do you really think I should permit the line from Richmond, via Mannassas [sic] Junction, to this city to be entirely open, except what resistence [sic] could be presented by less than twenty thousand unorganized troops?' This is a question which the country will not allow me to evade."[21] McClellan later reported that destroyed railroad bridges along the Orange and Alexandria as well as at Fredericksburg seemed to indicate that the Confederates had no plans for any thrust against the capital. He noted that Thomas and Hitchcock had substantiated that conclusion in their own report to Lincoln and Stanton. Years later he stated a bit more dogmatically: "I knew that they could not intend to return immediately, that they would never undertake the assault of the works around Washington, and that from the moment the operations by the lower Chesapeake were developed they would be tied down to the vicinity of Richmond so long as the Army of the Potomac remained anywhere near the James river. All they could attempt would be a raid in the Shenandoah." Whether or not Jackson's movements in the Valley comprised merely a "raid" seemed debatable to Washington officials. Yet, Confederate dispatches at this time—early April— indicated few offensive plans.[22]

Exaggeration may have been more the norm at this stage, both at McClellan's headquarters and at the White House. Poor intelligence evaluations led the army commander to ask for more troops than necessary for the Peninsula operation. Political and diplomatic considerations, whereby the national government's credibility hinged upon its ability to keep the capital inviolate, surely led Lincoln to emphasize the imagined dangers to that city. But, as the month of April slipped by, Confederate discussions and actual operations began to show signs of possible activity directed towards threatening the northern capital.

McClellan's threat to Richmond caused Confederate leaders to assemble for a planning session in the office of President Davis on April 14. Johnston advocated an immediate offensive against the Federal force on the Peninsula. G. W. Smith advanced the notion of abandoning the Peninsula and Norfolk, concentrating near Richmond and then attacking McClellan, or simply placing a siege garrison in the capital while the rest of the army struck out offensively beyond the

Potomac. Smith thought this invasion might carry all the way to Philadelphia or New York before McClellan could capture Richmond. Washington and Baltimore could be threatened. James Longstreet, who was also present, ostensibly had the same idea in mind, but the conference, led by Davis and supported by R. E. Lee, became preoccupied with the more immediate concern for Richmond. Offensive plans on the grand scale were never fully developed, even though Johnston apparently alluded to them as late as two weeks after the conclusion of the conference.[23]

Meanwhile, the Federal situation was well represented by two events. Wadsworth labored to build up the Washington garrison during April, and he found that while his raw levies of infantry made progress, the artillery continued to lack sufficient horses, and the cavalry were equipped only with sabres. An inspection of the southern forts on March 29 disclosed varying local conditions, ranging from Fort Barnard where the Fourteenth Connecticut had everything in good order, to flooded magazines at Fort Woodbury and Fort DeKalb where the garrison comprised an ordnance sergeant and two sentinels! A mock alarm exercise ordered by Stanton for April 19 to test the state of readiness in the defenses disclosed that 4,100 men when rushed to the southern perimeter from north of the Potomac had varying amounts of ammunition and arms; the southern forts lacked sufficient cannon shells; and the one effective mounted unit had just returned from arduous service in the Shenandoah. Wadsworth resorted to impressment of horses from disloyal Virginians, confiscation of quartermaster teams for his artillery, and continued pleadings for better support from the War Department.[24]

McClellan could be found at the other end of the spectrum, conducting a time consuming siege of inferior Confederate forces on the Yorktown-Warwick line. He telegraphed on April 28 that he would like to have the 30-pdr. Parrotts in the works around Washington sent to him at once since he was short "of that excellent gun." Lincoln replied on May 1 that such a request dismayed him—largely because it indicated procrastination on McClellan's part— but probably also because it continued to show that the general failed to appreciate Lincoln's very basic concern for the capital's safety.[25] Still, the President gave way under McClellan's prolonged bombardment for more troops, and by mid-May, he had ordered McDowell to march southward along the Richmond-Fredericksburg railroad to cooperate with McClellan as long as his movement left Washington covered. It was about this time that Stonewall Jackson in the Shenandoah Valley once more unhinged Federal plans.

The Confederate high command realized that it could stave off disaster before its own capital only by preventing reinforcement of McClellan from Federal forces elsewhere in Virginia. Thus, orders went out to Jackson to increase his activities in the valley. The side effect would naturally cause great consternation in Washington. Exactly that happened as Jackson's operations befuddled official Washington, unnerved Banks who was left in the Valley with little more than a guard force, and unglued McClellan's grand plan. The crowning blow came on May 23 and 25 when Jackson destroyed major elements of Banks's command piecemeal at Front Royal and Winchester and swept the Shenandoah clear of Federals. Stanton immediately wrote Assistant Secretary of War John Tucker at Fort Monroe: "Our condition is one of considerable danger, as we are stripped to supply the Army of the Potomac, and now have the enemy here."[26]

To be precise, monthly returns showed at least 101,252 effectives available for containment of Jackson—if effectively coordinated and commanded. But the "great panic," as this episode of the war was termed, created anything but concerted effort. Rumors floated about that Jackson was ready to cross

the mountains and besiege Washington with numbers ranging from twenty to forty thousand "foot cavalry." A worried Lincoln informed McClellan that he thought the enemy
thrust on the Potomac was a general and calculated drive, and
one which could not be mounted if the Confederates were really concentrating on a last ditch defense of Richmond. He added: "I think the time is near when you must either attack
Richmond or give up the job and come to the defense of
Washington."[27]

McDowell's southward movement was suspended as he
was directed to rush troops to the valley to destroy Jackson.
He calmly protested that his people could do little to save
Banks given the time it took to march to the Shenandoah. He
also tried to soothe Lincoln and Stanton that the immediate
defenses of Washington were adequately manned and, furthermore, the whole business would only paralyze the delicate
cooperative movement with the Army of the Potomac. But
Washington authorities were adamant; the sudden crisis
developed the full implications of divided command with
McClellan, McDowell, Banks, and John C. Fremont all in
charge of armies working independently of one another, and
the best that Lincoln could do was to attempt to be the active
commander-in-chief and fight the battle for Washington in
the distant recesses of the Shenandoah, via the telegraph. The
result was close to disastrous.[28]

McDowell and Fremont were ordered to close a cordon
around Jackson. Northern governors received urgent injunctions to rush forward all possible volunteer and militia units;
and while the courtier Wadsworth tried to dissuade Lincoln
and Stanton from both courses of action, he too participated
in the frantic hustle surrounding troop shuffling from
Fredericksburg to the upper Potomac. One moment he was
at the Alexandria docks supervising troop movements; later
he served as middle man between the Valley and McDowell's

headquarters, reporting on conditions as they unfolded. Finally, he dispatched a force upriver to sink the boats at the ferries and to guard the fords. Such alarm was contagious and spread to the troops garrisoning the defenses around the city. One young soldier at Fort DeKalb behind Alexandria wrote his sister that his unit heard reports of Lee as close as Manassas and Fairfax Courthouse, and that their "cannon are all loaded and shotted ready, the men are numbered so that each man knows where to go so there will be no confusion if we were to be attacked." He assured her that "there is not much danger of that" even though the rebels were in behind the main army and their object undoubtedly was to take Washington or Baltimore. "I only wish they would try it," he proclaimed boldly.[29]

Such panicky actions did not prevent one group of irate citizens near Tenallytown, D.C., from protesting vehemently about the target practice by nearby Fort Gaines. Apparently they were more concerned about Federal than Confederate shells. But, one hundred miles to the south of Washington, the Confederate authorities could sense the dislocation of the Federal efforts in northern Virginia. The time had come to seize the initiative away from McClellan. Johnston attacked at Seven Pines on May 31, and, while receiving the wound which ultimately cost him command in Virginia, effectively reversed the trend of the Federals' spring offensive.

Elsewhere, the attempts of Lincoln and Stanton to conduct the war themselves foundered on divided command and poor communications. The story has been recounted often of Jackson's Valley campaign, and while historians such as Allan Nevins contend that the administration had no reason for its alarm, since troops could be brought from Baltimore and other neighboring points for the capital's defense, such observations miss the essential point.[30] McClellan might have been correct at some point in thinking that the best defense of Washington was an all-out attack on Richmond.[31] But the Lincoln government could not take a chance of leaving Washington vulnerable to attack once Jackson's fast moving army ranged unchecked in the valley. McDowell tried to assure a worried Lincoln that there were sufficient troops around the city to guard it, and, anyway, transportation facilities being what they were, his own force could do little to affect the outcome in the Shenandoah Valley. But Lincoln and Stanton wanted the battle for Washington fought far from the environs of the city. Ironically, they achieved their aim in May and early June as Jackson eluded the trap, defeated the forces sent against him in detail, but evacuated the Valley when Richmond authorities decided that McClellan's threat to their own safety required the return of the valley force. In Jackson's wake lay a completely dispersed and worn out series of Federal contingents which would never be of much value to McClellan.

Early in June, elderly General Hitchcock resigned his position as "Military Adviser," at least partially because of his dissatisfaction at being blamed for the way the war in the east was being conducted, partly because of ill health, and mostly because Lincoln and Stanton did not seem to take his advice regarding the absolute necessity, in his view, to retain enough troops to defend Washington. He explained to his old friend Winfield Scott, now in retirement, that he had repeatedly urged retention of Blenker's division of Banks's corps from Fremont's force on the upper Potomac, to better serve the immediate defense of the capital. In his mind, Jackson's brilliant strokes in the Valley were a direct result of the administration's failure to listen to him. As Hitchcock later told the McDowell court of inquiry:

I have attached very great importance to the possession of Washington, not so much as a military point but from its political position. It is the capital of the United States. The government is here. The archives of the nation are all here. It is the depository of the original Declaration of Independence and of the Constitution of the United States. It is the residence of the foreign ministers. These and many similar considerations give to this city a peculiar character. Its possession by the enemy, even for a short time, would injure the cause of the country more than the loss of many battles at a distance.[32]

As McClellan recoiled from the standoff at Seven Pines and Jackson gave a final display of tactical brilliance over Federal forces in the valley, Lincoln finally realized the game which the Confederates had been playing. Thus, he ordered Stanton to reassemble McDowell's army in order to have it cooperate with McClellan. He sensed that while Washington had been saved, Jackson had eluded his poorly coordinated pursuers, and that Federal strategy was in complete disarray. French newspapers were trumpeting the latest in Federal miscues, and the French Foreign Minister Thouvenel once more began to talk of mediation between North and South.[33] A quick remedy was in order.

As usual, McClellan took his time in regrouping, only to discover that he no longer held the initiative. The battle for Washington which took place in the Shenandoah, combined with McClellan's own inertia, had cost the Federals a chance to easily capture Richmond. Such hopes were completely dashed when Lee, Johnston's successor, used the Richmond defenses as a pivot from which to launch the Seven Days maneuvers that eclipsed McClellan's thrust on the Peninsula.

Meanwhile, as McClellan and Lee slugged it out on the Peninsula, reorganization of the Federals in northern Virginia took place. On June 18, the forces in and around Washington were grouped into a corps under Brigadier General Samuel D. Sturgis, and Wadsworth reverted to merely military governor of the District of Columbia. Sturgis had told Stanton the day before that "with proper attention and vigilance in the drilling of the men at the guns in the various forts, and a well organized movable column, such as we may have, the defense of the district can be made good in case of an attack until reinforcements can arrive.'' Eight days later Lincoln created the Army of Virginia, composed of Sturgis' corps and all troops in the so-called Shenandoah, Rappahannock, and Mountain departments.[34] The purpose of Major General John Pope's new army was to move by land to Richmond—part of an overwhelming convergence upon the Confederate capital by Federal land power. But, as usual, Lincoln wanted this new army to also screen the Union capital.

The possibility remained that Lee might turn northward and attack Washington after Seven Days. McClellan telegraphed Lincoln about it on July 4. Stanton feared it, and it was in the thoughts of such dissimilar men as Secretary of State Seward and Quartermaster General Meigs. Even some northern columnists projected such gloomy forebodings. The army commander naturally wanted reinforcements to prevent such an event, but Lincoln had told him on June 28: "If you have had a drawn battle, or a repulse, it is the price we pay for the enemy not being in Washington. We protected Washington, and the enemy concentrated on you; had we stripped Washington, he would have been upon us before the troops sent could have got to you." There didn't seem to be any reason for changing his mind after Independence Day as Pope substantiated the view by citing 23,000 available troops for service in the Shenandoah; 19,000 in McDowell's corps dispersed at Fredericksburg and Manassas; and Sturgis' small force in front of Washington—"they number about 17,000 men mostly raw recruits & fragments of broken regiments in no condition for service." Furthermore, he told the Committee on the Conduct of the War: "It is not necessary . . . in order to protect the capital, that I should interpose myself between the enemy and the place itself."[35]

As McClellan's men relaxed about their camp at Harrison's Landing in the July heat and Pope worked to band together his army, Lincoln decided upon further reorganization. Largely upon the advice of old Winfield Scott, the President ordered Major General Henry Halleck to assume the post of general-in-chief of all Federal forces. The main issue was the Army of the Potomac, as powerful voices argued for McClellan's dismissal. But the army was situated close to Richmond, and, perhaps, one final offensive might capture the place.

McClellan wanted to concentrate all available Federal forces on the James and capture the rebel capital by moving to the Southside and cutting communications with the rest of the Confederacy—much as Ulysses S. Grant was to do two years later. But union intelligence reports once more inflated Confederate strength around Richmond; a subtle political charade was going on in Washington, fanned by distrust of McClellan as well as great hopes for the new man from the west—John Pope; and both medical and engineer officers thought it wise for the army to move quickly from the malarial James Valley. Halleck had favored this course all along, and, with Lincoln's blessing, ordered McClellan to transfer his base back to Aquia Creek on August 3. Speed was imperative, for Lee, released temporarily from responsibility for Richmond's defense, would certainly strike out for northern Virginia. Alone, Pope might not be able to contain him.

McClellan protested bitterly against any retirement from the Peninsula. On August 4, he wrote to Halleck that directly in front of his army lay the heart of the rebellion and there should be collected the resources to determine the fate of the nation. A decided victory there, he declared, and the military strength of the rebellion would be crushed. "It matters not what partial reverses we may meet with elsewhere here is the true defense of Washington. It is here on the banks of the

James River that the fate of the Union should be decided,'' proclaimed Little Mac.[36]

Halleck painstakingly replied that he considered the Army of the Potomac really was split into two parts with the entire enemy force in between. Neither part could reinforce the other in case of attack. Pope could not be sent to the Peninsula, hence the unification would have to take place midway, namely at Fredericksburg, where both Richmond as an objective and the defense of Washington as an alternative could be effected by the united field force. In Halleck's view: ''If General Pope's army be diminished to re-inforce you, Washington, Maryland, and Pennsylvania would be left uncovered and exposed.''[37]

In fact, this was exactly what many senior officers in the Army of the Potomac tacitly desired. They, not Pope's force, would be called upon to save the Union, and so speed was hardly in their vocabularies. Attorney General Edwin Bates noted a criminal tardiness and bickering among army leaders, and McClellan's clique was quite perturbed about so-called malevolent incompetents in Washington and their chief competitors in the Army of Virginia. After all, didn't Pope have plenty of men, they asked, and his July returns, in truth, showed 70,000 men available, with 9,226 alone servicing the 554 guns in the forts of Washington.

Most of these garrison troops had found little to do all summer but practice with their fortress artillery, drill and countermarch between various forts and redoubts in the heat, curse the diarrhea, typhoid, and typhus, but, if lucky, catch a quick off-duty swim in either Rock Creek or the Potomac. They were men of the First Maine Heavy Artillery, Sixteenth Maine, One Hundred and Twentieth and One Hundred and Seventeenth New York, One Hundred and Thirty-First Pennsylvania, and Thirty-Second Massachusetts—all infantry and the Ninth and Tenth Rhode Island. Greenhorns, latecomers to the conflict, they certainly impressed veterans of the Peninsula as unlikely candidates for any battle which Pope might fight against Lee. After the Confederates had bested the pretty-boys of the Army of Virginia, then the true soldiers of McClellan would step in and save the capital—or so they thought.[37]

Lee was already on the move. He gambled on McClellan's inertia by sending Jackson's 12,000-man corps off to Gordonsville even before Halleck had assumed his duties. By the middle of August, before McClellan's people had even departed from Harrison's Landing, the Confederates had fully 55,000 men poised on the Rapidan river ready to destroy Pope. By the time McClellan awoke to the fact that Lee's people were leaving rather than strengthening Richmond's defenses, it was too late. Washington authorities had determined on a concentration of Pope, and the Army of the Potomac. Everyone, inlcuding McClellan and Pope, had to admit that Lee held the initiative and Pope's army covering Washington rather than Richmond was now the objective of the conflict in the Virginia theater.

Those hot August days were spent in intricate maneuvering which took the contending armies ever closer to the Federal capital. On August 14, Barnard was assigned to the command of the fortifications surrounding Washington. On August 22, Halleck explained to McClellan that the object was to hold the line of the Rappahannock until sufficient forces could be gathered to take the offensive. Any retreat would be a fighting one, step by step back to Manassas and the Occoquan; new levies were to be kept in the Washington forces as a reserve. By August 27, Jackson had executed his famous flank march around Pope. His men lay devouring the riches of the Union supply base at Manassas. His position behind Pope, and astride the Orange and Alexandria, was only thirty miles from Washington—one long day's march—and officials in the capital knew only that the telegraph had gone dead.[38]

McClellan reached Alexandria on the evening of the 26th to find a quiet town with Sumner's and Franklin's corps preparing to disembark from their transports. While corps and division commanders debarked their troops with due deliberate speed, there seemed to be no air of crisis or rush at the Alexandria wharves. But the situation changed drastically during the final days of the month as Lee, Longstreet, and Jackson pinned Pope down to a conclusive battle on the old battleground of Bull Run. Jackson's appearance at Manassas caused officials in Washington to scrape together a task force to try to save the railroad bridge over the creek; but that expedition ended in disaster, and shuffling of garrison forces in the fortifications continued apace on the 27th. McClellan wanted to concentrate as many of the Army of the Potomac units as possible immediately in front of Washington's forts; Lincoln and Stanton thought they should be sent forward to help Pope.[39] Once more there was great confusion in top circles of Federal command.

Such divergence of opinion among Union leaders only added to the problems surrounding the two days of Second Bull Run. Later controversies over McClellan's role have clouded the matter of whether anything was accomplished at all in the close-in defenses. It remains unclear whether or not McClellan actually dallied so that he, not the westerner, could save Washington. But if he remained reluctant to rush forward men from his own command to help the Army of Virginia, he did pursue matters which he knew something about. His basic defense lies, perhaps, in the dispatch he sent to Halleck on August 27, in which he suggested Pope's retirement behind Bull Run to Fairfax and relinquishment of the railroad for "The great object is to collect the whole army in Washington, ready to defend the works and act upon the flank of any force crossing the Upper Potomac."[40]

BATTERY
RODGERS

ITS
15-INCH GUN

Guardian of the Potomac Approach—Battery Rodgers
(National Archives and Records Administration, Washington, D.C.)

Meanwhile, McClellan took it upon himself to analyze the immediate situation in Washington's defenses, since "no one in Washington appears to know the condition of matters, and I have a fancy for finding them out for myself." He effectively suppressed rumors like the one, on the night of the 28th, that Lee with 150,000 men was moving directly on the Chain Bridge. He told his wife that he was avoiding Lincoln, Stanton, and the Washington scene, preferring to remain on the Virginia shore, admitting: "What I am doing now is rather a volunteer affair—not exactly my business but you know that I have a way of attending to most other things than my own affairs." Thus, during the period of Second Bull Run, a flurry of dispatches issued from McClellan's headquarters tent, all directed toward insuring that the close-in defenses of Washington were in the best possible shape. McClellan inspected the line of forts on the southern perimeter in person, insuring that Upton's Hill, for example, was secure. He was in close touch with Barnard about such matters as adequate garrisons for the northern perimeter and active cavalry patrolling north of the river towards Rockville and Frederick. Furthermore, he studied the statistics of the garrisons, searching for weaknesses.[41]

These strength figures were deceptive. Barnard noted a force of nearly 30,000 men was carried on the rolls of the District and Defenses of Washington for August. Yet, he complained to Halleck on August 28: "I feel called upon to state that against any serious attack I have no means of holding the line of fortifications from Fort Richardson along the front of Arlington to Fort Corcoran, nor the line on this [District] side of the Potomac." Furthermore, one inspector general reported that most of the 10,026 men stationed along the Virginia line were new men and imperfectly trained in using fortress artillery. Similar complaints came from Barnard regarding units stationed east of the Anacostia, and, apparently, many of the garrisons had been sent into the field that previous week, leaving only token cadre in their place, a fact that greatly distressed the engineer. Still, McClellan, Barnard, and others knew very well that the garrisons were merely the pintle around which the field army would maneuver. Their aim to preserve trained, first-class garrisons in the forts for any eventuality was commendable. However, in retrospect, their distress calls seem to have only added to the manifold problems besetting GHQ during those trying days of August. As McClellan wrote dejectedly to his wife on August 29:

> No means to act with, no authority, yet determined, if possible to save the country and the capital. . . . I do not know whether I shall be permitted to save the capital or not. . . . I am heartsick with the folly and ignorance I see around me.[42]

Second Bull Run, like the first battle, ended in a resonant Federal defeat, but this time there was no rout. Nevertheless, the question of the integrity of the capital remained in the balance. Some of Washington's fortification troops moved out by rail to block any Confederate thrust via the Orange and Alexandria through Fairfax toward the capital. Eben Gilley of the First Massachusetts Heavy Artillery reported marching past the courthouse "but didn't see any rebels," although the next day one of his comrades was wounded by "friendly fire" of a trigger-happy New Yorker in an adjacent unit. The comrade and attending doctors were soon captured by Confederate cavalry, paroled, and rejoined the Union forces which meantime had retired back to Cloud's Mill closer to Alexandria. If Second Bull Run did not form the "battle for Washington," then the fighting which occurred on September 1 at Ox Hill, or Chantilly, certainly provided the climax. The confusion surrounding that day has clouded its importance in terms of defending Washington.

[126]

Pope's force was seeking to avoid encirclement and make its way back to the protective fortifications. Various components of the Army of the Potomac were moving to join Pope or heading for the defenses of the city and no one seemed to know quite what to do with still others. Pope at least entertained some idea about a renewal of the offense and Lee was seriously considering how to cut off Pope's Army of Virginia from Washington and destroy it in detail—then, perhaps, to move against the rest of the dispersed Federal forces and possibly break them up before they could reform under the shadow of the fortress guns at the capital.[43]

Chantilly ended in a tactical stalemate during a thunderstorm with two Federal generals—Philip Kearny and Isaac Stevens—dead on the field, and the Confederates convinced that they could not outflank and catch the Federals in a trap. The battle ended Pope's ambitious plans for renewing the offensive, and at 7:30 A.M. on September 2, he hinted strongly that the entire Union command ought to be withdrawn into the safety of the defenses of Washington. Yet, this indecisive action had preserved the integrity of Pope's army. Had Lee succeeded in cutting off major portions of the command and destroying them piecemeal, then the Union high command would have been in serious trouble. As it was, Chantilly taught Lee that he could not do anything more against Pope and McClellan unless he was willing to send the Army of Northern Virginia against the strong defensive works and reorganized Union forces on the banks of the Potomac.[44]

The twenty-four hour period after Chantilly proved decisive for both Union and Confederate authorities. McClellan assumed command of the defenses of Washington and all troops protecting the city on September 2. Clerks and government employees were organized for defense of the panic-stricken city. Engineer authorities remained pessimistic about the ability of the defenses to contain an enemy assault.

Allowing for the exaggeration in McClellan's memoirs, even Halleck and Stanton despaired of saving the capital. They had ordered evacuation of arsenal stores, and a warship stood offshore in the Potomac to carry the President and his cabinet to safety. The situation appeared ominous.[45]

Only Lincoln and Welles projected any measure of calmness in the face of catastrophe. The latter thought Halleck and Stanton were overly apprehensive and he recorded in his diary for September 2:

> The military believe a great and decisive battle is to be fought in front of the city, but I do not anticipate it. It may be that, retreating within the intrenchments, our own generals and managers have inspired the Rebels to be more daring; perhaps they may venture to cross the upper Potomac and strike at Baltimore, our railroad communications, or both, but they will not venture to come here, where we are prepared and fortified with both army and navy to meet them.[46]

Welles continued to deplore idle gossip on September 3 and 4. He pointed to the twenty-five vessels of the Potomac Flotilla under the command of Commodore Charles Wilkes (hero of the *Trent* affair), as a deterrent to Confederate capture of the capital.

Meanwhile, McClellan was under fire from his opponents for neglecting Pope during the Second Bull Run campaign, but his abilities for seizing control of a disorganized army and welding it into a fighting force again temporarily surmounted the criticism. As Samuel Heintzelman put it: "Whatever mistakes he has made he has the confidence of the troops. If we are attacked under Pope we fear another defeat. McClellan would restore confidence to officers & men & he would be received with enthusiasm by the whole Army."[47]

Thus, it was almost by default that McClellan received responsibility for defending Washington early in September. He positioned his old corps and divisions at strategic locations along the southern defense perimeter—Porter at Upton's Hill with McDowell nearby, Franklin in front of the works at Alexandria with Heintzelman in support, Darius Couch in the area around Fort Corcoran and upriver toward Chain Bridge, and Sumner in reserve from Fort Albany toward Alexandria. Then, McClellan rode among the returning soldiery and rekindled their confidence; even panic in the streets of the District subsided with his appointment. It was not an idle boast when he recalled years later that by dawn of September 3, the troops were all in position to repulse attack, and Washington was safe.[48]

But was this really true? The initiative still lay with Lee, resting his army near Chantilly. In nine short weeks he had transferred the war in the East from the doorsteps of Richmond to the threshold of Washington and completely reversed the tide. The Federals still did not know his intentions, although Pope, Porter, and others all warned Halleck to watch the fords across the Potomac. The Confederate chieftain realized that the fought-over territory of northern Virginia could not support his army in any protracted siege of the Federal capital. He wrote Davis on September 4: "I had no intention of attacking him [the enemy] in his fortifications, and am not prepared to invest them. If I possessed the necessary munitions, I should be unable to supply provisions for the troops. I therefore determined while threatening the approaches to Washington, to draw the troops into Loudon, where forage and some provisions can be obtained, menace their possession of the Shenandoah Valley, and if found practicable, to cross into Maryland.[49]

Lee had displayed a superb adeptness at judging the reaction of Federal generals to a given situation, and he had taken the fullest advantage of Washington's sensitivity on the subject of the defense of the capital since assuming command of the Army of Northern Virginia in June. But he was too shrewd to push his luck; consequently his plans did not at any time contemplate a full-scale rush on the Washington defenses. Yet, McClellan, Halleck, Stanton, and Lincoln had no certain knowledge until September 4, when 55,000 grayclad soldiers splashed across the Potomac north of Leesburg. Even McClellan admitted that as late as a week after the Confederate crossing " . . . whether it was their intention to cross their whole force, with a view to turn Washington by a flank movement down the north bank of the Potomac, to move on Baltimore, or to invade Pennsylvania, were the questions which at that time we had no means of determining." He freely admitted that if Lee had remained before Washington, he would have preferred to rest and regroup the merged Union armies preparatory to giving battle. But his hand was forced; accordingly when ordered to organize a field force to pursue Lee on the 3rd, he moved the II and XII corps to Tennallytown, and the IX corps to the northern suburbs on the Seventh Street road, with cavalry pounding the roads toward Poolesville and the Potomac fords.[50]

The Army of the Potomac now stretched from the Potomac at Poolesville, across country to New Market, and by September 10 covered both Washington and Baltimore. The strategic situation remained as hazy as the sultry days of early autumn. McClellan's ponderous pursuit of the Confederates was fed in part by faulty intelligence provided to Halleck and Halleck's own dispatches between September 9 and 16, which warned the army commander about exposing Washington to a sudden attack. Halleck continued to fear that Lee might draw McClellan too far to the north towards Pennsylvania, then slip back down either the northern or southern bank of the Potomac and attack Washington.[51]

[130]

The army commander parried such reports since he knew that defense forces left around Washington numbered 94,000.[52] Banks had been left in charge of the immediate defenses of the capital "during the absence of the major-general commanding," and his engineers and staff scurried about strengthening exposed points in the defense system, eg., the Fifteenth New Jersey constructed Fort Kearny in the northern defense line between Second Bull Run and Antietam. In addition, new barriers of sandbags were erected, ordnance shifted to better sites, stragglers were collected, and the local troops actively scouted the Virginia countryside for signs of the rebels.[53] Barnard, pessimistic as always, felt the defenses east of the Anacostia lacked continuity and "an enemy in force, . . . may make a sudden effort that way and break through the intervals." Lack of troops, copious copses of woodland, uncertainty of armament, reluctance of veterans of the Peninsula to wield a spade—all clouded the picture for the engineer officer, and he recommended stocking the forts with food so that they might simply serve as rallying points during a siege.[54]

Even Heintzelman, charged with the southern defense perimeter, recorded in his diary on September 8, "We have not got everything quite in shape yet. The removal of Franklin's troops leaves an opening in our picket lines." But otherwise, Banks's forces were rather imposing with 46,800 men of the combined veteran corps of Heintzelman, Porter, and Sigel, 15,515 garrison troops, 6,500 from Wadsworth's so-called "Metropolitan Guard," and Daniel Casey's provisional brigades of 4,500. Most of the officers and men would probably have agreed, at least tacitly, with E. O. Wentworth of the Thirty-Seventh Massachusetts, who wrote to his wife from Arlington on the 16th: "We have a large force within signal call, and such is the strength of our fortifications that we can repulse a vastly superior force. Washington cannot be

[131]

taken by any force advancing upon it from the west."[55]

The overall situation received great attention in European court circles. Indeed, the much coveted recognition of the Confederacy hung largely upon what Lee was doing in Maryland. The American minister in France, William Dayton, warned Seward of the impact upon the French government of Washington's danger and the invasion of Maryland. Foreign Minister Lord John Russell noted on September 13: "The whole Federal Army has fallen back behind the fortifications around Washington," and he privately told the British minister in France to test the French government as to future cooperative diplomatic action. To the British prime minister, Russell cited October as a momentous time for cabinet decisions, and Lord Palmerston replied that if Washington or Baltimore should fall then it might be appropriate to intervene in order to effect an armistice.[56]

Such fears were partially obviated by the stalemate at Antietam in mid-September. The contest showed that Lee's invasion was not dependent on the Leesburg-Manassas operational axis, although some Washington officials continued into September to fear reoccupation of the Confederate position at Manassas. Furthermore, the battle so weakened the Confederate army that it had to retire to Virginia, and it chose to do so via the Shenandoah valley. If McClellan's lack of pursuit was striking, so too was the lack of any concerted thrust from the Washington sector into the area beyond Bull Run, as a cooperative venture to capture the Army of Northern Virginia. Local officials were preoccupied with preservation of Washington both as capital and the proper base of operations for the future. Neither Lincoln, Stanton, Halleck, nor subordinate commanders like Banks or Heintzelman appeared capable of doing anything more than sending weak reconnaissance forces to probe the Virginia countryside, guard the Potomac crossings below Point of

Rocks (Halleck continued to fear that Lee would sideslip past McClellan and attack the capital), and dispatch piecemeal reinforcements to the Army of the Potomac from the huge garrison force at Washington.[57]

When McClellan proposed crossing the Potomac and pursuing Lee via the Valley, Halleck telegraphed on September 26: "Will not this line again expose Washington, and compel us to keep a large force here? The enemy is repairing bridges on the Rapidan and Rappahannock, preparatory to throwing a force on Washington, if it should not be properly protected. Cannot your army move, so as to cover Washington, by keeping between it and the enemy?" The army commander replied rather cavalierly: "I have no fears as to an attack on Washington by the line of Manassas. Holding Harpers Ferry as I do, they will not run the risk of an attack on their flank and rear, while they have the garrison of Washington in their front."[58]

Halleck remained adamant, although he allowed twenty regiments or 18,667 men to be stripped from the Washington defense force and rushed to the Army of the Potomac, Heintzelman, Banks, and others protested this subtraction from the defenses, and such moves definitely hampered reconnaissance operations in northern Virginia. Despite the reinforcements, McClellan continued to tarry although he was beginning to understand when Halleck told him flatly "it seems to me that Washington is the real base of operations, and that it should not under any circumstances be exposed." Still, said McClellan, the cavalry was exhausted, the infantry was without clothing and disorganized, and the whole army needed reconstitution. The theme was familiar to Lincoln, and on October 6, he ordered the Army of the Potomac to cross the river and give battle. Seven days later he instructed the army commander that his best recourse was to move east of the mountains on a direct line for Richmond with supply routes fanning

out to him from Washington. Such a procedure would naturally insure the city's safety.

At that point Stuart's raid into Pennsylvania unhinged
the equilibrium. McClellan dallied once more; the Confederate
cavalry swept close to Washington in mid-October, causing
an additional panic among the citizenry. Everyone feared a
sudden dash into the city. Troops were placed on constant
alert. As usual, interceptor forces of Federal cavalry and infantry were everywhere but in the right place. As Heintzelman
observed from the southern perimeter: "If I had been allowed
to have sent a Divis. [sic] to Leesburg some weeks ago this
rebel Cavly & 6 pieces of Arty. would not have been able to
make their escape." But the inept handling of the Federal
forces permitted Stuart to slip back across the Potomac to
the embarrassment of all concerned.[59]

Despite the fact that McClellan finally moved slowly forward to the vicinity of Warrenton by early November, Lincoln's patience had run out. The onset of winter weather, the
voices of northern politicians, and the continued prospect of
a long stalemate in the east all appeared clearly to the president. As Halleck told Heintzelman on October 28, the chief
executive had actually controlled military operations for the
past four weeks and he was at wit's end. On November 5, Lincoln ordered Burnside to supersede McClellan in command
of the Army of the Potomac. The long and bloody story of
defending the capital in 1862 reached its conclusion. Perhaps
J. G. Barnard best summarized the experience when he wrote
on October 17: "The commanding general of the active forces
in Virginia would always be the best judge of how many men
are required in Washington, and it is for want of harmony
and concern between those who controlled the forces near
Washington and the commanding general of our principal active army that we owe in part recent disasters."[60]

CHAPTER SIX

Cavalry Raids and Gun Drill

The Quiet Period, 1862-1864

Washington by late 1862 was a fortress city. Surrounded by a chain of fortifications, connected by lines of earthworks mounting the most powerful guns of the period, the Nation's capital had changed greatly since Inauguration Day, 1861. In reality it had its own army—the garrison of artillery, cavalry, and infantry, always in readiness to man the works or if necessary to take the field in an emergency. The city itself was evidence of a wartime transition from the overgrown Southern village of 1860 to the bustling governmental center of later decades. The streets were now deeply rutted from hard usage by army wagons and cavalry horses. Officers and soldiers swarmed the sidewalks and crowded the hotels by day and night. Hackmen were gouging soldiers $6.50 for one-way trips to camp. Congress was practically in permanent session and contractors, camp followers, and curiosity seekers—even occasional Confederate parolees—could be found in the galleries of the bars such as those in Willard's and Ebbit hotels. Bedlam and pandemonium blended together as business and the conduct of conflict resolution preoccupied the war lords of Washington.[1]

Out in the suburbs and across the Potomac and Anacostia rivers stood the forts—some fifty-three enclosed works and twenty-two batteries. Their clay sides were naked of grass, and both in front of and behind them stretched acres of fields—strewn only with random brush piles and tree stumps. Cleared to improve fields of fire for the artillery, they were all that remained of noble forests that had covered the area before the war. Fence rails and prosperous farms had long since passed into the oblivion of soldiers' cooking fires and living huts, or abandonment to the "necessities of war." The few local inhabitants who remained were either relocated inside the defense lines or eked out an existence in the "no-man's land" between Federal protection and Confederate guerilla control. Convalescent camps, garrison barracks, stables, depots, and flotsam of guard posts, contraband huts, and stragglers' tents covered the rear areas. What impressed Noah Brooks, newly arrived war correspondent from the "shores of the Peaceful Sea" or California, was the martial aspect of the capital.[2]

Still, this martial aspect could not hide the fact that the mere presence of the grayclad host less than fifty miles from the city in late summer and early fall had caused more than usual official concern about the city's security. Unmaneuverable artillery in the fortifications, wide gaps between individual works, and the need for better river defenses were among the more obvious deficiencies. As the gray tide receded from the Potomac valley, Federal leaders once more called for reevaluation of the state of Washington's protection.

J. G. Barnard apparently precipitated the matter early in October when he wrote Army headquarters: "As everything connected with this subject of the fortifications is left to my individual will, I take this occasion to state what I am doing, and what, I think, is required." The engineer officer was piqued over a dearth of labor to work on the defenses. He recited briefly the history of the effort to date: special purposes for isolated works before Bull Run which "doubtless exercised an important influence in deterring the enemy from following up his success by an assault upon Arlington and Alexandria"; construction of the thirty-five-mile system after Bull Run "through a country extensively wooded and of intricate topography"; all executed under the pressure of an enemy in front. He cited the weakest part of the system—from the Potomac to Fort Massachusetts on the Seventh Street Road—as the most likely point of enemy attack after Second Bull Run. He mentioned the pitiful state of the lines east of the Anacostia, where heavy woodland and difficult topography all but obviated the viability of the works from Fort Meigs to Stanton—a line designed to prevent an enemy from shelling the navy yard and arsenal. Finally, since "if the enemy attack Washington, it will be with a large force and numerous artillery," Barnard felt that more adequate bomb-proof shelter was necessary in the various works, and that the 24- and 32-pounder seacoast guns which had been quickly emplaced in the works from the Washington arsenal should be replaced with field and siege guns of more manageable quality.[3]

Several weeks later Barnard pointedly asked for appointment of a study commission for the defenses by Secretary of War Stanton. Noting that cost estimates for completing the work that he had been doing on the forts were necessarily

BLOCKHOUSE GUARDING AQUEDUCT BRIDGE
(Library of Congress)

imprecise, the engineer told the secretary that "there is scarcely any limit to the amount of work which may be bestowed on it, and the practical limit will depend on varying circumstances and individual judgement." He pointed to recent events as justification for the defense system, however incomplete and imperfect. Recounting his own involvement with the project from its inception, and noting that "everyone in authority is too busy to give any attention to this matter," he respectfully suggested appointment of a commission of three or four high ranking officers to lend a consensus to any recommendation for improvements, alterations, or continued maintenance of the defenses. Stanton ordered establishment of this commission on October 22.[4]

The commission labored on the problem for two months. Meanwhile Barnard and his close associate, Lieutenant Colonel Barton S. Alexander, strove to clear more firing lines, strengthen escarpments and revetments, and mount 100-pounder rifles on center-pintle carriages in prominent fortifications. Labor problems continued to be among the most frustrating and unresolved questions as can be discerned from a letter that Alexander wrote to his chief on December 21, pointing to deficiencies at Chain Bridge, where only hired men and contrabands worked on the several fortifications. As Alexander pointed out, only he and Barnard possessed precise information on the needs of the defense system, and should either of them be called to other duties, then their replacements might incur serious errors of judgement in selecting the true line of defense. He was aware that all previous requests for work parties had met refusal, but he pleaded with Barnard to place the matter again before the general-in-chief or the secretary of war. The Chain Bridge works were essential to the city's safety, he said, and it would be folly to suppose "that our enemy would fail to take advantage of such serious blunders in engineering," as had accompanied their original rapid erection. Showing some appreciation of the direction being taken by land warfare after two years of fighting, Alexander contended:

> Commanding officers of troops are ambitious to have a showy command. They always reply, when requisitions for working parties are made, that the troops must drill; that they must learn how to handle their muskets and march. At the same time these troops are putting up the works that are necessary for the defense of this city they are attending the very best school in the land to teach them the duties of engineer soldiers, and acquiring knowledge which is not less than important than the ABC of the profession, and which they will all be called upon to practice before we can hope to reduce any of the enemy's strongholds.[5]

The commission to examine the defenses of Washington submitted its report the day before Christmas and six days later Barnard placed it before Secretary of War Stanton. The commission approved the work that had been done upon the vast defensive network, noting with pride the 643 guns and 75 mortars in the system. They suggested numerous additions and changes to existing works, and construction of five or six new forts. They also proposed to add a new feature to the defense system by the construction of works to defend the river from naval attack. They stressed the need for more wells in the forts, improvement of surrounding rifle pits for supporting infantry and perfection of the lines of communication via roadway construction along the defense perimeter.

Upon due deliberation the Commission announced that 25,000 men were required for infantry garrisons. They calculated upon computations of two men per yard of front perimeter, and one man per yard of rear perimeter. The board of officers also estimated a need for 9,000 artillery (three reliefs for each gun), and 3,000 cavalry—or a permanent garrison of 34,000 men. Yet, Barnard and his colleagues did not think it necessary to keep the infantry in the works at all times. They could camp nearby, drill rigorously, and be available in case of emergency. Artillery men, whose training took more time, were to be stationed in each fort or battery. Thus, once the gunners had learned the technical handling of the guns, range finding, and disposition of the armament, they would remain on permanent assignment in the defenses, or so thought the Commission.

Maintenance of a maneuver force appeared as a key element in the Commission's report. This force, to number no less than 25,000 men, was to operate outside the defenses against enemy attack columns. The Commission hastened to add:

> Against more serious attacks from the main body of the enemy, the Capital must depend upon the concentration of its entire armies in Virginia or Maryland. They should precede or follow any movement of the enemy seriously threatening the Capital.[6]

Barnard's covering letter specified cost figures. He noted that $550,000 had been expended on the defenses of Washington before the Peninsula campaign. He felt the expenditure was justified, for it had gone into "upwards of fifty forts and a number of batteries with large dimensions, and extensive bombproofs." He once again reiterated his work, the work done following the army's return from the James, citing the high costs accompanying employment of "a large number of civil assistants, superintendents, and overseers, to supervise the works and troops and laborers employed," as well as hiring of laborers, purchase of building materials, and sundry expenses. He thought that $100,000 additional had been spent during the last five months of 1862. He suggested that $200,000 more might be required to complete the work suggested by the Commission but noted that the famous lines of Torres Vedras had cost $1,000,000 "in a country where labor commanded one-tenth of what is paid in this country."[7]

The suggestions of the Commission were strenuously pursued during the early part of 1863. No immediate danger from Lee's main force threatened the capital as the Army of the

Potomac floundered through ill-fated campaigns near Fredericksburg. Still, numerous cavalry raids and guerrilla incursions emphasized the continued threat to Washington and occupied the attention of garrison forces for much of the succeeding year.[8]

The first of these activities came as the Commission was deliberating on the fate of the fortifications and may have spurred their conclusions. The raids of J. E. B. Stuart's cavalry before and after Fredericksburg were directed mainly at Burnside's communication line along the Telegraph Road from the Occoquan to Falmouth. But such raids invariably moved beyond the axis of the old northsouth highway and into that buffer zone between the Occoquan-Bull Run line and the southern defense perimeter of Washington. Encompassing Fairfax and eastern Loudon counties, this area was an extremely sensitive locale for Federal authorities. Picket posts, camps for railroad guards, sentinels at road junctions, as well as early-warning lookouts were spotted throughout the area at such places as Centreville, Fairfax Courthouse, and Fairfax Station, Union Mills, and Dranesville by late 1862 and early 1863. Forward positions for the main defenses of Washington, they bore the brunt of skirmishes and alarms as mobile columns of Confederates sought to disrupt and pin down isolated contingents from the main Federal effort farther south.[9]

The raids of Wade Hampton in late November and mid-December caused much consternation among Federal authorities. Hampton's troopers captured supply wagons, pickets, and much other booty, reaching the banks of the Occoquan itself before being turned away by overwhelming numbers of Federal infantry from Sigel's XI corps advancing from Fairfax Courthouse to reinforce Burnside. But Hampton's raids were mere preludes to a larger attempt by Stuart just after Christmas to dislocate Federal plans. Taking 1,800 men and 4 guns, Stuart raided up the Telegraph Road but with meager results. Rather than turning back from the Occoquan to the Rappahannock, the always optimistic Stuart was persuaded by favorable scouting reports to press beyond the Occoquan toward the Orange and Alexandria railroad.

Hampton was directed to demonstrate toward Accotinck, and Stuart's main column pressed on toward Burke's Station on the rail line. By this time the alerted Federals were suitably confused and fumbled toward interception. Their humor was not improved by receipt of Stuart's famous telegram to Quartermaster General Montgomery C. Meigs concerning the quality of Union mules which Stuart's telegraph operator sent from Burke's on the night of December 28. But at least the Union command knew where the enemy lay, and Heintzelman, commanding the Defenses, ordered subordinates, such as Brigadier General John J. Abercrombie, to send columns to stop Stuart's incursion, while alerting the outlying commanders in Fairfax county to be on guard against attack. Still, Federal commanders misjudged Stuart's route of march. Although in truth finding, as Heintzelman reported later, "every point so well guarded and all our troops on the alert that they could only seek an outlet for escape," Stuart's people defied the Union supposition that they would "attempt to retreat between Alexandria and Fairfax Court-House."[10] Instead, the grayclad troopers moved northwestward, brushing the Federal posts at Fairfax Station and the Courthouse swerving around pockets of heavy resistance before turning westward at Vienna. Heintzelman's units seemed to be content to deter rather than intercept, and the Confederates passed beyond the sensitive area west of Washington, retiring to the Rappahannock line via Middleburg and Warrenton.

Although Stuart overestimated his success at destroying Burnside's direct line of communication with Washington, he had in fact scattered Union cavalry on the Occoquan, rendered necessary the dispatch of large bodies of blueclad cavalry to patrol in Fairfax and upper Prince William counties, and created the impression that another raid into Maryland was afoot. His raid had fatigued Union cavalrymen and horses during the cold and snowy season, and while some Federals rejoiced at having stopped the rebels at Fairfax Station, their superiors became all the more concerned with proper stationing of railroad guards, patrol columns, and fortified strongpoints west of Washington. From the fall of 1862 onward, the forward lines of the Defenses of Washington were pushed outward from the main fortifications near the city. More than ever the early warning system for Washington could be found along the line of small campfires and picket posts beside Bull Run or out towards Leesburg.

Perhaps more important for the future of the war on the outskirts of Washington was the little group of irregulars left behind by Stuart to conduct what amounted to guerrilla operations in northern Virginia. Styled "partisan rangers" and led by Major John Mosby, this elusive mosquito band wrought havoc on the outfringe of the defenses of the capital. More glamorous in legend than effective militarily, Mosby's men nonetheless occupied Heintzelman's subordinates by capturing pickets (and in one case a brigadier general), raiding supply trains, and in general denying effective Federal control over Fauquier, Loudon, Clark, and portions of western Fairfax and Prince William counties in 1863 and 1864. In the winter and spring of 1863, the official reports overflowed with skirmishes and "affairs" at colorful little Virginia hamlets like Herndon Station, Aldie, Snicker's Ferry, Dranesville, and Chantilly. Such was Mosby's work; he did it well; and his men generally baffled Union columns sent to suppress such activities under the shadow of the capital.[11]

Meanwhile, by early 1863, Heintzelman was having other problems in his command. Problems of funneling troops to the field and organizing his own units, difficulties with sutlers

[144]

and deserters from Burnside's army, discussions with Dorthea Dix about the convalescent camp at Alexandria, were all compounded when Hooker replaced Burnside as commander of the Army of the Potomac. Heintzelman told Halleck privately that he would not serve under a man whose reputation had been acquired while his subordinate. But, for the record, he wondered if his command could not be constituted as a separate department, claiming that it stretched from Piscataway Creek on the Maryland shore below the capital to Annapolis Junction, northwestward to the mouth of the Monocacy, and on the Virginia side along Goose Creek, out to Aldie and the Bull Run Mountains, then back along Cedar Run to the Occoquan. As Heintzelman observed:

> There does not appear to be much connection between the Army of the Potomac and the troops for the defense of Washington. Scarcely an order issued from the headquarters of the Potomac applies here. On the contrary, the commander acts under orders from the General-in-Chief.[12]

Halleck cautioned patience, but on February 2, the War Department issued orders reconstituting the Defenses of Washington as the Department of Washington and the XXII corps. Aggregating 61,979 officers and men present for duty on January 31, the defense command also numbered 654 pieces of heavy artillery and 204 field guns. The reorganization reflected both the expanded physical perimeters of the defenses and the increasingly complex strategic considerations. Halleck implied as much when writing to Burnside on January 7: "In all our interviews, I have urged that our first object was not Richmond, but the defeat or scattering of Lee's army, which threatened Washington and the line of the Upper Potomac."[13] Confederate operations in 1862 had forced a reevaluation of the limits and role of the huge expenditure of men and ordnance and land space which defended the national capital.

Late in February 1863, rumors of a raid by Jackson and Stuart into Maryland created a flurry of excitement. Stoneman blunted what amounted to another Confederate cavalry raid north of the Rappahannock, and Heintzelman's department once more settled into its normal routine. Additional rumors and alarms continued into March as Hooker and the Army of the Potomac prepared for spring campaigning. In the defenses themselves, new senior officers came and departed with regularity (Major General Julius Stahel was sent to bolster cavalry forces), the naming of the forts around the city to honor Union war dead occupied great time and attention, and, at the end of March, Chief Engineer Barnard took stock of the situation once more.[14]

Barnard had approached Secretary of War Stanton on February 2, concerning the $200,000 appropriation needed from Congress "to carry out the recommendation of the Commission, to connect with the system of defenses already established forts and batteries for the defenses of the Potomac." On March 31, he sent an extensive analysis of the armament, garrisons, and fortifications of the so-called Defenses of Washington. At that time, Barnard noted some 26,725 artillery and infantry in the garrisons (as compared to 56,221 officers and men, and 506 heavy and 262 light artillery pieces in the department). He supposed that the numbers of additional troops required were directly proportional to "the circumstances and force of the attack, and . . . the condition of the Potomac, i.e. in speculative figures anywhere from 35,000 (if only the southern defense line were attacked) to 50 or 60,000 if the river was low, and the enemy held both shores." Barnard repeated the words of the Commission that ultimate security would depend upon Washington's field army, the Army of the Potomac. In general, reported the engineer, construction and repair work was progressing slowly, 100 rounds of ammunition per gun was stockpiled in each fort, and Barnard generally believed that full garrisoning of any section of the defensive perimeter was to be effected only as a specific threat became apparent.[15] Two weeks later, Barnard clarified his interpretation of the need for such a sizable force to defend the capital. He cited the need to protect not only Washington itself but also Alexandria, the Chain Bridge, the reservoir of the Washington aqueduct, and the heights across the Eastern branch or Anacostia which enfiladed the navy yard and arsenal.[16]

Meanwhile, reinforcements for the Army of the Potomac drained manpower for the Department of Washington. Statistics showed that by the end of April, total forces present to defend Washington were down to 44,223 officers and men although 824 pieces of heavy ordnance and 386 field guns were counted in the department. While Mosby continued to irritate the pickets on the fringes of the perimeter, and Hooker blundered through the ill-fated Chancellorsville campaign, Barnard and Heintzelman faced the ever-present shortage of labor. The work force for the defenses normally relied upon troop details, contrabands, or, as a last resort, hired laborers. But the withdrawal of potential combat troops left the engineers shorthanded. In addition, many artillerists like those of the Second Pennsylvania Heavy Artillery on the northern defense line, refused to wield the spade. Barnard was forced to employ 1,000 hired civilians to complete work recommended by the Commission. Many such workers were recruited as far away as New York city, and the cost of travel and daily wages of $1.00-$1.25 per day for common laborers, and $2.50 for foremen measurably reduced the $200,000 appropriation earmarked for improvements to the defenses. Fiscal pressures coupled with apathetic soldiers, convalescents, or small-pox-ridden contrabands, and the result was usually the same—poor workmanship, shortage of manpower, and ill-kept standards of maintenance. By the May 22, Barnard was complaining loudly to Heintzelman.[17]

GUNS WHICH PROTECTED WASHINGTON
(National Archives and Records Administration, Washington, D.C.)

Barnard told the commander of the defenses that lack of troops south of the Potomac had forced him to suspend work on that side of the river. He had spent over $30,000 in payrolls for hired labor in April alone, and he had but $14,000 left from the $200,000 appropriation, with expectations of little over $10,000 remaining at the end of May, and much unfinished work on the books, including interior work on works such as Fort Craig, bombproofs needed in Forts DeKalb, Woodberry, Cass, and Tillinghast, and other labor needed at Chain Bridge, Fort McDowell, and the river batteries. Barnard reflected how tired he was of the work on the latter and "the probable allegation that it is endless may be frankly admitted." He concluded: "It is extremely difficult to keep up a large force of hired laborers, and as to contrabands, of which there are multitudes somewhere, cultivating Arlington or employed by the quartermaster, I have never been allowed to get any number."[18]

Heintzelman was more than sympathetic to the engineers' problems. By mid-May, Stanton and Halleck were beginning to worry that Hooker's defeat was the prelude to another Confederate offensive. They decided to investigate the defense plans for the capital. Hooker himself contended that various Federal contingents from Washington and Baltimore to the upper Potomac were all out of position to help him, and he asked for reinforcements. But Heintzelman countered such requests with the claim that Washington should not be stripped of any more troops. He told Halleck on May 17 that the department's morning report of the previous week showed the aggregate manpower strength present for duty to have been 52,629 but when those detailed to special or other duty, sick call, or in arrest and confinement were tallied, the number shrank to 32,982. He then proceeded to demolish even this figure by a detailed rundown which illustrated just how thin the departmental manpower was stretched in 1863.[19]

Heintzelman pointed to 1,530 men at headquarters, on railroad guard between Washington and Baltimore, or in the reserve of artillery camps of instruction. Fort Washington added another 118 officers and men, as did 5,324 socalled "city guards" of Washington and Alexandria. 1,117 personnel of the Corps of Observation stretched along the northern bank of the Potomac to the mouth of the Monocacy, and Camps Convalescent and Distribution contributed an equal number. Stahel's cavalry division numbered 3,739, and garrisons from the Chain Bridge to Fort Greble comprised 5,329, while 5,988 personnel were included in the southern defense line. This left Abercrombie's force of 8,581. But the first brigade of Pennsylvania Reserves—1,524 strong—held the depot at Fairfax Station and furnished laborers to load and unload cars and provided railroad guards. "General Abercrombie sends one regiment to picket on the Occoquan, where, on account of the wooded nature of the country, I only use cavalry, and cannot send a wagon to the depot without a strong escort, or it will be captured by the guerrillas," claimed Heintzelman. Even Abercrombie asserted that he usually stationed two regiments at Wolf Run Shoals; two regiments at Union Mills guarding the Bull Run railroad bridge; four regiments at Centreville; two regiments at Chantilly; and one regiment stretched along the Orange and Alexandria from Bull Run to Cedar Run, where connection was made with cavalry of the Army of the Potomac. Heintzelman thus decided that for sundry reasons no troops could be withdrawn from any of the main garrison posts or forts, and as far as Abercrombie's division was concerned:

> To withdraw this would compel the abandonment of the Occoquan, Bull Run, and the railroad to the defenses in front of Alexandria, and the quartermaster's station at Vienna. It would be virtually giving up to the enemy all the country up to the fortifications on

the south side of the Potomac, and much closer than they were at any time two winters ago, when their flag waved for so many weeks in sight of our Capitol. Our cavalry would be powerless to prevent incursions even between our forts.

Heintzelman noted that north of the Potomac there were fifty-six forts and batteries and south of the Potomac, sixty-two forts and batteries, but that "our cavalry would be powerless to prevent incursions even between our forts, as all the rifle-pits would be unoccupied" should any more troops be withdrawn. He concluded:

The Army of the Potomac operating so low down the Rappahan-nock as Fredericksburg, should we remove the troops that now hold the fortifications of Centreville and the positions in the vicinity, would throw open to the enemy all the country on the Upper Rappahannock and the Valley of the Shenandoah, permitting them to send troops without interruption to operate as far as the Potomac on our defenses south of that river, and still preserving to themselves a secure line of retreat beyond the Blue Ridge. I am decidedly of the opinion that no more troops can be spared from the Defenses of Washington.[20]

Halleck concurred with Heintzelman's conclusions as he forwarded the situation report to Stanton. In a rather lengthy memorandum on May 18, he outlined various options open to both Hooker and Lee, and he suggested that Federal forces would probably remain immobile on the Rappahannock line for some time. Lee might be expected to either attack Hooker, move to regain Norfolk while demonstrating against Washington, Harpers Ferry, or Maryland, or more probably, reverse the priorities of the latter and strike northward. Halleck felt this course posed the greatest argument against reduction of the defense force for the capital.[21]

The pesky raids of Mosby's guerrillas and even larger cavalry units apparently continued to cause great concern as

[151]

Stanton again queried Halleck on May 23 about the proper cavalry protection for Washington and nearby supply and transportation lines. Conferring with Heintzelman and Quartermaster General Montgomery C. Meigs, Halleck concluded that little improvement could be made by the people in the Department of Washington and much depended upon dispositions of the cavalry of the Army of the Potomac. Heintzelman and the garrison forces had cut down trees to block roads, and they had further barricaded and fortified the bridge approachs and strengthened picket posts around the city. Departmental cavalry manned the early warning system beyond the defense lines, and in general, Halleck's memorandum to the secretary of war placed more burden of preventing raids or countering those that occurred upon Hooker's cavalry than upon the mounted force of Heintzelman. Implied in the dispatch was the ever-present note that the commander of the Army of the Potomac was not making the best use of his forces and not keeping higher headquarters apprised of his plans.[22]

The probability of Halleck's deductions about Lee's plans was more reality than speculation by early June. Lee had discussed the merits of going north once more with Richmond authorities in mid-May. He pointed to the attractiveness of an invasion of the war-weary north, seizure of some great northern city, and a victory in battle on northern soil. Furthermore, such a move would break up Federal plans for the summer campaign, and, if combined with bringing forces from North Carolina, and concentrating them under Beauregard for a diversionary move on the Culpeper-Manassas line to Washington, then the success of the mission seemed assured. Davis and Postmaster General John H. Reagan argued that Lee should send men west to help in Mississippi, and Beauregard was never ordered north against Washington. Still, the fright caused by Lee's main movements in June and July brought a measure of initial success to Confederate arms.[23]

Interestingly enough, Lee experienced the same frustrations with his civilian superiors concerning the safety of Richmond as the succession of Federal commanders faced with the Lincoln government involving Washington. The Federals in June 1863 were staging diversions of their own. Union forces under Major General John A. Dix on the lower peninsula moved toward Richmond in what Lee took to be merely another raid. But the Davis government decided to withhold reinforcements from North Carolina scheduled to help the Army of Northern Virginia. The usual lack of coordination of Federal armies, timid expeditionary officers, and offsetting concern in Washington for that city's safety all dissipated the peninsula operation. But the effect nicely counteracted Lee's design for Beauregard although he continued to urge that plan before the Davis government as late as June 25.[24]

At the very moment that Lee was thus writing to Davis from Williamsport, Maryland, his presence on northern soil was naturally causing consternation in Washington once more. At the time, strength figures in the Department of Washington showed fewer than 50,000 effectives with 913 pieces of artillery available for defense. Repeated dispatch of reinforcements to the Army of the Potomac worried Heintzelman, especially as he received excited reports from Barnard and his engineers about continuing weak chinks in the capital's armor. The engineers complained loudly that fort commanders were removing abattis, and erecting ineffective and poorly placed barricades and stockades to block roadways against cavalry raids as well as blockhouses for railroad protection. Concern for such matters was highlighted by daily reports of incursions by Mosby's guerrillas. When Hooker sought to have Stahel's cavalry patrol the Shenandoah valley, Stanton and Halleck supported Heintzelman's opposition on the grounds that the 5,397-man cavalry division, based on Fairfax Court House, was the only mounted unit in the department, and "if it be removed there will be no force in front to give notice of enemy's raids on Alexandria or Washington."[25]

Hooker was facing great difficulties of his own. Lee was moving northward, his intentions unknown. Behind Hooker lay a rather confused and somewhat hostile command situation in Washington. Hooker's initial response to Lee's activity was to propose a movement across the Rappahannock against the Confederate rear and then on to Richmond. This suggestion was vetoed by Lincoln and his advisers, who wanted Hooker not only to adhere to earlier instructions to cover Washington but in so doing to strike the Army of Northern Virginia—the true objective—now strung out from Fredericksburg to the Potomac. Lincoln deplored Hooker's constant call for reinforcements and the army commander discovered that he could not peremptorily order the various miscellaneous commands of Heintzelman, or Daniel French at Harpers Ferry, and Robert Schenck in the Middle Department, to strengthen the main army. The roadblock was Halleck, Hooker's opponent from as far back as prewar California, but many critics also pointed to Hooker's rather petulant response to the pursuit of Lee.[26]

The facts show that Hooker's army moved ponderously northward, keeping roughly between Lee's army and Washington. Union cavalry pricked their opponents' cavalry screen as the blueclad footsoldiers encamped successively at Centreville, Fairfax, and Dranesville before passing into Maryland. The capital seemed safe for the moment as its field army, reportedly in good spirits, moved less than fifty miles to the west. But the Federal command functioned in its usual erratic fashion with Lincoln, Stanton, and Halleck communicating with Hooker in a somewhat confusing and contradictory manner; Hooker continually overestimating the strength of the enemy and seeking reinforcements; and Heintzelman and Schenck providing numerous cries of alarm for the safety of the two cities they were assigned to defend. Everyone seemed to have a different notion of duty and responsibility. All too many individuals were offering too much advice to higher headquarters. The main Federal field force, the real defenders of Washington, Baltimore, and Philadelphia, was commanded by a general who lacked the confidence both of his superiors and of his troops, and he did not evidence much awareness of what he wanted to do anyway. One general officer in the Army of the Potomac, Brigadier General Alpheus S. Williams concluded: "In this case there is a momentous issue, for if we are badly defeated there is but little hope, I think, of saving Washington. The troops held so sacredly about that 'corruption sink' would make a poor show before the victorious Rebels.[27]

Part of the trouble came from the nature of the vantage point of Washington itself. Lincoln, Stanton, and Halleck were much closer to the pleas and complaints of Heintzelman, Barnard, and others than they were to Hooker. Given the continuing focus of the politicians and Halleck's personal peculiarities, it remains difficult to see how the vital question of defending Washington in June 1863 could have resulted other than in confusion. Perhaps Heintzelman summarized the majority feeling most aptly when he recorded in his diary: "The whole north is aroused & Lee's army will not escape if our Generals are worth the parchment their commissions are written on."[28]

As the month of June turned into its final week, Heintzelman's problems seemed only to escalate. His strength figures of 48,824 men and 926 guns slowly dwindled to 32,644 by the last day of the month. Picket posts on the Occoquan line were reduced and then abandoned as the Army of the Potomac swept up outlying garrisons to swell its own ranks, and both the divisions of Brigadier Generals Abercrombie and Samuel W. Crawford went off to Hooker during the latter

[155]

part of June. In the words of one historian: "There is no doubt that reinforcements for the Army of the Potomac stripped the defenses of Washington of practically all of their mobile units, which were composed largely of veteran troops." Apparently the vast majority of some 25,000 men sent to Hooker by Heintzelman and Schenck came from the Washington garrison. In addition, Heintzelman's department dispatched manpower and equipment to Dix's expedition on the peninsula and the defenses of Suffolk. It is little wonder that Heintzelman complained loudly to Halleck about the situation. This in turn radically affected the Union high command and its impressions of Washington's protection and Hooker's intentions.[29]

Hooker sent Major General Daniel J. Butterfield to Washington and Baltimore to gather still more troops, but his chief of staff ran into stubborn opposition from Halleck and even Lincoln. He should not have expected otherwise for Heintzelman trumpeted, "As all my cavalry has been taken from the other side, should the Army of the Potomac move from my front, the first indication of the approach of the enemy would be their appearance at our works." Even Barnard chorused that same day, "I understand that not only are there no troops left to man the rifle-pits and to support the artillerymen of the forts, but that even the number of artillerymen is not up to the standard." The engineer pointed as usual to the Commission report of 1862, and he believed that quartermaster employees and "citizens and transient persons in Washington" should be organized into a supplementary force since the enemy was nearly at the city's gates.[30]

Two days later Heintzelman's contention proved to be true. As the Army of the Potomac moved across the Potomac, Confederate cavalry under Stuart followed in its wake. The "Plumed Knight," stirred on by Mosby's intelligence reports as well as the distinct possibility of added glory, persuaded

[156]

Lee to let him cut loose from the main army in the Shenandoah valley and stage what amounted to a separate invasion of Maryland and Pennsylvania. His direction cut between Hooker's army and the Washington defenders. Swinging around the Union outposts at Centreville, Stuart's men watered their horses in the coolness of Bull Run at Wolf Run Shoals, then struck briefly at Fairfax, Annandale, and Dranesville on June 27. That night they crossed the Potomac and rested the next morning in the lush fields above Rockville.

By now Heintzelman was beside himself with frustration. His meager remaining mounted detachments were brushed aside and panicky personnel at headquarters spread alarm on the streets of the city. Then the grayclad cavalry dashed into Rockville at noon on June 28, amazing churchgoers and enraptured school girls from a local academy at the county seat. More unnerved, however, were Union quartermaster authorities, when a supply train of 150 wagons lumbered up the pike from Washington only to fall into the waiting hands of the alert rebels. Stuart's troopers chased some of the teamsters and wagons back to the defense line at Tennallytown. But the full bag of prisoners included over several hundred teamsters, as well as 125 wagons, 900 mules, forage, whiskey, bacon, hams, and sugar. Such encumbrances proved embarrassing to Stuart's column as it moved much more slowly than before northward into Maryland. Nonetheless, he still managed to cut telegraph contact between Washington and the Army of the Potomac, to destroy small portions of the railroad west of Baltimore, and to increase the fears of defenders of that Maryland city and of the national capital.[31]

Historians have claimed that Stuart's antics cost Lee the battle of Gettysburg. But for a time, the Southern cavalrymen baffled and enraged Stanton, agitated Halleck, and gave Lincoln deeper concern. In the absence of any large unit of Federal cavalry, the Confederates escaped unscathed. As Meigs rue-

[157]

fully told Quartermaster Rufus Ingalls of the Army of the Potomac: "All of the cavalry of the Defenses of Washington was swept off by the army, and we are now insulted by burning wagons 3 miles outside of Tennallytown." Ingalls rejoinder that even an escort could not have avoided the disaster was probably meager balm to Meigs.[32]

Stuart shared Lee's healthy respect for Washington's fortifications no matter how understrength the garrisons. Furthermore, he was supposedly on an intelligence gathering mission, not one of attacking the capital. But those warm, anxious days in the Potomac valley found newly erected barricades in the streets, quartermaster employees and black units organized for defense, and Washington citizenry fretful about their close call. In Georgetown mills had to close for want of cargo vessels as Stuart cut the canal to the west; coal yards were empty; vessels stood idle at the wharves; and local "Secesh" rejoiced behind closed shutters. Heintzelman fumed about the cavalry he had lost to Hooker earlier, although Percy Wyndham collected a composite command of 3,000 stragglers after Stuart had departed the immediate area. When Heintzelman rode out toward Chain Bridge for a pleasure jaunt on the 30th, touchy sentinels mistook the blackberry-picking party for Confederates. Even the cannoneers at Battery Cameron sent shells over the heads of the party and into the canal—such were the fears in Washington during the crisis.[33]

Hooker by this time had come to the end of his period as leader of the Army of the Potomac. Unable to secure as many men from Heintzelman or Schenck as he wanted—not especially helped by the presence of Confederate cavalry at the doorsteps of the two cities—his inability to incorporate the men at Harpers Ferry into his army led directly to his relief. At 3 A.M. on June 28, Major General George G. Meade succeeded Hooker in command of the army. He had similar basic orders as Hooker—find and fight Lee, but cover Washington!

Stanton questioned Halleck and his subordinates on June 30 about the value of "planting batteries at the avenues of approach and at different points in the city." Halleck replied that earthen batteries in addition to the regular forts already existed, but that there were insufficient garrisons for them. Reports from subordinates such as Colonel H. L. Abbott, commanding the Third brigade, Defenses South of the Potomac, noted that the garrisons were spread too thin to really stop any determined attacker and charging: "Fort Worth is too high to command the road [Little River turnpike] by night by artillery fire, and my infantry is too bad to be trusted to protect even a section of the light artillery there, where there is no retreat from cavalry."

Halleck further counseled Stanton against putting ten or twelve batteries of mounted artillery along the main line of fortifications (ostensibly part of the original scheme of defense of the city), for that would "expose them to almost inevitable destruction" and would not enable them to concentrate, with whatever infantry was left, upon a particular threatened point. He concluded: "More batteries could be organized, but we have no artillerists to man them. I know of no available military means which have not already been employed to prevent a rebel raid on this city."[34]

Stuart's cavalry was gone by this time and anxious sentinels were peering into the haze on the horizon in vain. Convalescents, paroled prisoners, detachments of Pennsylvania Reserves, railway guards, city guards, and meager fortress troops remained. When officials extended the draft, the engineers complained bitterly that laborers and foremen were swept up and "men cannot serve the country in both ways at the same time." Scouting parties, however, disclosed that the rebels had gone from the Washington area. The telegraph soon brought news of the great battle raging at a small Pennsylvania crossroads town called Gettysburg. The fate of the capital had passed beyond the control of Washington observers.[35]

The Union victory at Gettysburg concluded the threat to Washington, Baltimore, and the northeast. The importance of that battle may have been appropriately summarized by the American minister in Paris, John Dayton, who wrote home to the secretary of state on July 10: "If Lee should take Pennsylvania and drive the government out of Washington, the effect would be immediate recognition from all of the European states." But such did not take place, and, while Longstreet had visions of a superb tactical sweep around Meade's left flank and imposition of a Confederate force between the Federals and the capital, nothing of that sort occurred. The rainy national birthday on the fourth witnessed Lee's retreat toward the Potomac, as well as momentary fright that the rebels might strike across South Mountain toward Washington via Frederick. But the race for the Potomac showed neither Lee nor Meade capable of lightning thrusts at this point. Even before the Confederate army escaped across the river, Lincoln appropriately noted the problem to Halleck on July 6: "These things all appear to me to be connected with a purpose to cover Baltimore and Washington, and to get the enemy across the river again without further collision, and they do not appear connected with a purpose to prevent his crossing and to destroy him."[36]

Both Hooker and Meade interpreted their mission of containment and protection too unimaginatively. Ingenuity and the drive to annihilate were simply not part of either's makeup. When Barnard could blithely report to higher headquarters on July 7, that he needed an additional $100,000 to complete the work recommended by the Commission the previous fall, such a request merely illustrated that while the sacred cow, Washington, remained inviolate, so also did the main threat. By late summer and fall of 1863, both the Army of Northern

[160]

Virginia and the Army of the Potomac were back in the Virginia piedmont. The more things changed, the more they stayed the same.[37]

As the Army of the Potomac returned to the axis of the Orange and Alexandria, depredations on that road resumed. Again Heintzelman's troops engaged in guerrilla chasing and guard duty on the railroad. Again he complained that his forces, numbering only about 34,000 effectives with 978 cannon, were inadequate for the various tasks demanded of them. By late August Heintzelman was settling into a routine which was highlighted only by daily reports of Mosby's activities, random artillery reviews, and occasional jaunts with cabinet members to forts around Washington. One such excursion took the department commander with Lincoln, Stanton, Barnard, and other local officials to newly built Fort Foote commanding the Potomac on Rozier's Bluff. Here Lieutenant Colonel Frederick Seward's Ninth New York "Heavies" were putting the finishing touches upon the most intricate and most sophisticated of any of the works in the defenses of Washington.[38]

There were no major conflicts in the eastern theater for a while after Gettysburg but mainly much cleaning-up and sparring activity in Virginia. Meade missed an opportunity to destroy Lee at Manassas Gap and was outmaneuvered and forced to retire behind Bull Run in the so-called Bristoe campaign; the two armies feinted with one another along Mine Run in the late fall. Meade, like his predecessors, felt that Washington officials interfered in offensive moves, and Lincoln and his advisers considered Meade too dilatory in closing with the enemy. But the Army of the Potomac kept carefully between Lee and the capital while, at the same time, Meade never fully grasped Lincoln's subtle logic contained in such enjoinders as: "If the enemy's sixty thousand are sufficient to keep our ninety thousand away from Richmond,

[161]

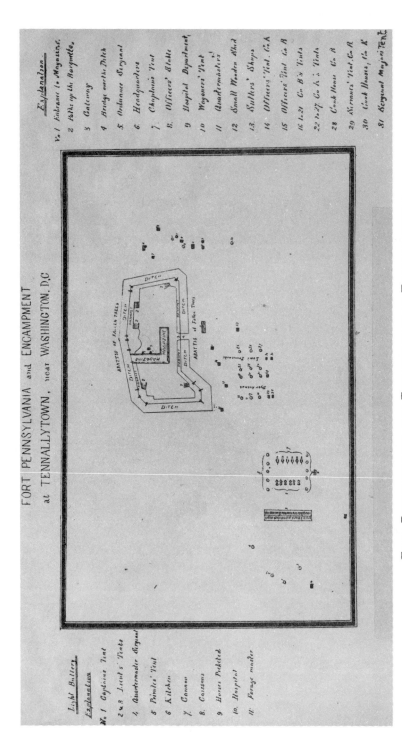

FORT PENNSYLVANIA AND ENCAMPMENT AT TENNALLYTOWN
(Drawn for Mr. George Baker by W. E. Cushing, Providence, R.I., 1862)

why, by the same rule, may not forty thousand of ours keep their sixty thousand away from Washington, leaving us fifty thousand to put to some other use."[39]

At the same time, Lee no longer had the strength for offensive moves, and while he found it relatively easy to force Meade all the way back to Centreville and Fairfax in mid October, he admitted to President Davis: "It is easy for him [Meade] to retire under the fortifications of Washington and Alexandria, and we should be unable to attack him advantageously." Meade concentrated on a compact, intrenched line fronting Bull Run. It stretched from the lower fords, through Centreville and Chantilly to Fairfax Court House. Meade's mediocre talents—as Gideon Welles classified them—may have caused much consternation in Washington, but Lee's attempt to effect another Second Bull Run was thwarted, and even Lincoln told northern citizens that he felt Washington was in no danger that autumn.[40]

Immediate defenders of the capital never exceeded 35,000 effectives that fall, although Meade's 80,000 veterans formed the first line of defense. Heintzelman and, after November, his successor C. C. Augur, spent most of their time worrying about Mosby and E. V. White and their guerrillas, as well as listening to complaints from the engineers. The story was always the same—burning wagon trains, captured couriers, telegraph lines cut, isolated pickets and patrols routed or destroyed. One frustrated Union cavalry colonel summed up the situation in late 1863 in northern Virginia: "I can clear this country with fire and sword, and no mortal can do it in any other way. The attempt to discriminate nicely between the just and the unjust is fatal to our safety; every house is a vedette post, and every hill a picket and signal station." In his mind, Attila the Hun had adopted the only method that could exterminate such citizen soldiers.[41]

Equally troublesome to War Department administrators were the engineers working on the forts. They were seldom silent in their demands and ardent desire to make the capital city impregnable. J. G. Barnard chose the acme of the Bristoe fright to approach Stanton about the continued weakness of the water approach to the capital—a subject to which he would return often in 1863 and 1864. The chief engineer had been actively surveying the condition of the defense system all summer. Appointed to head a small examining board on the fortifications guarding the aqueduct—Washington's water supply—the persistent Barnard wrote to the Secretary of War several times in September concerning the river batteries. Spurred on, perhaps by the inspection tour of the British minister, Lord Lyons, and Admiral of the Fleet Sir Alexander Milne and his staff, Barnard sent Stanton a strong note on October 13 urging development of river obstructions in concert with the shore batteries. Noting Confederate success at Charleston (but somehow neglecting the role of the U.S. Navy on the Potomac), the landsman cited Federal tests with underwater obstacles at New York, and the relative nakedness of Washington "if we should get into a war with a maritime power while the rebellion is yet powerful." The sixteen heavy guns in Battery Rodgers and Fort Foote could not compare with shore batteries protecting Boston and New York. Timber hulks would be unavailable in an emergency and the Washington Navy Yard would not be able to furnish the amount of cables required to hold the hulks together. Barnard never mentioned what role the navy might be expected to play—he merely requested Stanton to seek $300,000 from Congress and designate $150,000 from departmental contingency funds for these obstacles.[42] Stanton responded favorably, but the whole matter awaited the return of Congress to a new session in 1864.

Fearing that he might be pushing too hard, Barnard

nevertheless followed on October 14 with yet another dispatch to Stanton. He painstakingly recounted all the progress on the main works in the system, and this time he noted that $300,000 should be appropriated for "completing and rendering more permanent the defenses of Washington." Alluding to an old railroader maxim that "when the cars can go over the road it is half done," Barnard told Stanton that the forts were essentially in condition to render the services expected of them, "as a railroad over which the trains began to pass is brought to a condition to do the service expected of it," and, like the railroad, it was likely to turn out that they were really but half finished. Barnard claimed to have no disposition to magnify the work. "I am ready to leave it at any moment," he said, adding humbly, if somewhat inaccurately, "I relinquished command and the more exciting duties of the field at a moment when they would have brought me more palpable recompense, to carry out the works, because I felt that the security of Washington demanded their perfection, and that the security of Washington meant the security of the nation's cause, and that I was the man upon whom the duty fell."[43]

Late in the month Barnard suggested establishment of an ordnance board to examine the status of the fortress artillery in the defenses. He was especially concerned with simplification of the variety of calibres, additions and reductions which might make the artillery more effective, and whether or not guns on barbette carriages should be further reduced in number. The board was constituted on November 9, with Barry, Barnard, and G. W. Cullum—all from the 1862 commission which had studied the system—joined by G. A. De Russy and Barnard's assistant, B. S. Alexander.[44]

As winter once more descended on the Potomac valley, random cavalry and guerrilla raids on the Orange and Alexandria (once more the lifeline of the Army of the Potomac)

[165]

bothered officials in the Department of Washington. But relative calm returned to the locale. The Army of the Potomac and the Army of Northern Virginia settled into winter camps, eying one another warily and wearily across the Rappahannock near Culpeper—sixty miles from the northern capital.

CHAPTER SEVEN

Attack on the Capital

Fifty years after he had served in the defenses of Washington, Thomas Lounsbury noted that he had always regarded the extensive works at Centreville as a "humbug—a gigantic imposition upon the credulity of the American people." Of value only against frontal attack, utterly powerless to resist an assault from the flank, these works seemed to him to be the playthings of civilians, scenes of drudgery for the soldiers who built them, and bastions of tediousness for those garrison troops who served in them. As Lounsbury observed: ". . . it seems never to get through the heads of some men that the strength of a position depends not so much on its fortifications as it does on the number and spirit of the soldiers who hold it, and the ability and resolution of the officer who commands it." Lounsbury served on the outer defense perimeter. But he might have appropriately applied this same judgement to the main system of Washington forts. By the winter of 1863-1864 the line of security for the capital still contained weak points, and more importantly some of these weaknesses were human. "Uncle Abe's pets," the paper-collar troops of the defenses, were dedicated but hardly battle-tried. They were profoundly tired of gun drill and of polishing brass shoulder scales for inspections and parades, and many of them probably wished they could fight something besides the "gray ghosts" of Mosby's guerrillas, escaping convalescents or draftees, or merely their own boredom.[1]

Duty in the camps and fortifications around the nation's capital had become reasonably static by this stage of the war. Drill, guard mount, fatigue details, and inspections comprised the soldier's day. Writing letters home, visiting friends in other units transitioning the Washington area en route to the front, collecting delicacies from loved ones at the express office in the city, or fretting about terms of enlistment and the fortunes of the Army of the Potomac seemed to fill the thoughts of the fortress soldiers as expressed in letters and diaries of the time. For most men the time passed pleasantly enough, "each day shortening our term of service." There were variations in the daily routine from unit to unit (including "zouave drill" in some cases), but experiences of the Third Massachusetts and Fourth New York heavy artillery regiments, stationed north of the Potomac, provide a composite picture of garrison activities.[2]

A typical day began at 5:40 A.M. At reveille the guards ceased their challenge calls and the men had twenty minutes to fall in for roll call. Police and patrol assignments were made at roll call and the men had until 7:00 to attend to personal cleanliness before the bugle call, "Peas on a Trencher,"

Modern Views at Fort Ward Park, Alexandria, Va

summoned them to breakfast. Surgeon's call came at 9:00 to the tune "Come and Get your Quinine, Come and Get Your Whiskey," and guard mount followed sick call. The most neatly dressed soldier was picked for orderly at the captain's quarters, with company drill following guard mount at 10:00, after which "some of the boys did nothing but loll around . . . others smoked, washed their clothes and polished their firearms, or if they were lucky went down to Washington on passes." Noon meal to the bugle call of "Roast Beef" was followed by crisp notes of "To the Colours" at 2:00 P.M. signalling battalion drill. "Retreat" called the men to dress parade at 4:00 or 4:30. Supper call, again "Peas on a Trencher," was sounded at 6:00 and then the men passed the time until "Tattoo" at 8:30 or 9:00. "Taps" came at 9:00 or 10:00 and camps and forts became quiet as the men fell asleep "to awake to another peaceful day or to receive orders to march to the front." Occasionally, the boys might get a bit unruly as at Fort Slocum in late March 1863 when despite the poor health of the Eleventh Vermont everyone apparently got into a hot snowball fight according to S. B. Bruce of that unit.

The complex command structure of the defenses and the passage of so many general officers in an out of the department caused countless problems for efficient management of the garrisons. In order to discourage too frequent inspections and to preserve authority over the commands in the forts, officers like Barnard and Heintzelman periodically issued orders outlining the chain of command and, on one occasion in early 1863, General Orders 45 restricted each general officer to one prearranged cannon salute per year. Although ostensibly designed to conserve ammunition, this order was also intended to discourage unnecessary inspections. Regular inspections took place often enough anyway, with a major inspection every Sunday morning and troops excused from drill on Saturday afternoons to clean and polish weapons and accoutrements.[3]

Drill usually lasted from four to six hours per day, and both infantry and artillery drill were practised regardless of the branch represented by a specific unit at a specific fort or camp. In the case of the Tenth New York Volunteer Heavy Artillery, drill included heavy and light artillery exercises, as well as infantry and bayonet practice. The garrisons drilled as companies, battalions, and brigades, and artillery practice was conducted twice a week at specified times. The target was generally an old tent or log, or in the case of Fort Greble, a buoy in the river. Naturally, the overly zealous local commanders sometimes found abandoned buildings or other targets worthy of their aim, but records of the firing were always sent to the chief of artillery of the defenses.

Some of the more monotonous chores by mid-war were household in nature. Cutting brush and timber from the approaches to the forts, sodding and trimming fort embankments, cleaning the guns, laying of gun platforms, manufacturing gabions, and the ubiquitous policing of the area were included in this category. The officers' duties were more varied than those of the enlisted personnel since there were numerous reports, details to be supervised, and what apparently proved to be the most irritating chore—participation on court martial boards. Lieutenant Colonel George E. Chamberlin of the Eleventh Vermont complained from Fort Totten in mid-1863: "I believe I am destined to spend the most of my term of service in military courts & boards of some kind." Even the usually indefatigable Barnard complained dejectedly to the War Department in January 1864:

It is proper to state that I had intended on the close of the campaign of 1862 to ask to be assigned to duty with the troops believing that after serving two years as an Engineer Officer I was entitled to share with my Juniors the advantages in the way of promotion attending the command of troops and the still more important

advantage of instructing myself by actual practice in all the duties
of the soldier, convinced that such practice was important to me
even for a complete knowledge of my duties as an Engineer.[4]

Surely the diets of the soldiers must have become slightly tedious after awhile, although proximity to Washington
markets and regional tastes may have enabled the fare to vary
somewhat. An officer at Fort Totten in 1862 reported the diet
there included smelt, Irish potatoes, apples, mutton, ham, tea,
coffee, and milk. The Seventeenth Maine ate baked beans
every Sunday morning. Troops at more outlying posts in
Virginia were often able to procure turkeys, chickens, and
vegetables which they confiscated from the surrounding
countryside, and melons, peaches, and apples in season were
brought from Negroes and sutlers who came to the forts daily in order to sell produce. Whiskey and wine made their way
surreptitiously into camp and fort, and passes to Washington
offered the opportunity to consume much esteemed oysters
in the city's restaurants—although the soldiers' pay probably
rendered such opportunities relatively rare.[5]

Washington continued to be the principal attraction for
leisure time activities although a $6.50 cab fare from Virginia
to the District of Columbia may have daunted some enlisted
men. Other local sites such as Arlington, or local belles like
Edmund Brooke's daughters Maria and Anna residing in
northwest Washington near the camp of the First Maine Heavy
Artillery, or the Unionist daughter of the Woodworth family
near Lewinsville where the Tenth Rhode Island was posted—all
attracted the curious young soldiers from the north. But the
concentration of troops around the city also posed a threat
to the peace and quiet of the locale, and pro-Southerners often
clashed with the blue-coated volunteers. Some units were
privileged, and the Tenth New York heavies which garrisoned
Forts Mahan, Dupont, and Davis, east of the Anacostia, had
relatively free access to the city. The Tenth was "privileged

to come and go without the usual restraint on troops here. A lady or anybody seeing their number on the streets are insured against insult and feel a sense of security with their presence here that cannot be said of some.''

For those individuals and units less fortunate than the New Yorkers, leisure time in the forts could be spent in many ways. Sleeping and eating took on new significance for those unused to military life. Daily journals and ''scientific notes'' from the last excursion were kept by the young volunteers. Books were took bulky for troops at the front, but compact disposable publications such as *Beadle's* dime novels and the *Waverly Magazine* were popular around Washington's camps and forts. Many soldiers simply whiled away the time by viewing the surrounding countryside from the high ground occupied by the forts. There was a race course within a half mile of Fort Stevens on the Seventh Street road. The beneficial aspects of leisure time were recalled by the regimental historian of the First Maine Heavy Artillery when he recorded after the war: ''Some of our younger officers, who had been students before entering the service, went far beyond the ordinary drill in their studies of engineering, field works, and field fortifications, permanent earth works, ordnance and gunnery, theory of projectiles and artillery practice, studies which made them useful in their after service and especially so during the siege of Petersburg.''[6]

Holidays meant a full day or half-day relief from duty for the enlisted men. Regimental histories note Thanksgiving, Christmas, and New Year's Day as special holidays, in this regard. Vermont Captain (later Major) Aldace F. Walker wrote home from Fort Massachusetts (later Stevens) how he missed being with the folks on his first Thanksgiving there in 1862; the next year he noted the absence of a ''Vermont Thanksgiving,'' but a month later sounded more upbeat suggesting: ''We had quite a time Christmas Day. A Holiday—

and some twelve dollars in prizes were distributed for wrestling, running, jumping and climbing. We had a good deal of fun over a blindfold wheelbarrow race by the First Sergeants, and a greased pole. The officers ran a race—the one who touched a fence last to treat—the fast ones put in, and the slow ones did not touch the fence at all, so that the joke was on a Second Lieutenant, who was not in the secret." Preservation of the sabbath and strong religious feelings of the era also meant a lighter schedule on Sundays although Church parade and the presence of officers' ladies in camp set a more formal tone that day. If the Nineteenth Maine was at all indicative, the chaplain and regimental commander vied with one another in the pulpit on qualities of patriotism, religion, and temperance. Walker joined other officers from Forts Slocum, Totten, Stevens, and Slemmer in attending services religiously at the Episcopal Saint Paul's church, Rock Creek parish near the northern line. Still, this future Congregational minister pointedly commented that "the church is small, the service odd, the choir ignorant." Just about everyone appreciated the various regimental bands—the First Maine and the Second Pennsylvania Heavy Artillery Regiments noted as having the best—and the Fourth New York "heavies" staged a "Columbiad Ministral" show to relieve its tedious service at Fort Corcoran.[7]

Nearly all the officers were attended by servants, many of them recruited from the plethora of homeless blacks hovering around the camps and forts. Prejudice and exploitation of the Freedmen could be found in nearly all letters and diaries, and Aldace Walker opined in January 1863: "I hear the President has issued a Proclamation of Freedom, but I have not seen it. I am convinced that the negroes cannot take care of themselves so that they will be otherwise than a nuisance to the community. Want them freed, but should demand instant colonization if I was big enough to have a public voice," he told his father. Indeed, no better account of the "life and times" of junior officers in the wartime defenses of Washington remains to us than the copious letters of this Vermonter home from 1862 to 1864. Middlebury College graduate, postwar minister and regimental chronicler for his unit the Eleventh Vermont (First Heavy Artillery), Aldace Walker's letters capture a saga of a young rural American thrust into a position of responsibility commanding other young volunteers even before he reached his majority in life. Walker's experiences embraced the typical military duties of sitting on courts martial, perfecting the proficiency of his unruly men, and bracing camp life of lice and flies, sickness and poor weather, while obviously relishing both avoidance of battle strife and the vibrancy of service near the nation's capital.[8]

At first, Walker wrote glowingly of dress parades and pomp which brought an influx of influential visitors to camp and fort. In September 1862, Secretary of State William Seward conveyed a delegation of British dignitaries (Walker called them "English sprigs of nobility) to see the Vermonters' parade. An English officer in the party pronounced The Green Mountain boys' appearance "far surpassed that of a British regiment he just saw arrive in Canada," recounted Walker. But a year later, the weekly round of inspections and dress parades which forced the Vermonters to congregate at Fort Bunker Hill—several miles' march from other posts they garrisoned—dulled the enthusiasm.

Walker's letters home regaled kinsmen with stories of the flow of Yankee volunteers through Washington en route to the front. He noted sojourns to the wartime capital—"a very easy, plain city . . . the avenues are rather promiscuous like . . . none of any consequence, however save Pennsylvania and there is hardly another street of mark in the city; cars go every four minutes." But, later, he dismissed the unfinished Washington monument (he called it "the National

Monument") as inconsequential and doubted its much ballyhooed grandeur even if ever completed (which he also doubted). The Vermonter seemed happiest when intruding himself into the households of local Unionists such as the Blagden family for their musicales, or riding out the Seventh Street road from Fort Stevens to drop by Francis Preston Blair's Silver Spring country home. Here, Walker could talk politics with the old politician and newspapermen and his son Montgomery, Lincoln's postmaster general. He particularly delighted in hearing the younger Blair's daughter play her Chickering piano. Union pickets were always stationed by the estate's gate to ward off unwanted guests, but Union soldiers and officers never numbered among the latter. Walker declared that the people of the locale were perceived to be "secesh" generally, but the soldiers on the northern defense line found sufficient kindness from families like the Blairs and Blagdens to forge close ties with the neighborhood (despite periodic forays into chicken coops and gardens for dietary supplements to army rations).

Walker's letters read more like those of a normal peacetime garrison soldier of the prewar and postwar army than those of a wartime veteran. Construction details of winter barracks, sodding of the magazine inside Fort Stevens, road work on the famous military road linking the forts (and still serving as one of Washington's major streets), or sneaking away to a cool dip in Rock Creek at Pierce's Mill to offset summer heat in tropical Washington fill his missives. Friendly rivalry with their partner unit in the northern lines—the Second Pennsylvania Heavy Artillery—kept the Green Mountain boys on their toes. Camp diseases like measles, pneumonia, and diptheria decimated the rural New Englanders and even spread to officer families carrying off the little ones, several of whom also found final resting places in Saint Paul's graveyard. Still, everyone lived well as Walker noted that:

"We are very well situated here—store nearby which furnishes us butter, eggs, sugar, potatoes, &c. and a patch of tomatoes, a quarter of an acre in extent, joining my tent; turnips, beets, apples, vegetables of all sorts handy by." Only fresh meat was a problem, he conceded, but in all, it was a far cry from "hardtack and coffee" which fueled soldiery in the Army of the Potomac. Windstorms and mud and snow were worse enemies, it seemed, and the infrequent alerts when Confederates and guerrillas ventured too close to the city's perimeter. Then, Walker and his men stood round-the-clock guard in their forts, somewhat dispelling the caustic notion of "Uncle Abe's pets."

Walker occasionally bridled at the criticism of the men guarding Washington. He told his father on January 16, 1863 that he wanted to "put in a plea in response to the slur civilians love so well to cast upon the officers of the army, in relation to the 'throng that crows the streets of Washington.' " Most of them came from the myriad of hospitals and supply facilities about the area. "And when we remember that every officer in this portion of the United States is dependent on this city for all clothing and equipments, that many are assigned here on the various court-martials in session, and that every officer prompted in the Army of the Potomac has to visit Washington to be mustered in on his new commission," said a petulant Walker, the wonder was that the streets contained so few, in reality. Walker and the others thought they were doing their duty, heartily snubbed the bounty men and draftees who came down later from Vermont to fill the ranks, and readily admitted the absurdity of being issued white gloves and brass shoulder scales—the mark of heavy artillery units in the forts.

As the months passed, Walker's letters dealt increasingly with daily chores of training the men and fretting about officer promotions. Winter quarters offered an opportunity for special instruction in military affairs, while an active social whirl attended visits to old school chums working in the city or en route to other units. The Vermonters, like the other garrison regiments, became more like families with communities and activities of their own, tied to the field armies only by what they read in the newspapers or what they could learn from the telegraph line which ran out from the War Department downtown to Fort Stevens. Walker marveled at the continuing praises sung on McClellan's behalf, long after he had departed the scene. He wrote his father at one point: "I think it may almost be regarded what that Pennsylvania fellow imputed to Cameron—that Southern independence is certain—to be true. He did not think it treason to express this thought, adding, "I don't know but it is darkest before dawn, but I can't see as we can subjugate the South, and what is worse, the Army of the Potomac can't see it either." Walker explained that he had talked with men in the streets and in hospitals, "and all though all are willing to fight for their country, still the idea of the 'best attainable peace' will be a talking one, and I fear will prevail—who knows?"

Walker turned twenty-one during his service at Fort Stevens, but marked the occasion only by noting his amazement at having commanded an eighty-four man company of men even before that landmark date. The rambunctuous Vermonters took advantage of his youth, apparently, for several times he wrote of having "got my foot down again, and mean the men shall see I am in earnest. We have had a pretty easy time for the last few weeks, and things have got to running pretty loosely, but I have brought up one or two of them with a yank." He enjoyed his new found responsibilities, his ability to learn and lead fellow soldiers, and like the whole generation of American young men who experienced national service in the war, Walker realized such training would never have occurred in peacetime.

Walker eventually weathered the doldrums of drill and waiting for better firearms, standing inspection, and reprimanding wayward enlisted men and junior lieutenants. He, like the others, was quite ready for new adventures when the call came in late April 1864 to leave the Washington forts and join the main fighting army. By this time, Walker had been twice promoted and ended his tour in the lines by commanding Forts Saratoga and Thayer near Fort Lincoln. That his experience with this part of his military service had left its mark seemed clear in a letter written to his father on November 8, 1863 from Fort Stevens. Therein, he told his father: ''I have been all through the two brigades from Fort Lincoln to Chain Bridge, some fifteen miles, lately; find some bigger forts than ours, and better situated, but none where so much taste has been shown, or care and pains taken; our camp is ahead of all, and when all are done we shall be not ashamed of ourselves at any rate.'' Ironically, Walker and his Green Mountain boys would find themselves back at Fort Stevens the following summer, helping to train the guns and man the earthworks when the Confederates made their most serious attempt to threaten—and possibly storm—the bulwarks of the nation's capital.

The Army of the Potomac considered duty at Washington as ''soft,'' and postwar accounts are filled with nostalgia for the carefree days of garrison duty. But some aspects of this duty proved to be distinctly unpleasant. Crowded living quarters or duty in rain and snow could be as injurious to health as enemy bullets, while the summer often brought malaria and typhoid caused by unsanitary conditions. Bathing and washing of clothes polluted most of the streams around Washington, leading Orange and Alexandria officials to complain that soapsuds from troops picketed on Bull Run were fouling the boilers of the locomotives. Furthermore, the regimental historian of the One Hundred and Fiftieth Pennsylvania noted:

The scattering of the regiment and the breaking up of the camp at Meridian Hill were doubtless beneficial to the health of the command, which had suffered frightfully from the unwholesome conditions prevailing in that locality. Between the height and the city proper, at no greater distance from the position occupied by the 150th, was a wide belt of vacant ground, marshy in places, but at other points sufficiently firm to form a dumping-place for refuse of every description from the outlying portions of the capital. Various forms of malaria speedily developed among the men, its ravages being especially noticeable in the country companies, nearly one-third of whose numerical strength was presently in the hospitals.[9]

In addition to measles, dysentery, and other diseases, the weather could also make the men just as miserable in garrison as in the field. There were of course the usual grumbles about mud, rain, and snow. But periodic windstorms blew down tents to the discomfort of the occupants before more permanent wooden barracks were constructed near many of the forts in late 1862. Overcrowding in tents and barracks increased the incidence of disease. In 1864, for example, authorities recommended that the men, at least some of them, should sleep out of doors in decent weather. Life was generally more pleasant in the forts in the summer when the major annoyances were merely insects and dust.[10]

If disease claimed more lives than enemy bullets in the Washington garrison, picket duty could still prove hazardous to the health. One soldier at Fort Greble wrote, " . . . standing guard on a freezing, drizzly night brought as many imaginary foes and discomforts as in after winters . . . when we knew the enemy was right over there within gunshot." All around Washington occasional brushes with dissident citizenry made dangers more than illusory. Certainly the southern defense lines and those on the Rockville pike were more dangerous than those located beyond the Anacostia. But the civil-military relations in the area were generally predicated less on overt hostility than upon the encroachment of Federal troops on personal property and daily lives. Before the end of the war military authorities made no effort to compensate owners of land upon which the forts were built or who had lost timber and fencing; J. G. Barnard, for one, thought upwards of 1,000 claimants made the chores quite impossible. That a few stray shots were aimed in the direction of blue-coated soldiers by irritated property owners rather than true Confederates might be suspected from General Order 23 of the Department of Washington, which was issued in April 1864:

> The General Commanding has learned with surprise and regret, that there is a disinclination on the part of farmers in the vicinity of the city to cultivate their gardens and farms based on an apprehension that their fences will be torn down and their crops destroyed by soldiers near them.[11]

In fact, the quiet period from the end of the Gettysburg campaign until Grant's movement forward in the spring of 1864 produced a sense of false security for the defense forces, local citizens, and public officials. Barnard continued to battle the bureaucracy over such questions as ordnance for Fort Foote and Battery Rodgers and congressional procrastination on appropriations "for completing and rendering more permanent" the defense network. Both the cost-conscious legislators and Barnard's own military superiors undoubtedly wondered why an additional $300,000 was needed, for the demands of the armies in the field seemed more important. Yet, even the secretary of war went along with appropriation of one-third of that amount by late January. At that time nearly 40,000 troops were situated in Major General Christopher Augur's department, augmented by 789 heavy and 246 field guns, and as one historian has commented, although much of the command was inexperienced with actual warfare "almost all [had] arrived at a very creditable state of discipline."[12]

Mindful, perhaps, of the difficulties experienced at the beginning of McClellan's campaign in 1862, Stanton ordered a full-scale inspection of the defenses of Washington in March by Brigadier General E. R. S. Canby, then on assignment in the city. The inspection uncovered numerous minor discrepancies in the strength of the works and garrisons, and led to shifts in units, construction of stockades to prevent cavalry incursions on the Aqueduct, Chain, and Long bridges, employment of repatriated Confederate deserters on work crews, and other administrative reforms. The engineers continued to fret about the insufficient timber for fort repairs, and emergency logging details were sent into western Fairfax and eastern Loudon counties. They also insisted that troops not actually on guard or picket duty should be employed as construction crews, and the unit commanders remained equally adamant that they should not. But by late March, more important matters portended as a new general-in-chief arrived in Washington with very definite ideas about the spring campaign.[13]

Ulysses S. Grant, newly promoted to the rank of Lieutenant General because of victories in the western theater, undertook his new assignment on March 9, 1864. He promptly decided to travel with Meade's field army rather than command from a desk in Washington. His primary focus became Lee's army and the need to destroy it on the ground between the Rapidan river and Richmond. The continuing question of manpower and supplies for the field army immediately became paramount. Units in the Department of Washington and Middle Department, which embraced Baltimore, became targets for requisition and were alerted for possible field duty. But overall hung the stigma that until Grant and Meade could actually prove to President Lincoln, Stanton, and even Halleck that the Army of the Potomac was capable of containing Lee and preventing him from threatening Washington, wholesale stripping of the Washington and Baltimore garrisons remained out of the question. Random units of infantry, artillery, and cavalry were dispatched to the field army in March and April, but internal reassignment, and replacement with Veteran Reserve contingents of convalescents, light artillery troops outfitting at the camp of instruction, and 4,500 dismounted cavalry at the cavalry depot took effect and the basic garrisons for Washington remained inviolate. The main heavy artillery units continued to train on fortress artillery and the new replacements were all able to take positions as infantry in the rifle pits in order to prepare for any emergency.[14]

The capital was in fact strongly protected as Grant and Meade embarked on the spring campaign of 1864. Strength figures at the end of April showed an increase of 5,000 men and sixty-two field guns (only partially offset by a decrease of eighty-one heavy artillery pieces) in the Department of Washington. Attorney General Edward Bates even speculated in his diary on April 25: "I have no certain information, but I conjecture that Burnside with his army [the independent IX corps] will be charged with the defence ot this capital; and that the army of the Potomac (relieved from that embarrassing and paralyzing duty) will, henceforth be free to devote itself to all exigencies of the war farther south." Furthermore, Assistant Adjutant General James A. Hardie of the Department of Washington reported on March 8 that the ammunition, communications, water supply, and condition of the earthworks were generally good and that manpower, while theoretically not providing three reliefs of gunners nor a reserve, "is deemed sufficient" since forts on fronts not attacked might provide the larger proportion of their garrisons to the support of those threatened. He concluded:

The general impression on my mind, produced by the observations of the last seven days, is that the city is provided against attack with a system of fortifications calculated to inspire confidence as to the result. This, viewing the system as intended to resist an assault of the enemy, and to compel him to resort to a siege, or to detain him until we can accumulate our resources for defense.[15]

The Washington garrison was called upon to provide manpower for Burnside as Halleck directed Augur to organize an infantry regiment from the swollen heavy artillery units such as the Second Pennsylvania—numbering alone 1,846 officers and men. Halleck told Grant that the available forces for Washington's safety, in terms of numbers, stood up well when tested against the 1862 strength figures suggested at the time of McClellan's embarkation for the peninsula. He stressed that:

I have always considered this line of defense too long, but very able officers are of a different opinion. The evil, if it exists, cannot probably be remedied now. Perhaps the forts south of Anacostia Creek might be abandoned. If so, as they bear on the arsenal and navy-yard, they should be dismantled and the guns and ammunition removed.[16]

The manpower situation became more serious as the Army of the Potomac absorbed enormous casualties in the Wilderness, and at Spotsylvania and Cold Harbor. Grant suddenly became "the Butcher" rather than "the Hammerer" in the eyes of many Unionists. Young First Lieutenant Edgar S. Dudley of the Second U.S. Artillery told sorrowfully of his trip by water to Washington in May upon a boat nearly swamped with the carnage of the battlefield—"The cabins and the decks were piled with wounded, not a bit of space that could be occupied was vacant." But Grant was tenacious and he was determined not to yield the relentless pressure on Lee. Suddenly men, horses, and equipment in the Washington area became premium commodities as the high command was persuaded to commence the wholesale stripping of the capital's garrison. To soldiers like those of the Second New York

Heavy Artillery, it was difficult "to go away from the forts we had learned to love so well, the huge walls of which had been cemented with the sweat from the brows of most of the men." Eben Gilley of the First Massachusetts Heavy Artillery wrote his mother on May 7, that "I am very glad that did not re-enlist and it will be a Happy day when we get Orders to get ready to start for Massachusetts." Instead, orders came to go downriver to join the Army of the Potomac. Within the month, Gilley wrote home to Marblehead from a camp near Gaines Mill, not far from Richmond. Likewise, Elias Babcock of the Tenth New York Heavy Artillery, who had complained bitterly to his wife in late March about having to march fifteen miles circuitously from Fort Carroll across the river from Alexandria to a new post at Fort Willard just south of the town—"a distance by bee line about 5 miles"—found himself hoofing it even greater distances with the Army of the Potomac. Yet, Babcock and others expressed great confidence in Grant's ability to gain victory. Writing to his wife back in Adams Center, Jefferson County, New York just before leaving Fort Willard, Babcock noted that Grant was doing the "tallest fighting the World ever saw" and the news was most cheering. At this rate, said Babcock, the Civil War will soon be over, this Campaign so far has opened the best of the war, and may God help the right." He noted thousands of troops going down the river to the front with the Potomac full of troop transports going to and from the battlefield taking down the soldiers and bringing back the wounded. "It is a dreadful time," he said, with "everybody has run mad," as "Grant has opened the grand ball and is fast driving Lee into his last ditch, let us take courage and pray that this Rebellion with its supporters may be numbered among the things that were."[17]

Meanwhile, Mosby raided Grant's communication lines beyond the boundaries of the department. This relative calm in the Washington suburbs allowed responsible officials to carry on their daily tasks, worrying more about replacements of Veteran Reserves and Stanton's call for militia mobilization than anything else. Barnard continued to parry the claims of citizens for reimbursement for land taken to build the fortifications, and his subordinates continued to badger local garrison commanders for neglect of abatis, and for allowing cannon to rest for months at a time, thereby damaging traversing circles, pintles, and other equipment. By June 7, Halleck told Grant that he had forwarded 48,265 men from the Department of Washington to the field army since the beginning of the campaign. Murmurs of continued Federal ineptitude in the Shenandoah valley reached Lincoln's ears, but defenders of the capital feared random cavalry and guerrilla raids on the defense perimeter more than any consummate thrust by the Army of Northern Virginia. After all, was not Lee and his ragged force now penned up inside its own defense line covering Richmond and Petersburg?[18]

Pulses began to quicken toward the end of June as the war near Washington became more active again. Mosby increased his activities as Department of Washington strength figures dipped to 33,289 officers and men (mostly convalescent troops), with 950 heavy and only 39 field guns. Lieutenant General Jubal Early had effectively stopped Major General David Hunter's thrust in the Shenandoah valley at Lynchburg and driven him out of the area into West Virginia, thereby uncovering the sensitive corridor of the Valley. Suddenly there was great fear that Early might move on the capital itself— although both Grant and Meade, relying on faulty intelligence, assumed that Early's Confederate force was still in the Richmond-Petersburg lines.[19] By early July, however, there were definite indications that a sizable Confederate army was moving northward through the Shenandoah valley, and moving fast.[*]

*For a fuller account of Early's summer operations, see the author's JUBAL EARLY'S RAID ON WASHINGTON, 1864 (Baltimore, 1989)

MAJOR GENERAL C. C. AUGUR
(National Archives and Records Administration, Washington, D.C.)

Lee had been awaiting a chance to again carry the war northward ever since the winter. He had written to President Davis in February expressing the desire to seize the initiative and: "If I could withdraw Longstreet secretly and rapidly to me [from southwest Virginia] I might succeed in forcing Genl Meade back to Washington & exciting sufficient apprehension at least for their own position, to weaken any movement against ours." He continued to urge a buildup in Virginia long after Grant had come east and the Federals had seized the initiative. By late spring the overwhelming Union combat power in the area had forced Lee back upon the defensive to protect Richmond. But the pressures upon him became so desperate by June that Lee gambled on the tactically dangerous move of dividing his forces in the face of a superior enemy. He dispatched Early with fifteen thousand combat veterans to sweep Hunter from Lynchburg, open the Valley once more to the Confederacy, and threaten Washington. Early took with him men of Jackson's old corps—itself only a shadow of its former striking power, but still capable of rapid, audacious movements. By early July Early's new "Army of the Valley" had accomplished its first two objectives and was sweeping northward, down the valley, toward the Potomac. The Federals possessed little with which to oppose Early. Scattered detachments guarded the Baltimore and Ohio railroad against guerrillas and Hunter's reserve under Franz Sigel was soon pushed by Early from Martinsburg to Harpers Ferry and finally across to Maryland Heights. By Independence Day the raiders were across the Potomac and into Maryland, having "got the 4th July Dinner" which the Federals had gathered for themselves. Private T. E. Morrow of the Eighth Louisiana wrote home: "They had all kinds of fruits, preserves, sardines, oysters, wines & Liquors, & any amount of meats, our boy's enjoyed the delicacies as well as the substansials, [sic] it was a great treat." Northern authorities took alarm that something more than cavalry or guerrillas was causing the trouble. Hagerstown and later Frederick were both ransomed for gold, and there seemed to be little opposition between Early and either Baltimore or Washington. Early learned from Lee on July 6 that some vague attempt would be made to free the Confederate prisoners at Point Lookout, far down the Potomac, and that he should cooperate in the endeavor. Thus, on July 9, as his men marched through Frederick, Early detached Colonel Bradley T. Johnson's cavalry to destroy the rail link between Baltimore, Washington, and Philadelphia and then move on toward Point Lookout. Only the Confederate general and his associates really knew what was going on up to this point.[20]

Frankly speaking, Federal authorities had been caught napping. As Attorney General Bates later contended: "How an army so great could traverse the country, without being discovered, is a mystery. There must have been the most supine negligence—or worse." It seems that everyone expected someone else to act—Halleck claiming it was Grant's prerogative, Lincoln placing somewhat sublime faith in Grant's prudence, and both Grant and Meade remaining unaware until July 6 that Early had been detached from Lee's main army. The Gideon Welles diary entry for that day may have best expressed the thinking in Washington at this stage of the conflict:

> We always have big scares from [the Shenandoah] and sometimes pretty serious realities. * * * I have sometimes thought that Lee might make a sudden dash in the direction of Washington or above, and inflict great injury before our troops could interfere, or Grant move a column to protect the city. But likely Grant has thought and is prepared for this; yet he displays little strategy or invention.[21]

Far too much was expected of Ulysses S. Grant at this point. New to the theater and the wiley ways of Lee, he undoubtedly expected too much from his eastern subordinates,

Henry Halleck included. Furthermore, his principal responsibilities lay with overall direction of Union military operations throughout the south. He could not be expected to understand the paranoia of Lincoln and his cabinet concerning the national capital. Some precautionary measures were taken at Washington early in July, although not all of them tended to help matters. On July 2, eight batteries of artillery were about to start for the front when Halleck stopped five of them and sent them to Harpers Ferry the next day. They arrived in time to be bottled up with Sigel's forces on Maryland Heights. On July 4, cavalry forces were organized from random detachments at the depot across the Anacostia and dispatched under Lieutenant Colonel D. R. Clendenin of the Eighth Illinois cavalry to follow the artillery upriver. It too passed beyond the area of immediate usefulness for the defense of the capital although it ably served Major General Lew Wallace, commanding the VIII corps or Middle Department, with headquarters in Baltimore, in his subsequent operations along the Monocacy river. Meanwhile, inexperienced militia and 100-day men in the forts of Washington on the northern side of the river set to work training on the big guns and cutting brush which had overgrown the field works. Barnard and Augur fretted about their troop strength—during the first week in July, Lieutenant Colonel Joseph A. Haskin commanded the entire northern perimeter from Fort Reno, on the Rockville pike at Tennallytown to Fort Lincoln, on the Bladensburg pike, and while he had 411 heavy guns and three nominal brigades for garrisons, these actually numbered less than 4,000 men on duty, or hardly ten men to a gun. Still, Halleck and Stanton did not feel any great alarm, and it was not until the sixth of July that various responsible officials began to realize the true state of affairs. Halleck immediately called for reinforcements, especially heavy artillerymen to sprinkle among the militia. Stanton asked the governors of Pennsylvania,

New York, and Massachusetts for additional 100-day men. Grant dispatched Major General James B. Rickett's division of the VI corps to Baltimore, and the confusion and feverish activity mounted.[22]

Early's destination remained unclear, and it was actually the abrupt action of an unsung departmental commander that uncovered the Confederate's intention and seriously dislocated his timetable. Lew Wallace acted without the knowledge and approval of the War Department in trying to determine whether Baltimore or Washington was Early's real objective. Martialing forces along the Monocacy in the western sector of his command, Wallace went in person to supervise the defense preparations, especially to protect the valuable Baltimore and Ohio railroad bridge across that stream just south of Frederick, some forty miles west of Baltimore. Scraping together a composite force of infantry, cavalry, and artillery (later supplemented by the arrival of Rickett's contingents from the VI corps), skirmishing with Early's advance guard began west of Frederick on July 7.

Wallace subsequently withdrew his outposts behind the Monocacy and took position astride the highways to Washington and Baltimore as well as the Baltimore and Ohio railroad where it crossed the stream. On July 9, he defied Early to give battle. Outnumbered better than three to one, and spread too thinly along the banks of the river, Wallace's force was soon outflanked by the veterans of Major General John B. Gordon's division. By evening the Federals had been swept from the field after a stubborn fight. But, some of Early's crack brigades had been badly bloodied, and Louisianian T. E. Morrow wrote his father: "Our Brigade lost a good many in killed & wounded, in fact our Regt. lost more men according to the number carried in than any other fight with the exception of Sharpsburg" noting two-thirds of his own tiny company had been shot down. True to their departmental

[191]

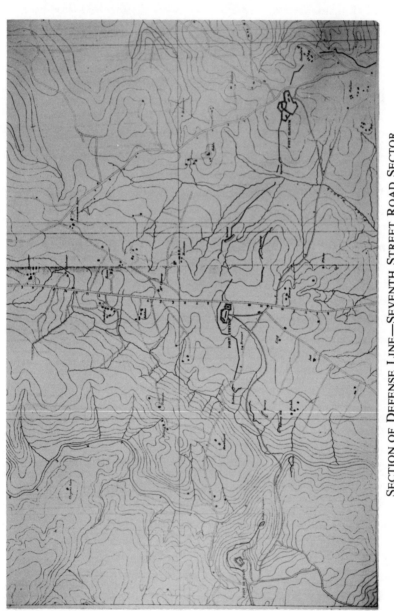

SECTION OF DEFENSE LINE—SEVENTH STREET ROAD SECTOR
(Barnard's Defenses of Washington Report)

mission, Wallace's disorganized troops retreated toward Baltimore—although some later historians have thought that his men should have harassed the Confederates even after the battle and perhaps continued to contest the way leading to Washington. But Wallace's delaying action held up Early for a full day, and as early as July 8 the Confederates' movement upon the Federal left disclosed their objective to be the national capital and not the Monument City.[23]

News of Monocacy astonished officials as refugees poured into Baltimore and Washington. Governor Augustus W. Bradford's home was destroyed within four miles of the Maryland city. Baltimore's railroad communications with Harrisburg and Philadelphia were cut and two trains were captured by hard-riding Confederate troopers, some of whom carried away Major General William B. Franklin, who later escaped. Maryland citizenry panicked and called upon Lincoln for aid; Wallace upon his return to Baltimore found alarm bells tolling and loyal citizens assembling to defend the city. The situation was no better at the capital—as Assistant Secretary of War Charles Dana telegraphed to Grant—and throughout Maryland, and Pennsylvania, local organizations were mobilizing to thwart Early's raid. In Washington proper the defense of the city north of the Potomac rested upon 1,819 infantry, 1,834 artillery, and 63 cavalry—for a total of only 3,716 effectives. South of the river were positioned 4,064 infantry, 1,772 artillery, and 51 cavalry for an effective total strength of 5,887 men. There were some additional 8,300 garrison troops spread throughout Washington and Alexandria; 627 men organized into six field artillery "regiments" training at the Artillery Camp of Instruction; a "brigade" of 800 cavalry based on Fall's Church and Annandale for protection against Mosby; and 1,200 assorted cavalrymen awaiting equipment and mounts at Camp Stoneman. Total forces—heavy artillerymen, national guardsmen or 100-day men, militia, city guards, clerks, veteran reserves, and random veteran volunteer units—constituted a hodgepodge of roughly 20,400.[24]

As the crisis increased in intensity, special preparations were made by citizens and local organizations to defend Philadelphia, Wilmington, and Baltimore, as well as the roads between these cities. Halleck directed Major General George Cadwalader to sweep the Philadelphia hospitals of walking wounded and send them to Washington. The D.C. militia were called out; Quartermaster General Meigs organized employees and clerks of his department and marched them to the forts; scouting parties were kept active in Fairfax county and along the Potomac; and arrangements were consummated for destroying the bridges across the rivers should the need arise. At last, even the President himself felt constrained to appeal directly to Grant for aid and the general-in-chief decided to start the remainder of the VI corps and portions of the XIX corps, then arriving at Fort Monroe from the Gulf, for Washington.

The weekend of July 9-10, 1864 was one of misery in the capital. Refugees from Maryland poured out lurid tales of Rebel depredations and contributed to an already tense situation. Mosby's rangers terrorized a party of picnickers near Falls Church and eluded pursuing Federal cavalry. Citizen humor equaled the weather, hot and sultry, and Lincoln suggested to one group of hysterical Baltimoreans, "Let us be vigilant but keep cool. I hope neither Baltimore nor Washington will be taken."

Meanwhile, Augur and his staff bustled about shifting troops from the southern forts to the threatened defense line. Lowell's cavalry—1,000 strong—were concentrated as scouts out towards Rockville and Silver Spring; and ever-changing command arrangements were symbolized by an influx of general officers all seeking to be of help, but mainly getting on each others nerves. Colonel J. M. Warner (First Vermont

Heavy Artillery) was assigned the brigade centered on Fort Reno. Brigadier General Martin D. Hardin took command of a "division" which extended from the Potomac to Fort Slocum. Major General Alexander McCook reported to Augur and took charge of a reserve camp with authority over the whole line of the northern defenses of Washington. Major General E. O. C. Ord was shipped to Baltimore to take charge there. The snarl of disorganized command was fully represented by the fact that while Augur commanded the department, Halleck had ordered Major General Quincy A. Gillmore to come and save the city; Stanton brought McCook in for similar duties; and Ord was Grant's man, sent to help repel the invaders. By Monday noon, the crucial moment in the crisis, the full impact of Halleck's impatience was delivered upon an unsuspecting brigadier, spoiling for honors, who had telegraphed his availability for service from the comfortable parlors of the Fifth Avenue Hotel in New York. Halleck rather testily observed to him: "We have five times as many generals here as we want, but are greatly in need of privates. Any one volunteering in *that* capacity will be thankfully received."[25]

Nor was Grant any better informed on the actual state of affairs as he told Halleck not to wait for reinforcements from City Point but to "get into Early's rear and destroy him." Halleck immediately telegraphed back:

What you say about getting into Early's rear is probably correct, but unfortunately we have no forces here for the field. All such forces were sent to you, long ago. What we have here are raw militia, invalids, convalescents from the hospitals, a few dismounted batteries, and the dismounted and unorganized cavalrymen you sent up from James River. With these we hope to defend our immense depots of stores and the line of intrenchments (extending 37 miles) around the city. But what can we do with such forces in the field against a column of 20,000 veterans? One-half of the men here cannot march at all. The only body fit for the field was Ricketts' Division, which has been defeated and badly cut up under Wallace. If those remains can hold Baltimore till re-enforced, I shall be satisfied.[26]

[195]

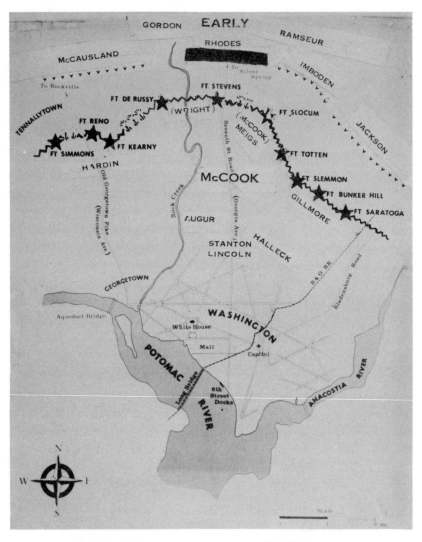

BATTLE MAP—EARLY ATTACKS FORT STEVENS
(Defending Washington Files, Fort Ward Museum, Alexandria)

Thus, at the very moment when Washington officials were preparing for a last ditch defense, and Union veterans were streaming northward in relief, Early's main body was passing through Gaithersburg and Rockville toward the capital. Johnson's cavalry moved past Reistertown, Cockeysville, and Parkton, near Baltimore, and reportedly appeared on the York road scarcely seven miles from the Monumental City. Here, however, the heat of July and the dust of Maryland highways, together with the delay experienced at Monocacy, changed the course of events. Early began his march toward Washington on July 10 at 3:30 A.M. with John McCausland and Robert E. Rodes in the van followed by Stephen Ramseur, John B. Gordon, and J. Echols with the army train and Armistead Long's artillery intermixed with the infantry. The day was excessively warm, the roads thick with dust, and the straggling soon became epidemic.

Early's army was forced to move into bivouac near Gaithersburg by late afternoon having marched twenty miles that day. Washington lay approximately the same distance ahead of them. The night proved to be oppressive and officers and men got little rest. The next morning promised no relief from heat and dust, and as the day progressed, more and more of Early's veterans dropped by the roadside. Early and his officers constantly pleaded and badgered their soldiers to close ranks and move on, but, by this stage in the war, genuine physical breakdown was taking place among the underfed, ill-clothed Confederates. Harassed by Colonel Charel R. Lowell's Union cavalry, the Confederate column moved slowly on and when the head reached Rockville, McCausland's cavalry proceeded south on the Georgetown turnpike toward the Union defense line at Tennallytown. The main column, with Rodes's division in the lead, plus a small cavalry detachment, took a left turn at Rockville, proceeded to Mitchell's Crossroads and Leesborough, where the Confederates then turned right onto the Seventh Street road, which led straight south past Silver Spring into the heart of the city. Cavalry skirmishing preceded both columns.

Early arrived before Fort Stevens shortly after noon. He immediately noticed the weakly held Union lines. His problem was now one of mustering sufficient troop strength for an attack, and much of the afternoon of July 11 was spent by the general and his staff in urging forward and into a line of battle the fatigued men in the ranks. The spirit was willing, but thousands of bodies were not, and Early did not mount the important and decisive attack on that afternoon simply because months of arduous campaigning and the heat of July combined to prevent it. Broken down and exhausted troops (Early's entire force probably comprised little more than 11,000 or 12,000 men, given battle losses, straggling, and desertions), insufficient artillery strength (mostly 12-pdr. Napoleons and horse artillery), lack of intelligence from the supposedly numerous Confederate sympathizers in Washington—all caused Early to pause. Many of the Confederate rankers found local liquor supplies and the cooling waters of the fountain pond at "Silver Spring," far more inviting than beating the Yankees in the forts. Even Mosby failed to coordinate any effort to pin down Federal troops in the defenses south of the Potomac. Early's pause proved fatal in the race for the capital.[27]

Union commanders were just as desperate as the Confederates to win that race. An illusion of strength was created as the fortress artillery went into action and militia skirmishers swarmed out front of the entire defense line from Forts Simmons and Reno eastward to Fort Totten. But the focal point of the action was between Forts De Russy and Totten. Rock Creek offered a particularly attractive area for the enemy force to attempt a *coup de main* (something which Major General J. C. Breckinridge, among others, urged throughout Early's

[198]

attack). Just to the eastward, the Seventh Street road, commanded by Fort Stevens and ancillary batteries, soon witnessed the greatest amount of combat action. Both sides sought to concentrate decisive firepower and men at this point in the defenses. As the skirmishing swayed back and forth during the afternoon, on report trickled back to Union headquarters downtown that the Confederates had moved to within fifty to one hundred yards of the works. Despite the veterans' derisive comments about Ohio militia and 100-day men, and other random units from New York and elsewhere, these contingents proved to be sufficient for bluffing and blunting the probing attacks of Confederate skirmishers. They were incapable of containing any all-out thrust by Early's main force, and even the heavy artillery fire seemed somewhat laughable to more experienced veteran gunners. Still, the 100- and 32-pounder cannon, the mortars, and the various lighter guns in the works did break up more sizable concentrations of Confederates that afternoon, and they drove sharpshooters from various structures left standing beyond the works. July 11 witnessed mostly a holding action, a desperate attempt by the Federals to buy time for Grant's promised reinforcements to arrive on the scene.[28]

The long wait ended about 2:00 P.M. as transports began debarking the first units of the VI corps and later the 650-man vanguard of the XIX corps at the Sixth Street wharves. Lincoln was there to greet them, munching on a piece of hardtack as if nothing was amiss. Led by their corps commander, Major General Horatio Wright, the men of the VI corps first moved out toward Georgetown until Halleck realized the mistake and directed them up Seventh Street. Cheers of the local populace spurred the gaunt veterans onward until they came within sight of Fort Stevens. The militia skirmishers were being roughly handled at the time and Wright wanted to lead his own men into action immediately. McCook passed the

PRESIDENT ABRAHAM LINCOLN AT FORT STEVENS
(Contemporary Sketch from *The Soldier in Our Civil War*)

request to Augur, who demurred; then, to Wright's disgust, his troops were placed in reserve at Crystal Spring, about one-half mile behind the defense line. Moreover, Wright learned that the contingents of the XIX corps were being directed to Fort Saratoga, far to the right of the line and completely out of the danger zone. Wright protested so vigorously that Halleck and Augur gave way, and 500 men of Brigadier General Frank Wheaton's 1st brigade of the 2d division, VI corps, immediately took to the field beyond the line of entrenchments. These men, the Ninety-Eighth, One Hundred and Second, and One Hundred and Thirty-Eighth Pennsylvania veteran volunteers, quickly restored the crumbling front, and none too soon. It was their prompt action which convinced Early that veteran Federals had appeared on the battlefield. Night fell on the two contending forces as they occupied approximately the same positions they had held earlier in the afternoon. Early now knew that some of Grant's veterans had arrived, but the question was one of how many. His units maintained their positions well in advance of Silver Spring, and showed now signs of yielding. Union commanders reshuffled units, tried to out-guess Early's intentions, and maintained a skirmish fire throughout the night.[29]

That evening both senior commanders and their chief subordinates evaluated the situation. Wine and good cheer flowed at Early's headquarters in Francis Preston Blair's spacious Silver Spring mansion as Early, Rodes, Gordon, and Ramseur chided Breckinridge about reoccupying his old vice presidential chair in the Capitol on the morrow. Still, the Confederate command was worried. McCausland had reported the works to be too strong at Tennallytown; Union signal stations at Fort Reno, Fort Stevens, and the Soldier's Home were able to pinpoint every Confederate movement and thus counter Early's strength at any given point. There was the ever present danger that arrival of more of the Army of the Potomac might close off escape routes through South Mountain or via the fords of the upper Potomac. Old Jube laid plans for an immediate attack at daybreak. Then the disheartening news came from Bradley Johnson's column that his own intelligence sources reported two more Union corps en route to Washington from Petersburg. That settled it; Early suspended the planned attack, pending a daylight reconnaissance of the Federal positions.[30]

Meanwhile, Federal officials took stock of their own situation in the light of what had transpired that day. They enjoyed the advantage of interior lines and they could reinforce almost any threatened point at will—provided there were sufficient men. But observers of the scene later described both calmness and panic, confidence and uneasiness, with confusion as the sole nonvariable. Lincoln, Stanton, and Halleck all displayed much vigor and less panic than during previous crises of this type, with the chief executive and his close advisers actually present to view the action on the afternoon of the eleventh. Lincoln, always filled with curiosity, had even spent the previous night with his family at their summer cottage near Soldier's Home, until military authorities had persuaded them that the area was simply too dangerous for the president to be wandering about freely. Still, Assistant Secretary of War Dana complained by telegraph to Grant the next morning that there was "no head of things," adding revealingly: "General Halleck will not give orders except as he receives them; the President will give none, and until you direct positively and explicitly what is to be done, everything will go on in the deplorable and fatal way in which it has gone on for the past week.[31]

The Union's greatest problem, up to this point, may well have been the confusion as to the limits and relations of the various commands rather than the inexperience and number of troops. Forts, riflepits, skirmish lines, reserves, and city

guards seemed to have separate and largely independent commanders, and troops arriving at the wharves were moved to
positions by orders emanating from people other than the commanding general of the department. 1,500 Quartermaster
employees under Meigs, sailors and workers from the navy yard
under Rear Admiral Louis Goldsborough, even impressed
Negroes and refugees added to the melee, and one subordinate
Provost Marshal, Major William E. Doster, noted in his diary:

> Noticed this morning in *The Chronicle* that Major General George
> [C.] Thomas calls out the militia and Brigadier General Grocer
> [Peter] Bacon is to command them! Went into the grocery, but no
> headquarters visible. Asked Bacon's brother where headquarters
> were; answered, 'Damned if I know!' Augur don't know. Nobody
> knows. Bacon more intent on weighing out sugar than shells. Things
> seem to go on as usual.[32]

Indeed, confusion was somewhat "usual" for Washington
in crisis. Even Major General Samuel P. Heintzelman, former
department commander and now safely ensconced at Colum-
bus, Ohio, added: "What an excitement there must be amongst
the authorities. I supposed Gen. Halleck wants an alarm signal
fired upon and Mr. Stanton to have cannon planted on the
streets. I am glad I am not thus involved." War correspondent Noah Brooks, however, noted the availability of upwards
of 60,000 men under arms to defend the city that night. The
usually acidic Gideon Welles, returning from a ride to the battle
area where he had noted both a war-torn landscape and reassuring words of strength and determination from both Wright and
McCook, pronounced:

> I am satisfied that no attack is now to be apprehended on the city;
> the Rebels have lost a remarkable opportunity. But on our part there
> is neglect, ignorance, folly, imbecility, in the last degree. The Rebels
> are making a show of fight while they are stealing horses, cattle, etc.

through Maryland. They might easily have captured Washington. Stanton, Halleck, and Grant are asleep or dumb.[33]

There was little sleep for the men in the ranks during the hot night of July 11-12. Confederate troop movements convinced some Federal officers such as Hardin that a night attack was under way, and nervous firing and marching about occupied many moments for the weary fighting men. Union officers and enlisted personnel slept atop magazines and parapets in the fort, and in the fields and trenches below them. Occasional flickers from Signal Corps torches mingled with flashes from muskets on the picket lines, and there were a few anxious moments when one innocent officer in the lines to the right of Fort Stevens asked for the countersign of the night and the signal officer of that post thoughtlessly spelled it out to him by torch in full sight of the Confederates. But the whole episode passed without notice, and greater events beckoned as the hot rays of another day glanced off the capitol dome and the two armies commenced the second day of fighting for Washington.[34]

Daybreak on July 12 found Early up and about early, scanning the Union lines for tell-tale signs of weakness, and supervising attack preparations. He found the rifle pits from Fort De Russy to Fort Slocum thick with troops, troops wearing faded blue uniforms indicative of veterans. There was but one possible alternative—to hold and threaten for another day, then withdraw by night. Confederate skirmishers began firing at the Union defenders almost at once, although during most of the day this firing was sporadic at best. The main body of Confederates lounged in bivouac, played cards, smoked, rested—and waited. This watchful waiting allowed commanders on the Union side to take better control of the defensive situation. Barnard and Halleck feared that the Confederates were about to slip toward the railroad and the forts east of the Anacostia and urged reinforcement of that quarter. But the greatest accomplishment came when Union authorities finally introduced a measure of order into the chaotic command situation.[35]

Grant had finally responded to the situation about noon on July 12 when he ordered Halleck to get Wright's people outside the trenches and drive Early away. He foresaw no conflict with Augur since Wright would command the maneuver element while Augur still had control of all troops within the defenses. Washington received the message about 1:20 P.M., but Halleck unaccountably failed to see it until 4:00 on the thirteenth. Nonetheless, arrangements were worked out whereby Hardin took charge of all troops from Fort Sumner near the Potomac to Fort De Russy at Rock Creek; Quartermaster General Meigs was placed in command of the rifle pits and fortifications from De Russy to Totten; Gillmore commanded the line from Totten to Fort Lincoln (including XIX corps contingents as quickly as they arrived), while Major General Abner Doubleday had control over the defense line east of the Anacostia. Wright was told to hold the main body of the VI corps troops in reserve on the Seventh Street road, and Colonel M. N. Wisewell was made Provost Marshal General of the department and undertook immediate supervision of affairs within the city limits behind the lines. It was now possible for the Federals to apply concentrated offensive power to drive the Confederates from the gates of the capital.[36]

The major irritation for the defenders on both days of the action came from Confederate sharpshooters emplaced in several structures within 1,100 yards of Fort Stevens and adjacent trenches. The heavy artillery persistently tried to flush the sharshooters only to have them return and resume their fire. About 4:30 P.M. on July 12, Union authorities decided to stop the flow of civilian spectators into the area behind the fort and to begin preparations for an attack to clear the area from Fort Stevens to Silver Spring. It was about this time that President and Mrs. Lincoln were driven into the area, to be joined there by Secretary Welles and others. There had been the normal cabinet meeting that morning, and Lincoln wanted to see how things were going out at the front. After visiting the hospital at the fort, the group moved to the parapets. Wright and McCook were already present, and they suddenly realized that the tall man in the stove pipe hat was none other than the commander-in-chief. Enemy fire was peppering the earthwork with bullets and when a surgeon, Captain C.V.A. Crawford of the One Hundred and Second Pennsylvania, was cut down near Lincoln, Wright thought it was high time that the president take a less dangerous position. Wright ordered the parapet cleared; discovered that Lincoln had not paid attention and saluted his chief bluntly: "This is no place for you, Mr. President, you must step down at once." Lincoln wryly observed that if Wright could remain there why couldn't he also. Wright finally suggested that he could order a file of soldiers to bodily remove the uncooperative president. By this time Lincoln was highly amused, and he descended behind the parapet with a smile. Numerous legends grew up after the war about the incident including the probably apochryphal story that young Oliver Wendell Holmes, later Associate Justice of the United States Supreme Court but at the time only a junior officer, had shouted to Lincoln: "Get down, you fool!" to which the Chief Executive remarked drily, "My dear Colonel, I am glad you know how to talk to a civilian." There is no definitive evidence that the future judge was even present in Fort Stevens during Lincoln's visit, much less that he uttered the disrespectful words. Moreover, at least several other individuals (including "Aunt Betty" Thomas, a free Black whose property had been confiscated in the original construction of the fort) all stepped

[206]

forward also to claim various exclamations to cause Lincoln to descend from the parapet. Captain Aldace Walker, who had returned with his fellow Vermonters to the fort they had helped build, wrote his father: "The Generals and President and Secretaries, &c., were in the Fort looking on, Lincoln with a hole in his coat sleeve."[37]

With Lincoln safely placed where he might observe, but avoid danger, the Union attack could now begin. Wheaton receive orders between 5:00 and 6:00 P.M. to furnish an assault element—Colonel Daniel Bidwell's second brigade of the second division. The guns of Fort Stevens fired a thirty-six shell barrage and, by prearranged signal, the virgin colors of the Seventy-Seventh New York dipped to start the assault. Confederate resistance stiffened after the initial surprise, but reinforcements saved the day for Wheaton. Nearly one-quarter of the attackers were cut down, including all but one of the regimental commanders, and the spirited engagement lasted well after 10:00 P.M. under the light of a new moon. The Confederates were not at all convinced that they had been bested in a fray which had started as a mere cleanup operation but ended in a pitched battle between infantry and artillery. Artillery fire from Forts De Russy, Stevens, and Slocum was intense, and the First Veteran Reserve Corps regiment from De Russy staged a supporting attack on Confederates posted behind breastworks in that sector. Finally, as the Union drive sputtered and threatened to collapse, McCook directed a cessation of operations. The Confederates could match any Union effort on the battlefield, and the objective of clearing out the sharpshooters had been attained.[38]

Early withdrew his legions under cover of night and the gray dawn of July 13 betrayed only an occasional picket and the lowing of cows and braying of mules, suddenly unaccustomed to the silence. Cavalry patrols from the Federal lines roamed out towards Silver Spring and Rockville, and they

[207]

PRESIDENT ABRAHAM LINCOLN UNDER CONFEDERATE FIRE AT FORT STEVENS, JULY 12, 1864
(Bas-relief Sketch, Schwizer Artist, Lincoln Stone, Fort Stevens, National Park Service)

reported the Confederate positions were abandoned. Meigs caught the flavor of what they found: "The House of Postmaster-General Blair, two miles out Seventh Street Road burned; old Francis P. Blair's house on the farm turned topsy-turvey, all his liquors consumed, and his papers ransacked, and the enemy in retreat toward Rockville and the fords of the Potomac." Captain Walker also ventured out to Silver Spring, and he told his father: "In Mr. Blair's house I found a photograph of a young lady with this writing on its back. I replaced the carte [de visite] and took a copy. Taken from a pilgerer for old acquaintance sake with Miss Emma Mason, and left at 11 p.m. here by a Rebel Officer, who once knew her and remained behind to prevent this house from being burned by stragglers, as was the neighboring one. 11 p.m., and no light. July 12, 1864." Actually, Washington's defenders appeared to be too relieved to press Early—although Lowell's cavalrymen caused a few anxious moments before Johnson's troopers (who returned from the Point Lookout raid shortly after midnight) drove them off. Maryland Confederates serving with Early's force, such as Elgar L. Tschiffely of Darnestown in upper Montgomery county, made their last visits to kinfolks, and by July 14, the Confederates had escaped across the Potomac between the mouth of the Monocacy and Goose Creek and had gone into camp near Leesburg. The threat to Washington was over.[39]

Union authorities mixed their relief with irritation over Early's escape as well as the various depredations which took place on the war-torn landscape between Fort Stevens and Silver Spring. A great deal of attention was given to the damage to the Blair mansion, the obscene drawings covering the walls, and the plain allusion to retaliation for Yankee destruction in the Shenandoah. Halleck, Stanton, and Dana, among others, were extremely critical of Wright and McCook for failing to mount an immediate pursuit of Early. But pursuit was the same old story. Wright finally got moving (under Grant's instructions), but reached Early's crossing over the Potomac too late on the fourteenth as the Confederates were gone. He complained to Halleck about insufficient troops (his force numbered approximately 10,500), and orders from the absentee general-in-chief were certainly vague as Grant urged a helter-skelter pursuit by "veterans, militiamen, men on horseback, and everything that could be got to follow . . . ." During all this confusion, Wright finally crossed the Potomac and chased Early to the Shenandoah river, but Grant wanted the troops returned to the Petersburg operation, and eventually pursuit ended with Early once more toying with Hunter as well as George Crook in the valley, Washington safe but wary that Early was still a threat, and Grant complacently pleased that the whole affair was over. As Edward Bates recorded in his diary on July 14: "Alas! for the impotence or treachery of our military rulers! The raiders have retired across the Potomac, with all their booty safe! Nobody seems disposed to hinder them.[40]

The title "Battle of Fort Stevens" is something of a misnomer. There was no rolling up of a flank, no piercing of any line, no all-out attack, no real maneuvering, no rout, no pursuit, in that two day action. But there was a decisive confrontation, a nasty, sharp bit of blood letting, and a wise decision. There was, in one sense, a victor; on the other hand no one was really vanquished. For once, an enemy force had tested Washington's vaunted defenses with their static fortifications and maneuver forces. The deterrent had worked, but only because of the timely arrival of veterans from the main field army, and in spite of much maligned militia, and a thoroughly fouled command arrangement. Still, Washington and the North had been frightened; faith in the Union cause had been shaken by the audacity of such a raid and its near success when administration spokesmen were suggesting that the rebellion was on the wane. Observers contended that Early missed capturing the city by only one day! The *Times* of London concluded on July 25 that the Confederacy was more formidable than ever before, which has led one historian to suggest: "That so splendid a ruse had been achieved is perhaps the finest tribute to Jubal's raid." Finally, in one possibly apocryphal story a cocky Confederate from the Fifty-Eighth Virginia couldn't resist a parting thought for Union authorities as he left his bivouac opposite one of the Blair houses in Silver Spring. Union soldiers found a copy of Lord Byron's works (undoubtedly liberated from a Blair's library), with the inscription on the flyleaf:

> Now, Uncle Abe, you had better be quiet the balance of your administration. We only came near your town this time to show you what we could do, but if you go on in your mad career we will come again soon, and then you had better stand from under.
>
> Yours respectfully,
> "The Worst Rebel you efer Saw"

As Old Jube himself put it ". . . we haven't taken Washington, but we've scared Abe Lincoln like hell!" although at least one of his less enamored staff pointed out that Lincoln had not been the only one scared during the two day fight (especially during Wheaton's sortie on the second day). Early replied that while perhaps true, history would never acknowledge the fact.

Indeed, the profane rebel never captured Washington or the president, but he certainly added to the fables of the Civil War. Years after the conflict, a southwest Virginia captain who had served with Early's force told a Union veteran at one Richmond veteran's reunion why he always showed up in his faded gray uniform. Said the ex-Confederate:

[211]

I was offered a new and handsome black suit to wear on this occasion, but declined it. You see railroad accidents are frequent, and I might be killed in one of them. In this event when I appeared at the gates of Heaven, Lee and Jackson would charge me with having deserted my colors, and would turn their backs on me. Should I go to the other place, old Jube Early would spurn me in his usual emphatic language for the same reason.

In the end, rebel cockiness attended the Confederate retirement to Virginia. Pelican state soldier T. E. Morrow wrote his father from a camp near Darkesville on August 2: "From Frederick City we made a demonstration on Washington City. We had the 'Yanks' badly frightened. We got in sight of the Dome of the Capitol in about four miles of the Capitol. We had cannading & skirmishing with the 'Yanks' for part of two days & left. It was the intention of our Generals to draw the 'Yanks' from Grant's Army. We had no idea of takeing the place."[41]

CHAPTER EIGHT

Winding Down the Threat

Any real threat to Washington decreased sharply after Early's raid. Of course, so long as the Confederates maintained any sizable force in the Shenandoah valley and Mosby's rangers roved unchecked in northern Virginia, the Lincoln administration remained uncomfortable. Equally uneasy were the engineer officers who continued their interest in perfecting the formal defenses. J. G. Barnard especially criticized those forts east of the Anacostia as being quite weak. Surveys of the main system of fortifications, completed prior to Early's incursion, noted many deficiencies and a need for improvement at various individual posts. Such repairs as sodding and sloping of parapets, construction of bombproofs, as well as the cutting and clearing of undergrowth, required many man hours for several hundred laborers throughout the late summer and early fall. Under the impetus of Early's raid, local post commanders and engineer officials frantically worked to finish jobs that should have been done before the appearance of grayclad units at the capital's doorstep. Still, the greatest attention focused on the continued presence of Early's legions, temporarily thwarted but hardly annihilated, regrouping in the lower Valley. Indeed, as late as July 23, Lee was writing to Davis, if only wistfully: "A mounted force with long range guns might by a secret and rapid march, penetrate the lines south of the Potomac, and excite the alarm of the authorities at Washington, but if its approach was known, I fear the defenses south of the river could be manned in time to prevent it."[1]

Early's escape from the Washington suburbs resulted less from his own dexterity than from fumbling efforts by the Federal high command, as well as from the continued heat wave, which now bothered bluecoated pursuers just as it had the Confederate host after Monocacy. Strength figures showed 48,253 effectives in the Military Department of Washington and 58,845 effectives in the Department of West Virginia from which to draw a sizable force for the containment of Early. Still, the only effective pursuit forces were those of Wright and W. H. Emory, and while Wright had orders to try to overtake Old Jube, he soon decided that his 10,500 veterans were insufficient for this task. He chased Early through Snicker's Gap and skirmished sharply with Confederates at the Shenandoah river crossing, but then turned back toward Washington. His footsore and battle tested veterans complained bitterly about being "used up" in senseless countermarching. Furthermore, Wright and Emory were simply pawns in the frustrating command confusion on the Potomac which, even after three years of warfare, showed few signs of abating.[2]

[214]

Strictly speaking the snarl was bound to remain so long as the general-in-chief continued to travel with the main field army. When Bruce Catton described the situation after Early's raid as "all lines of authority were crossed, and the War Department was buzzing and fretting and issuing inumerable orders, taking time along the way to modify, alter, or countermand the orders other people were issuing," he merely reiterates the fundamental organizational problem which plagued the Union armies in the east, and especially regarding the defense of Washington, throughout the war. Grant recalled with admirable hindsight after the war that Halleck and Stanton appeared to be moving forces laterally between the capital and Early, "and generally speaking they pursued this policy until all knowledge of the whereabouts of the enemy was lost," without realizing both that this was normal at that stage of the war and that he only contributed to the malaise himself. Recognizing the difficulty and delay of communication between his headquarters and Washington, he told Halleck on July 26 to have "some one in Washington" give orders and make dispositions of all forces cooperating against Early. This was simply open sesame for interference and interloping by both Stanton and Halleck, whatever their good intentions. Grant might have better served the cause at the time of crisis by returning in person to Washington as soon as Early's forces appeared before Fort Stevens. Communications from people like Stanton, Halleck, and Assistant Secretary of War C. A. Dana only tended to muddy the waters for the absentee general-in-chief.[3]

Grant's view naturally focused on Petersburg. Everything apart from that operation in Virginia, at least, remained secondary. Spurred by the reports from Dana and others that Early's force had left the immediate danger zone around Washington, he wanted Hunter's forces in the valley to deal with the potential of any additional move by Early either

[215]

northward across the Potomac or toward the capital. The VI corps was to be returned to the primary mission of capturing Petersburg. He construed Early to be returning to Lee's main force, and enthusiastically, if a bit naively, suggested on July 14 that if the enemy had left Maryland, then his pursuers should "eat out Virginia clear and clean as far as they go, so that crows flying over it for the balance of this season will have to carry their provender with them."

Obviously Grant was too new to the theater to realize the acute fears of the Lincoln government as long as the Confederates found a sanctuary in the Shenandoah. On July 16 he told Halleck: "With Hunter in the Shenandoah Valley and always between the enemy and Washington, force enough can always be had to check the invasion until re-enforcements can go from here," and he even envisioned Hunter following Early to Gordonsville and Charlottesville. On July 17, he judged that: "If Early stops in the Valley or before returning to Richmond, with a view of going north again, I do not believe he will go to Maryland, but will attempt to go through Western Virginia to Ohio, possibly taking Pittsburg on the way." He told Halleck that Pennsylvania and Ohio should organize their citizenry for such a contingency, and that the great number of discharged veterans in the North would render great service in repelling or checking such an invasion. He concluded: "I think I will order back to Washington all regiments whose terms of service will expire before the 20th of August. This will give quite a force round which to rally new troops." The next day he proposed to Halleck that the departments of the Susquehanna, West Virginia, and Washington be consolidated under one chief, and he proposed retrieval of Major General William B. Franklin from retirement for the assignment.[4]

Grant's intentions for his subordinates and their ability to mount a large-scale pursuit and *coup d' main* against Early proved incompatible. In the first place Hunter hardly

[216]

enjoyed unqualified support from the Lincoln administration. He spent countless hours rationalizing his actions against Early and seemed as mystified by dispatches from Washington as by the enemy forces. Furthermore, Halleck was more aware of Lincoln's and Stanton's sensitivity about any uncrushed Confederates in the Valley than was Grant. After all, Halleck had been in the area far longer; Washington officials had seen and heard the din of battle at Fort Stevens; and they knew firsthand how close had been the city's brush with disaster. Early's force, to them, was no raiding party to be taken lightly.[5] If Grant wanted the defenses of Washington and Baltimore stripped of all mobile units for reinforcements, Halleck was less sure of the wisdom of such a move. He saw the confusion in the wake of Early's raid—the continuing attempts to sort out the various commands in the forts around Washington; the prompt but somewhat erratic dispatch of Wright's "Army of Operation" on July 13; and the continuing push of reinforcements to Wright and Hunter after that. If the confusion was just as bad in Washington as it was in the field, Halleck could well appreciate the observation of Colonel J. Howard Kitching of the Sixth New York Heavy Artillery to his father on August 17: "General Augur told me that I would find things in very bad shape, and indeed I do. There has been no system in the management of the command till everything has gotten wrong and foremost." Affairs in the later summer of 1864 regarding Washington's protection closely approximated the mess which had worried Lincoln, Stanton, and McClellan nearly two and one-half years before.[6]

It was not until July 19 that Halleck found time to record his own observations on Early's operations. He observed for Grant's benefit that as long as Meade's army was south of the James and Lee's force lay between it and Washington, "he can make a pretty large detachment unknown to us for a week or ten days and send it against Washington, or into

[217]

West Virginia, or Pennsylvania, or Maryland.'' Hunter's army was entirely too weak to hold West Virginia and the Baltimore and Ohio railroad while also containing any raids north of the Potomac despite the fact that it ''comprises all troops north of Richmond that can go into the field.'' Northern militia could not be depended upon for aid and the Washington and Baltimore garrisons consisted of troops unfit for the field. Only the timely arrival of the VI corps had saved both cities, wrote Halleck. In a statement which echoed three years of administrative experience with this problem, he observed:

> So long as you were operating between Washington and the enemy your army covered Maryland and Pennsylvania, and I sent you all the troops from here and the North which could take the field or guard your depots and prisoners of war. But the circumstances have now most materially changed, and I am decidedly of the opinion that a larger available force should be left in this vicinity.[7]

The final paragraphs of Halleck's dispatch displayed the chief of staff's great anxiety. Faulty intelligence due to lack of enough cavalry had deceived Washington authorities as to Early's true intentions in early July. But had the Confederates crossed the Potomac below Harpers Ferry and moved directly upon Baltimore or Washington, or had the VI corps been twenty-four hours later in arrival, the depots of supplies and political seat would have been in gravest danger. Halleck bluntly asked Grant: ''Is not Washington too important in a political as well as a military point of view to run any serious risk at all?'' Horses and manpower were in short supply, and Halleck summed up the seriousness of that situation when he concluded: ''Volunteering has virtually ceased, and I do not anticipate much from the President's call which has the disadvantage of again postponing the draft for fifty days. Unless

our Government and people will come square up to the adop-
tion of an efficient and thorough draft, we cannot supply the
waste of our army.''

Meanwhile, Grant had been pondering the situation on
his own and Early obligingly made matters worse by suddenly showing signs of activity near Winchester. Grant directed
that Wright and Major General William H. Emory, commander of the XIX corps, remain in operation against Early
and wondered why together with Hunter they could not press
the enemy and move southward toward Charlottesville and
Gordonsville. But the Confederates effectively toyed with the
Federals throughout late July until even Dana was forced to
admit that: ''The pursuit of Early, on the whole, has proved
an egregious blunder . . . .'' Halleck rather petulantly replied
that Franklin was politically unsuitable for the merged
command envisaged by Grant, and seemed aghast at the prospect of consolidating the departments at all. Once more it
seemed that the Washington clique was substituting its own
notions of authority and strategy for those of the army's top
commander.[8]

An exasperated Grant now took his case directly to the
president. Sending a dispatch on July 25 by his Chief of Staff,
Brigadier General John A. Rawlins, Grant reiterated his views
on departmental consolidation to Lincoln. He now recommended Meade as the commander of a so-called ''Military
Division'' to be formed from the departments of the Susquehanna, Middle, West Virginia, and Washington. He also
noted the delays and confusion surrounding communication
with the capital—it was taking two days for dispatches to reach
their destination—and he ordered Halleck to issue emergency orders directly. Secretary of War Stanton replied for Lincoln on July 27, and suggested a high level meeting between
Grant and the chief executive. Meanwhile, Early's forces
showed continued activity as they drove portions of Hunter's

command across the Potomac, and by the end of the month, McCausland's cavalry was off an a dash which would result in the burning of Chambersburg, Pennsylvania and another alarm in the population centers east of the mountains. To Lincoln and Grant the time seemed ripe to demand bringing these incursions to a halt permanently.[9]

Just as Early's movements in early July had baffled Union authorities, so also did those of a month later. Conflicting reports that the whole Confederate force was across the Potomac mixed with others which proclaimed that it was merely another cavalry raid. The lack of Federal mounted troops was a distinct handicap; Grant dispatched a cavalry division back to Washington to counter the problem, and in the end this may have been the reason why he selected Major General Philip Sheridan, the crack cavalry commander of the Army of the Potomac, to pull everthing together against Early.[10]

Grant's instructions to Sheridan were simple—"to get south of the enemy and follow him to the death." Such stark sentiments mirrored the hard-boiled approach which the fighters had assumed after several years of conflict. Lincoln told Grant on August 3 to get on with such business but warned him to reread all dispatches emanating from Stanton and Halleck to see whether "there is any idea in the head of any one here of 'putting our army south of the enemy,' or of 'following him to the death' in any direction." Years of frustration led the president to bluntly tell his chief commander: "I repeat to you it will neither be done nor attempted, unless you watch it every day and hour and force it."[11]

By this time Grant certainly realized that traveling with the Army of the Potomac handicapped him just as it had McClellan when dealing with the machinations in Washington. But he trusted Sheridan, and the very day that he heard from Lincoln, Grant traveled to Monocacy Junction—the staging area for the Federals mustering to destroy Early—where he met Hunter. He secured that officer's willingness to step aside; he directed the assembled army to move forward to Halltown at the lower end of the valley; and when Sheridan arrived on August 6, the general-in-chief told him what he wanted done and then departed for Petersburg. Sheridan took charge of the consolidated "Middle Military Division" the next day. On the horizon lay important elections which could determine not only the future of the Lincoln government but also prosecution of the suppression of the rebellion. Sherman's army lay stymied before Atlanta just as Meade's forces seemed to be pinioned before the Richmond-Petersburg line. The citizens of the north were weary of long casualty lists, and overall, the situation in Virginia, at least, appeared to many people to be little changed from the spring and summer of 1862 when McClellan lay dead in the water before the Confederate capital while a large and able rebel field force reigned supreme in the Shenandoah and threatened the national capital. It was clearly Sheridan's task to resolve this dilemma and quickly.[12]

Sheridan experienced the usual problems of organization and consolidation at first. Early's ability at bluff did not help the new commander and Mosby's guerrillas disrupted supply and communication lines, forcing Sheridan to detach sizable contingents to counter that threat. Everyone tended to overestimate the real strength of the Confederates. Sheridan possibly misunderstood the sharp emphasis in Grant's instructions to devastate the countryside in order to obliterate Lee's breadbasket (an endeavor which the Union forces pursued with some vigor during August and early September), and he probably felt like so many generals before him, that he could accomplish his assignment with minimal battles and casualties. But in the eyes of his superiors his first movements seemed overly cautious, and finally, Grant had to travel from Petersburg for another talk with Sheridan. The general-in-chief simply dismissed the numbers game and since six weeks had

[221]

passed and the shakedown period was over, he ordered Sheridan to get out and attack Early. Sheridan's 30,000 veteran Federals did just that in the famous Valley campaign of 1864 whereby Early's fighting force was virtually destroyed at Winchester, Fisher's Hill, and Cedar Creek. These first real Union victories in the Shenandoah valley accomplished the task of ending Confederate supremacy in the area and, together with Sherman's victories in Georgia, insured Lincoln's reelection and continuation of his war policy. No longer would the Valley provide a covered way leading north into Maryland and Pennsylvania or a screen for Confederate movements threatening Washington.[13]

A residue of Early's army regrouped to provide several additional tests for Sheridan's forces later in the autumn, but the clear-cut victories of September and October appeared to the Northern people to demonstrate that their capital was no longer in imminent danger of capture. Assistant Secretary of War Dana announced to Rawlins on October 29 that: "The active campaign in the Valley seems to be over for this year." Such a statement begged the question of what further measures should be taken to secure Washington by Sheridan's maneuver force. Grant was anxious that the VI corps be returned to the main army and that Sheridan move the rest of his forces back into active operations against Richmond by striking and destroying the Virginia Central railroad, lifeline for Lee's army, en route. Sheridan demurred since he was more aware of Early's remaining force and Mosby's marauders, and by implication, the necessity of guarding the upper Potomac crossings and approaches to Washington. Halleck, ever mindful of his contingency, lost no time in forcefully pointing it out, citing Mosby's intimidation of local Federal cavalry squadrons from the Washington garrison, and expressing his desire that "some point south of the Potomac should be fortified strongly enough to resist any *coup de main*, and garrisoned with a force which can operate against a rebel advance either down the Shenandoah or the Loudon Valley." He sent Colonel George Thom and Lieutenant Colonel B. S. Alexander of the Engineers to confer with Sheridan and his officers and examine sites for such fortified garrisons.[14]

Dispatches from Thom and Alexander to Halleck, as well as Dana's to Rawlins, in late October, all indicated Sheridan's reluctance to quit the Valley prematurely in order to undertake operations against the Virginia Central. Overextended supply and communication lines, burnt-over districts, and the continued presence of Confederates gave Sheridan pause, and he desired to post the bulk of his forces in a strong defensive position behind Opequon creek where a rebuilt railroad line could supply the augmented Army of West Virginia in covering the lower valley. Thom and Alexander therefore recommended formation of two separate and distinct armies of 10,000 men each. One army was to provide for the defense of the Shenandoah and the country east of the Blue Ridge, to be strongly entrenched on the Opequon near the Winchester and Potomac railroad with detachments at Winchester and Snicker's and Ashby's gaps. The second army—for the defense of Washington and the country east of the Bull Run mountains—was to occupy a strongly intrenched and advanced position on the Orange and Alexandria despite Sheridan's fears that it would require a full corps to protect the railroad.[15]

Sheridan withdrew his army to Kernstown on November 9, so that it might find better winter accommodations and a shorter supply line. The Winchester and Potomac railroad was rebuilt from rails used on the Manassas Gap line earlier that fall, and the cavalry was prepared for the Virginia Central operation. Then Early stirred once more, thus delaying release of the VI and XIX corps but not hindering operations against the subsistence base in the Valley. Finally, Lee's recall of the bulk of Early's army in early December led to a similar retrieval of the VI corps by Meade's forces. Cavalry operations against the Virginia Central sputtered and ran afoul of cold weather and stubborn Confederation opposition. At the close of the year, Sheridan retained only the XIX corps as his main infantry force, although the entire Middle Military Division comprised nearly 78,000 effective fighting men, as well as 834 heavy and 339 light artillery pieces. Sheridan's final decisive victory over Early at Waynesboro on March 2, 1865, concluded the war in the Shenandoah valley and completely fulfilled the purpose for which he had been sent there.[16]

Still, the region of Virginia adjacent to Washington was by no means completely pacified, and before Sheridan could send troops back to Grant and accomplish other tasks desired of him by the general-in-chief, he needed to tidy up affairs in Mosby's so-called "Confederacy." In fact, Mosby's operations continued apace throughout the fall despite various schemes for countering them. Small bands of Mosby's rangers raided the very outskirts of the city. Captain Walter Bowie, a native of Prince George's county, Maryland was killed near Rockville in October having perpetrated a robbery and other havoc in the Montgomery county neighborhood, to which Federal cavalry and citizen's posse had responded forcefully. The spectrum of ranger activities included harassing Sheridan's wagon trains and dispatch riders as well as countless expeditions into Fairfax county against picket lines and the Manassas Gap and Orange and Alexandria railroads. Even the Baltimore and Ohio was struck repeatedly by the small bands of gray-clad guerrillas until the Federal command regarded Mosby's people as little more than outlaws and the level of atrocities on both sides rose measurably. Neither the hard-riding cavalry of Colonel H. M. Lazelle, based on Falls Church, the ambuscade tactics of an old Indian fighter such as Richard Blazer, nor the more numerous mounted contingents of Sheridan's main force proved successful at dealing effectively with Mosby.[17]

Mosby effectively carried out two missions—harassment of Sheridan and tying down garrison personnel from Washington. The latter alone numbered between 26,000 and 30,000 effective troops and over 1,000 artillery pieces throughout the autumn. Despite Grant's urging that he do something as early as mid-August, Sheridan could not detach sufficient force against the guerrillas until after Cedar Creek. Finally, on November 27, he ordered Wesley Merritt's cavalry division to sweep the Loudon valley, the heart of Mosby's enclave, and destroy the logistical base for the guerrillas and capture or disperse the rangers themselves. Unsuccessful to a degree in pinning down the elusive band, Merritt's units temporarily dispersed the rangers and destroyed crops, barns, and livestock, sparing neither Unionist nor Confederate sympathizer. By December, Mosby was under orders from Richmond to dispatch part of his command to the Northern Neck, between the Rappahannock and the Potomac—to quarter them in that section of the state which had not been overrun by moving armies. The subsequent wounding of Mosby himself and the general winter lull in operations pointed toward subsidence, but not the ending, of this particular threat to Washington and its suburbs.[18]

Mosby's irritant continued up to the time of Lee's surrender, and the winter months caused Washington officials countless moments of anxiety when an ice-locked Potomac bottled up shipping where the raiders might once more effect a blockade of the water approaches to the capital. Ceaseless raiding in Fairfax and Prince William counties, numberless reconnaissance trips, fruitless chases and missed opportunities to stamp out the Confederate guerrillas marked the monthly activities for Federal outposts around Washington. Strength figures for the Washington defense force continued at a high level throughout the winter: 31,278 effectives (with nearly 37,000 on the rolls), in January; 28,347 effectives (with 34,000 on the muster rolls), in February; and 900 to 1,000 artillery pieces pinned down in the static forts. All signified that the Lincoln administration was still not convinced of the absence of enemy threat to the capital. Even Grant had to write rather peevishly: "If the returns I have of troops in the Department of Washington are anything like correct there need not be the slightest apprehension for the safety of the capital. At this time if Lee could spare any considerable force it would be for defense of points now threatened which are necessary for the very existence of his army."[19]

Grant went on to say that Lee could not possibly send off any large body of men without the knowledge of the Federals. He felt that Washington's departmental commander, C. C. Augur, certainly possessed sufficient cavalry for an early warning. In fact, Grant queried Halleck on the point of why so many cavalrymen were posted in the capital city itself," . . . wasted in duties in no way tending to the protection of the place." He concluded that until the roads improved there was no way for a Confederate force to blockade the Potomac, and he stated frankly: "On the whole, I think there is not the slightest need of apprehension, except from a dash of a few mounted men into Alexandria, and with proper watchfulness this ought not to occur."

If the threat to Washington had been minimized by early March, as Grant implied, why then were so many soldiers, civilian laborers, and vast funds involved with continued perfection of the defenses of the national capital? It appears that as late as February 26, Halleck expressed fears that Mosby's expansion of activities in the Fredericksburg vicinity, and the attendant drawing of Federal strength from the Potomac valley, left "Alexandria and the Maryland line too much exposed to rebel raids." Even Sherman's father-in-law, Thomas Ewing, wrote to Stanton asking where Lee might be expected to go should he evacuate Richmond, and answering

[226]

VIEW OF COMPANY F, THIRD MASSACHUSETTS HEAVY ARTILLERY, FORT STEVENS, AUGUST 1864.
(Library of Congress)

his own question with the observation that Washington was the logical target. "Is Washington so well guarded that it will resist the first onslaught?" asked Ewing. Lee might not hold it, but he might hope for something from temporary posses- sion of the capital "an insignia of sovereignty," ". . . and at any rate, if he fell, to fall with 'clat; and, indeed, he might hope to arouse the dormant energies of Northern sympathizers by so bold a stroke, if successful even for a day."[20]

So the engineers continued to plan, the laborers to dig, and the cavalry to patrol, and the strength figures for March 1865 still showed 32,500 aggregate present and absent for du- ty in the Department of Washington with 1,113 heavy pieces of artillery and 436 light guns. Some of the artillery buildup might be attributed to reconcentration of ordnance at Washington following de-escalation of Sheridan's efforts in the Shenandoah. Winfield Scott Hancock, recovering from his Get- tysburg wound, replaced Sheridan in command of the Middle Military Division, and he was anxiously planning a spring of- fensive in the valley, more perhaps to retrieve old military reputations than anything else.

Gang-warfare in Loudon had grown worse with the absence of the restraining cavalier hand of Mosby who was recovering from a recent wound. But life in the fortifications and camps around Washington remained much as it had been for three years during the various interludes between crises. In fact, many of the quasi-warriors such as George H. Kimbell, a clerk in the Quartermaster department, regaled a friend in the navy after Early's raid with a somewhat glamorous por- trayal of how the departmental employees were "organized into companies and Regiments and armed and equipped as the law directs, and uniformed in Uncle Sam's blue." Like the heavy artillerists, the quartermaster units suffered through countless parades and inspections, Kimbell deploring only that "it is outrageously hot and almost impossible to keep comfortable."[21]

Complacency or satisfaction never proved to be the forte of the engineer officers, however. The evolution of the formal defenses of Washington from simple field fortifications to semi-permanent defensive works by late 1864 brought attendant problems of maintenance and constant reevaluation of sites and fortification design. Private G. J. Clark wrote a lady friend back home in Niagara County, New York on November 18, 1864 that upon arriving in the defenses, his unit went to Fort Woodbury on the Arlington line which "we found very dirty and in bad shape," had just gotten it fixed up good when they transferred to Fort Ellsworth behind Alexandria and found it to be even worse. "It will take us two weeks to get it fixed up & by that time we will have to leave." The defenses provided a school of practice for their profession as they sought to contain erosion and counter ballistic developments with the new, improved rifled artillery. By the autumn of 1864, the engineers had learned to increase parapet thickness from the original eight- to twelve-foot thickness to twelve or eighteen feet. They discovered that rain and frost, after only a single winter, eroded the scarp and destroyed the berm of the earthworks. They proceeded to adopt a uniform slope of 45 degrees, extending from the exterior crest to the bottom of the ditch, and this exterior slope of the parapet was usually sodded.

Similarly, the original board revetments were replaced by vertical posts of oak, chestnut, or cedar, four to six inches thick, set in a vertical slope of six feet of vertical rise for every foot of horizontal. The sides of gun embrasures were revetted with turf-filled gabions, and magazines and bombproofs were also strengthened by replacing the wooden framework with one by nine foot timbers of oak or chestnut placed tightly side by side. Roof logs of the same size received a minimal covering of earth, ten feet thick, to protect the powder stores or men from projectiles.

[229]

The huge amount of timber required for replacements of original wood caused acute problems by late 1864. Gun platforms as well as other uses caused countless requests from the engineers for timber-cutting parties to be sent beyond the defense perimeter. By late in the war even the timber of loyal Virginians was subject to cutting, and there was always the risk that Mosby's band would capture men assigned to such details. Still, the defenses of Washington were strong because the military engineering combined with the heavy ordnance emplaced in the works.

Application of lessons learned elsewhere in combat led to continued implementation of armament beyond the first 24- and 32-pdr. ordnance mounted on seacoast carriages. Rifled cannon now varied from 4½-inch, 6-pdr. James, as well as 10-, 12-, 20-, and 30-pdr. Parrotts mounted on either field or siege carriages, to the huge 100- and 200-pdr. Parrotts positioned on center pintle iron fortress carriages. Smoothbore artillery included 6-pdr. field, 12- and 24-pdr. as well as 8-inch mountain and field, siege and seacoast howitzers, and 6-, 12-, 24-, 32-, and 42-pdr. field and seacoast guns, topped by the immense 15-inch Rodman guns mounted at Fort Foote. Mortars ranged from the 24-pdr. Coehorn to 8- and 10-inch siege varieties. By the end of 1864, the defenses of Washington may well have represented the greatest concentration of various types of Civil War ordnance in one locale.[22]

The statistics, contained in a report from Alexander to the Chief of Engineers in early October 1864, seemed quite impressive. In addition to asking for $500,000 for the coming year to complete bombproofs, military roads, and maintenance functions, Alexander, like his mentor J. G. Barnard, packaged the existing fortifications in a manner calculated to amaze a reader. He cited the thirty-three miles of military roads and recapitulated:

The defenses of Washington consist of 60 forts, 93 batteries, aggregating 25,799 yards, and 35,711 yards of infantry covered way. There are emplacements provided for 1,447 guns. The present armament is 762 guns and 74 mortars.[23]

More revealing for purposes of explaining the continued rationale for the huge expenditure of time, money, and energy lavished on defending the capital were other key passages in Alexander's report. Alexander noted that it should be borne in mind that while this system encompassed the "cities" of Washington, Georgetown, and Alexandria, it was only a single line of defense, and if it were once forced by an enemy, "we have nothing between him and the public buildings and archives but our reserves, with the chances of battle in the open field." This consideration seemed to indicate a need for either a second line of defense or of having at all times, where there was a possibility of attack, the forts well garrisoned with practiced artillerists and a strong reserve within the defenses. In other words, said Alexander, "if we should be attacked by a powerful army, Washington City would become, in a military sense, not a walled city with gates, but a great intrenched camp, requiring a large army for its defense, the defensive works standing for a certain number of men, enabling, perhaps, all other things being equal, 25,000 men in them to repel the attacks of 50,000, or 50,000 to repel 100,000, or 100,000 to repel 200,000."[24]

Perhaps by the fall of 1864 the engineers were looking past the Confederates toward the next war. At the same time they were utilizing such an experience as Early's raid to plan for conflict with some hypothetical "enemy" which would naturally involve a siege of the national capital. "No one would have believed twelve months ago," warned Alexander, "that within a year a large force of the enemy would encamp within sight of the Capitol, and that one of our forts would be seriously threatened." Still, claimed the engineer, if that

[231]

fort had not been built, or had been improperly constructed, there could be little doubt but that the enemy would have taken possession of the seat of government.

Alexander warned against a false security since "the works are passive, and of themselves have no strength, unless they are properly manned." Furthermore, "these being of perishable materials, like a railroad, require constant repairs; old magazines require to be repaired or rebuilt; new bomb-proofs are required in many of the works; decayed revetments must be renewed; worn-out gun platforms require renewal; decayed abatis must be replaced by new; the scarps require constant attention—they must all be sodded, or revetted with masonry before the works can assume a permanent character; all interior earthen slopes of traverses, magazines, bomb-proofs, camps, & c., should be sodded; besides, some additional redoubts and batteries should be built in order to render those already constructed more secure." The purpose of the engineer's remarks was obvious. History repeated itself, and the United States should keep its defenses in order so as to guard against such a contingency in the future.

Events of the final days of the war rapidly outpaced the wishes of engineers like Alexander and Barnard. Lee's surrender on April 9 and Mosby's disbandment late in the month culminated the purpose for which fortifications, troops, and artillery had been collected originally. The assassination of Lincoln caused a flurry of activity as troops around the city went on alert in order to apprehend the conspirators. The threat of possible trouble with France over Mexico received official attention, but by late spring the armies had staged their final reviews up Pennsylvania Avenue and, in the main, the focus of the Federal Union was turning away from the fighting and toward occupation and nation building in a postwar environment. G. J. Clark wrote his friend Lena Shaw from Fort Woodbury in late April how the forts were being dismantled and the heavy ordnance shipped to the Washington arsenal and turned in for storage. He noted sadly, however, that one of the men had been shot by a sentry for disobeying a challenge, being too drunk to obey the order to halt. Reorganization of the Department of Washington on April 26 pointed in that direction as the districts of Alexandria, Washington, the Patuxent, and the "Northern Neck" were instituted. At the end of the month, strength returns for the Middle Military Division showed 111,048 effectives and 1330 pieces of heavy and light artillery, with the Department of Washington accounting for 68,138 of the men and 1121 pieces of artillery.[25]

On May 6, 1865, Brigadier General Richard Delafield's letter to the secretary of war finalized the question of which formal defenses of Washington were to be retained in the future. The Chief of Engineers reiterated the fact that on that date the Defenses of Washington consisted of seventy-four enclosed forts and armed batteries, each having a guard or garrison, and armed with 905 guns of various calibres, with magazine stores of powder and ammunition amounting to about 200 rounds per gun, or 181,000 rounds total. But, since the rebellion had been suppressed, Delafield saw no necessity for the extensive system of temporary works. He recommended that fifty-one of the forts and batteries should be dismantled at once, and the artillery and stores of all types should be withdrawn and deposited either in the remaining twenty-three forts or at the arsenals and depots under the charge of the different military departments of the army. After disarming, dismantling, and withdrawing the stores, a guard should remain to protect the property from fire and injury, and measures taken to restore the grounds to the rightful owners. To this end, Delafield recommended liquidation of claims on the government for the uses and changes made to the property by conveying to the owners the right and title to the buildings

[233]

and fixtures, as well as timber in the bomb-proofs, magazines, and stockades. Any excess should either be sold to the public or stored for possible military service elsewhere.[26]

Delafield named those forts to be retained north of the Potomac as Forts Carroll, Stanton, Baker, Mahan, Lincoln, Totten, Slocum, Stevens, Reno, and Sumner; south of the river, Lyon and the three redoubts nearby, Ellsworth, Worth, Ward, Richardson, McPherson, Whipple, Morton, C. F. Smith, and Battery Rodgers were to be retained. Although the possibility existed of further reductions in the future, "these twenty-three retained forts and redoubts occupy and command thirteen positions or lines of approach by roads or cover the cities of Alexandria, Georgetown, and Washington; its navy-yard and arsenal, and the roads from the north, west, south, and east." Furthermore, these works would provide quarters and other accommodations for the 10,000-man garrison which Delafield supposed might be permanently stationed in and about the national capital.

Four days later, Alexander separated the fortifications into three classes of importance for planning purposes. On May 20 he requested some decision on the future of the defenses in the light of orders to "limit operations on the defenses to labor of garrisons or enlisted men" in eleven works then in progress. Delafield replied within a week that no changes in orders could be effected but that Alexander should survey Fort Washington for a new water battery in that locale. General Order 315 announced on June 19 that Stanton, Grant, and Augur had all agreed with Delafield's plan. Finally, eight days later, President Andrew Johnson directed the division of the United States into military departments and divisions, with the Department of Washington (Augur's command), embracing the District of Columbia, Fairfax county, and Anne Arundel, Prince Georges, Calvert, Charles, and St. Mary's counties in Maryland.[27]

WASHINGTON, D.C. AT THE TIME OF THE GRAND REVIEW.
(Library of Congress)

Life for those engineers, workmen, and garrisons charged with the dismantlement phase of the operations soon became routine again. Alexander found himself discouraged by inadequate funding for hiring laborers to tear up timber and move equipment. The rapidly shrinking supply of soldiers were more intent on going home than cleaning up the debris of war. Alexander's nominal work force shrank from 384 civilians and enlisted men in April to 17 hired civilians by November. By mid-summer he had to admit that it might prove necessary to reduce still further the number of retained forts and emplaced cannon. Nevertheless, he completed a survey of a possible new water battery at Fort Washington and discussed the opportunities afford by "the use of iron for the protection of gun and gunners." By the end of the reporting year—September 30—he could tell Delafield that all engineer property in the dismantled forts had been collected at the four engineer camps, public bids invited for the materials in the dismantled forts, and that while terribly important, nothing had been done about the $300,000 appropriation from Congress on July 2, 1864, for providing obstructions in the Potomac to render the shore batteries more efficient for the protection of Washington against maritime attack.[28]

Those officers and men still on garrison duty after Appomattox found the peacetime duty just as boring as that during the war. One soldier in the Eighth New York Heavy Artillery at Bailey's Crossroads captured the climate nicely when he wrote on June 3: "Today like any other has passed away—with the world at large it has had no particular historic interest as the anniversary of any great event." Yet, some veterans such as Captain George A. Armes found much to remember about the summer and fall of 1865 near Washington. Armes had grown up in Fairfax county and his assignment in June included placing the proper armament in those forts south of the Potomac. Stationed at Fort

Whipple, he witnessed the departure of the rapidly disbanding armies until "nothing but the guard of a few volunteer soldiers were left to protect the Government property until the few regular troops could be distributed to take their places." But the volunteers were proficient at dress parade and drill, to the amusement of various visitors and tourists. Armes was subsequently transferred to the Freedmen's bureau where he came in contact with the numerous cases of brawls between former Confederates and Federal soldiery, Negro squatters and former property owners, litigation over damages by the government during the war, and the general reconstruction of a devastated locale.

Washington City itself had been changed by the war. The wartime shock of massive influx of workers, soldiers, refugees, and freed slaves had created a morass of over 130,000 people. J. M. Hartwell had written to Lena Shaw of Johnson's Creek, Niagara County, New York on February 13, 1865 complaining about "this abominable hub of creation" as he called the capital. He felt that the concentrated essence of iniquity seemed particularly prone to take advantage of the Freedmen and women huddled in camps and present on the streets of the city. Yet, other visitors could look with awe upon the wartime capital at war's end. Andrew J. Boies of the Thirty-Third Massachusetts came away from Washington in mid-June 1865 fascinated by the public buildings, the navy yard, marine barracks, and such touches as the iron fencing around the new-completed Capitol building. "The improvements at this place are extensive, and substantial," he declared solemnly, "with storehouses, an armory, shops in which are made gun-carriages." Soldiers going to and from the war through their national capital had indeed "seen the elephant," and their lives would be changed forever by this as part of their wartime experiences.[29]

The area surrounding Washington showed distinctly the signs of the tragic conflict. As one account noted, the scene was one of desolation from Alexandria to the Bull Run battlefield. Observers of the dedication of monuments on that battlefield in June 1865 remembered that "a few decrepit houses and leaning chimneys" were all that remained around Fairfax Court House. The local men with "their homes ruined, their families beggared and themselves humbled" drew the sympathy of more fortunate city dwellers from Washington. Throughout northern Virginia: "Fences are utterly swept away . . . occasionally a small patch of corn or wheat is passed, but the whole face of the country is changed. Scrub oak and pine are springing up everywhere." Centreville was a desert and as late as 1914, Washington newspapers contended that "the war" had killed that "village of rare beauty."[30]

It was little wonder that former property owners of sites occupied by Federal forts during the war might seek recompense at the end of the conflict. The interaction between such civilians and Federal authorities may well have been the touchiest point in the immediate postwar period. Barnard surmised in 1864 that nearly 1,000 property owners in the area would desire compensation at war's end. Certainly the situation at the sites for Forts Dupont, Davis, Chaplin, and Mahan, east of the Anacostia, were illustrative. The former owners of the property received compensation mainly by the return of land to them. Selby B. Scaggs, owner of the sites of Forts Chaplin and Craven, claimed $10,000 in damages to his 400 acre farm. But he was permitted only to reclaim his land, one dollar in cash, and the engineer buildings at nearby Camp Franklin as well as the timber in the two forts. On August 15, 1865, Michael Caton, owner of the Fort Dupont site, received one dollar, the five quartermaster structures on the site, and the wooden portions of the work. Daniel F. Lee, who in 1864 purchased the ground upon which Fort Davis had been constructed, asked for $1,500 damages to his land, and claimed the barracks, officers quarters, guard house and mess hall—

but the chief quartermaster of the Department of Washington opposed his claim and the buildings were sold at public auction. Lee bought the abatis as a consolation at $33.87! Litigation about Fort Foote dragged on until 1872 and 1873 when the former owners of "Roziers Bluff" deeded the land permanently to the Federal government. Nonetheless, by November 27, 1865, Alexander could report to Delafield that nearly $13,000 had been realized by sales of properties pertaining to the Defenses of Washington.[31]

Fort reductions continued until in December survey plots remained only for Forts Foote, Carroll, Stanton, Lincoln, Totten, Slocum, Stevens, Reno, Sumner, Whipple, Ellsworth, and Battery Rodgers. As a new year opened, Alexander received orders to discharge everyone connected with the defenses and to report directly to Delafield. Finally, on July 14, 1866, he closed his accounts on the defenses with $582.67 still left on the ledger. Thus, the books were formally closed on the vast fortification system which had existed for five years.

Over the subsequent years the once proud earthen works crumbled before time and the elements. Barnards wartime report on the defenses of the capital was published as a professional paper by the Corps of Engineers in 1871. Other national crises brought fear for the safety of the capital, and for a time after the Civil War the army preserved various defensive positions at Fort Washington, Foote, Whipple (renamed Myer in honor of the founder of the Signal Corps), and Battery Rodgers. But military authorities never again constructed extensive field fortifications to defend Washington. Instead, the rise of modern naval power in the late nineteenth century and air power in the twentieth dictated the direction of future defense installations for the city. Engineers were reluctant to suggest elaborate and costly new works when budget constraints and technological changes would render them quickly obsolete. Then too, the concept of defense of the interior (where after all Washington was located), shifted back to the seacoast. There the nation's first line of defense—a battle fleet of the navy and the army's coastal guns and later airpower—might prevent hostile invasion of the nation's shores.[32]

In the years after the Civil War, Fort Whipple (Myer), became successively a cavalry post and later a signal corps installation. Less a fortification and more a garrisoned post, it closely resembled the Washington Barracks, formerly the Washington Arsenal on Greenleaf's Point, where infantry and engineers were garrisoned after the war. The situation was different for the river batteries. Battery Rodgers at Alexandria quickly fell prey to postwar budget slashes but Forts Foote and Washington reservations witnessed an almost constant cycle of construction activity, base closings, and regarrisoning. At Fort Washington, for example, an earthen battery for 15-in. Rodman guns was erected during the Seventies, and eight batteries of the type constructed during the Endicott period for 4-in. guns, were constructed between 1896 and 1905. The situation was similar upriver at Fort Foote, and under the stimulus of the Spanish-American war, positions on the Virginia shore known as Fort Hunt, in honor of the chief of artillery for the Army of the Potomac, contained four batteries for 3-, 5-, and 8-in. guns. By 1903, Engineer reports listed seven batteries mounting 6- and 10-in. guns, and 12-in. mortars as well as various rapid-fire pieces of smaller calibres for the Maryland shore as well as the Virginia sites. Underwater mines supplemented the land batteries. Among those troops garrisoning the posts in the years after the Civil War were elements of the Sixth and Thirteenth Cavalry, Third and Fourth Artillery, Thirteenth Infantry, and Seventeenth, Forty-Fourth, One Hundred and Fourth, One Hundred and Forty-Third, and One Hundred and Forty-Seventh companies of Coast Artillery. Fort Washington served as headquarters for the Coast Artillery's District of the Potomac early in the twentieth century.[33]

Army War College student planners actively addressed the problems of Washington's protection during the years between World Wars I and II. They concluded that adequate defenses existed to contain the naval threat to the capital, and that air and land threats would involve meeting enemy forces at some distance from the city by "aggressive open warfare methods." One committee, studying possible war with Great Britain in 1925, contended that no permanent fortifications should be constructed in time of peace for the immediate land defense of Washington, and "the permanent assignment of airplanes or anti-aircraft guns for the protection of any particular city, or locality, is impracticable." Nevertheless, in World War II, the Sixth Pursuit Squadron was given the primary mission of aerial protection of the national capital, and a succession of antiaircraft gun and NIKE batteries after the war continued the tradition of static defense of the city. The still pending issue of anti-ballistic missile defense (Sentinel, Safeguard, "Star Wars") in the nuclear age brings the issue to present day Washington.[34]

In retrospect, even today, the defense measures taken to protect Washington during the Civil War were impressive. The fortification system alone surpassed anything comparable in Europe at the time, according to their architect, J. G. Barnard, and he compared them with the lines of Torres Vedras and Lisbon from the Napoleonic period as well as Sevastopol from the Crimean war. The salient question remains, however, whether or not the $1.4 million spent by the Federal government on the defenses, or the average of twenty to thirty thousand men (the equivalent of several corps), held back from reinforcing the Federal armies in Virginia, were really worth it. Washington's defense system never received a concerted, sustained attack by Lee's entire Army of Northern Virginia. The city never found itself with a situation such as Vicksburg, Atlanta, or the Petersburg-Richmond lines. Still, the strategic enclave around Washington often provided a refuge for defeated Federal forces—the very critical element in the equation between any potential attacker and the static fortification system. Such was true in July 1861 and September 1862. Early's raid in July 1864 suggested that the defenses alone might not have withstood a determined attack by combat veterans in large force. Yet to the soldiers it was as author William O. Stoddard suggested tongue-in cheek in *Inside the White House in War Times*:

> Did you ever see such tremendous earthworks as are these we reach and pass? Well, nobody else ever did and it takes much riding and walking to really see all or one of them; but, after seeing, one can have a better idea of the true relations between one or all of these vast defenses and the White House that is protected by them. It was so terribly hard to believe that the Government of the United States lived in a fort![35]

Yet, if the defenses of Washington may be compared to a modern deterrent, both accomplished in a sense their respective missions without any conclusive test. Both proved to be expensive weapons systems but worthy of the price to both government and taxpayer. Certainly the mere existence of the defenses of Washington gave pause to Confederate notions of attacking the capital. While willing to attempt pressure tactics at times in order to secure tactical success elsewhere, Lee remained unwilling to commit his army to a headlong rush at the city. In this sense, the expenditures of dollars, the long man-hours of construction or upkeep, the weeks and months of drudgery, illness, frustration suffered by young volunteers in garrison, and the thankless work of the engineers—indeed, the sizable mobile defense contingents—all may have proved worth the price. Because of such factors, Washington— Symbol, Sword, and Shield of the Union—emerged unscathed from the test of civil war.

APPENDIX A

Washington's Forts Today

Public parks and a national cemetery scattered through the Washington area today commemorate the defenses of Washington. Several public thoroughfares bear the name "Military Road" in honor of their original purpose during the Civil War. The men and guns are gone, for the most part, and once proud ramparts have diminished with age. Yet some thirty-five major traces of the main fortifications remain, representative of a past grandeur. The works at Forts Stevens and Ward have been partially rebuilt in order to preserve historically a bygone era for the inquisitive visitor. Elsewhere, the remnants include:

North of the Potomac

Battery Cameron	1900 Block of Foxhall Road, N.W.
Battery Parrott	2300 Block of Foxhall Road, N.W.
Battery Martin Scott	5600 Block of Potomac Place, N.W.
Battery Kemble	Chain Bridge Road, N.W.
Fort Bayard	River Road and Western Avenue, N.W.
Fort Reno	Nebraska Avenue and Grant Place, N.W.
Battery Rossell	Grounds of Peruvian Embassy on Thirtieth Place, N.W.
"Battery to Right of Broad Branch"	5301-5303 Twenty-Ninth Street, N.W.
Fort DeRussy	Rock Creek Park near Oregon Avenue, N.W.
"Battery to Left of Rock Creek"	Beach Drive at Ross Drive in Rock Creek Park
Battleground National Cemetery	6625 Georgia Avenue, N.W.

[243]

Fort Stevens .... George Avenue and Quackenbos
Street, N.W.

Fort Slocum .... Oglethorpe Street and Kansas Avenue,
N.W.

Fort Totten .... Fort Place, off North Capitol Street, N.E.

Fort Bunker Hill .... Fourteenth and Otis Streets, N.E.

Battery Jameson .... Fort Lincoln Cemetery

East of the Anacostia

Fort Mahan .... Forty-Second Street and Benning Road,
N.E.

Fort Chaplin .... Texas Avenue, N.E.

Fort Dupont .... Alabama Avenue, S.E.

Fort Davis .... Pennsylvania and Alabama Avenues, S.E.

Battery Ricketts .... Bruce Place and Fort Place, S.E.

Fort Stanton .... Erie Street, Seventeenth Street, Morris
Street, S.E.

Battery Carroll .... Nichols Avenue and South Capitol Street,
S.E.

Fort Greble .... Nichols Avenue, S.E.

Fort Foote .... Fort Foote Road off Maryland Route 210

Fort Washington .... Fort Washington Road off Maryland Route
210

South of the Potomac

Fort Marcy .... George Washington Memorial Parkway

Fort Ethan Allen .... Glebe and Military Roads, Arlington

Fort C. F. Smith .... 2411 Twenty-Fourth Street North,
Arlington

Fort Scott .... Aurora Hills section, Alexandria

Fort Richardson .... Grounds of Army/Navy Country Club,
Arlington

Fort Ellsworth .... Behind George Washington Masonic
National Monument, Alexandria

Fort Ward .... City park on West Braddock Road, Alexandria

Fort Willard .... Belle Haven section, Alexandria

[244]

The U.S. National Park Service administers the majority of these sites although Arlington, Virginia includes some remnants within its city park system and Alexandria, Virginia maintains the restored Fort Ward and small museum facility for the public. Around the District of Columbia, Arlington, and Alexandria may be found historical markers describing individual forts, and Battleground National Cemetery near Walter Reed Army Medical Center in northwest Washington as well as the Grace Episcopal burial ground contain remains of the fallen from the battle of Fort Stevens. In this fashion these sites continue to serve the needs of the community and nation. In an era concerned with ecology, recreation, historic preservation, and parkland, the remnants of the Civil War defenses provide a refuge for new generations against urban blight and congestion. They will remain as silent sentinels—monuments to that drama which shaped the destiny of a united nation.(*)

* For fuller discussion of the forts, past and present, and a self-guided tour around the system, consult Cooling and Owen, MR. LINCOLN'S FORTS: A GUIDE TO THE CIVIL WAR DEFENSES OF WASHINGTON.

APPENDIX B

Regulations Governing the
Defenses of Washington

GENERAL ORDERS,   WAR DEPARTMENT,
                                   ADJUTANT GENERAL'S OFFICE,
No. 42   *Washington, February 2, 1864.*

The following Regulations for the care of Field-works and the government of their Garrisons, prepared by Brigadier General BARRY, Inspector of Artillery, U.S.A., are published for the government of all concerned:

1. It is the duty of the Commanding Officer of each work to provide for the care of the armament and the safety and serviceable condition of the magazines, ammunition, implements, and equipments; and, by frequent personal inspections, to secure the observance of the rules prescribed for this purpose.

2. The fixed armament, consisting of the heavy guns and those the positions of which are prescribed, will be numbered in a regular series, commencing with the first gun on the right of the entrance of the main gate. Where there are platforms temporarily unoccupied by guns, they will be numbered in the regular series. The ammunition will be kept in the magazines, with the exception of a few stands of grape, canister, and solid shot, which will be piled near the guns.

3. The gun-carriages will be kept clean, and all axles and journals well lubricated. They will be traversed daily, and never be allowed to rest for two successive days on the same part of the traverse circle. If the gun-carriage does not move easily on the *chassis*, the tongue will be occasionally greased. The upper carriage should not rest habitually on the same part of the chassis.

[246]

4. The *elevating screw* and its *box* will be kept clean and well greased. When the guns are not in use, the screw will be run down as far as it will go, the breech of the piece being first raised until the muzzle is sufficiently depressed to prevent water running into it, and kept in that position by a wooden quoin or block. The *tompion* should be kept in the muzzle, and the apron over the vent.

5. The piece is not to be kept habitually loaded. It will be time to load when the enemy appears, or when special orders to that effect are given.

6. The Commanding Officer will see that a shed is constructed for the implements and equipments. For each drill these will be issued to the gunners by the ordnance sergeant, or other non-commissioned officer acting as such, who will receive and put them away after the drill is over, and be at all times responsible to the Commanding Officer for their safety and serviceable condition, and that the supply is adequate. When sheds cannot be provided, the implements will be kept near the pieces, or in the bomb-proofs. The *equipments* (haversacks, tube-pouch, &c.) may be kept at the entrance of the magazine, where they will be sheltered. Platforms for projectiles will be laid near the guns; for canisters, a couple of pieces of scantling for skids will answer. A water-shed, made by joining two boards together at the edges, should be placed over them. When the wooden sabots become wet they swell and burst the canisters, so that they cannot be put into the gun. When this happens, dry the sabot until it shrinks sufficiently for the canister edges to be brought together and tacked.

7. When not supplied by the Engineer Department, materials for constructing the sheds and for skidding will be furnished by the Quartermaster's Department, on requisitions made to the Chief of Artillery.

8. The magazines must be frequently aired in *dry weather*. For this purpose, the ventilators and doors must be opened after 9 a.m., and must be closed, at latest, two hours before sunset. The ammunition for different classes of guns will be carefully assorted, and the shelves, boxes, or barrels containing each kind, plainly marked. When there is more than one magazine, the ammunition will be so distributed as to be near to the particular guns for which it is provided. Cartridges must be moved, and,

[247]

if necessary, rolled once a week, to prevent *caking* of the powder. In doing this, care must be taken not to pulverize the grains. *Friction primers* must be kept in the tin packing boxes, and carefully protected from moisture. They will be frequently examined, and dried by exposure to the sun. This must always be done immediately after wet weather of long continuance. The supply of friction primers for each gun must be fifty per cent greater than the number of rounds of ammunition provided for it. A dozen primers will always be kept in the tube-pouches in use at each gun. Three lanyards will be provided for each gun, one of which will be kept in store; the other two in the tube-pouches. As soon as received, the *hooks* will be tested to see if they are sufficiently small to enter the eye of the primer, and yet strong enough for use.

9. In order that practice may be had in the use of friction primers, authority is given to expend on drill five per gun each month. These primers will always be taken from those longest at the post.

10. There should be one lantern for every three or four guns; and two *good globe lanterns* for each magazine.

11. No person will be allowed to enter the magazines except on duty, and then every precaution against accidents will be taken. Lights must always be in glass lanterns, and carried only by the person in charge of the magazine. Swords, pistols, canes, spurs, &c., will not be admitted, no matter what may be the rank of the person carrying them. Socks or moccasins will be worn, if they can be procured; if they cannot, then all persons must enter with stocking-feet. No fire or smoking will be allowed in the vicinity when the doors or ventilators are open. *Too many precautions cannot possibly be taken to avoid the chances of an explosion.*
A copy of this paragraph, legibly written, will be conspicuously posted near or on the doors of every magazine.

12. Companies will be assigned to guns in such proportions as will furnish at least *two,* preferably three, reliefs in working them, and sufficient men in addition for supplying ammunition from the magazines. From fifteen to twenty men should therefore be assigned *to each gun,* and instructed in its use. Companies should habitually serve the same guns, each man being assigned a special number at the gun, and thoroughly instructed in all its duties. As occasion offers, all of the officers and enlisted men should be instructed at each of the different kinds of gun at the post, as well as in the duties of all the numbers at each gun. Every night at retreat

or tattoo, the men who are to man the guns in case of a night attack should be paraded at their pieces and inspected, to see that all their equipments, implements, and ammunition are in good order, and the gun in serviceable condition and easy working order. The men so stationed should "call off" their numbers before being dismissed. In case of alarm at night, all should repair at once to their posts, equip themselves, and await orders, without losing time by forming upon their company or battalion parade grounds.

13. Each gun should be under charge of a non-commissioned officer, and to every two or three guns should be assigned a Lieutenant, who will be responsible to the Captain for their serviceable condition at all times. The Captain will be responsible to the Commanding Officer for the condition of the pieces, and the instruction of the men of his company. Artillery drills will be frequent until all of the men are well instructed, and there will never be less than *one artillery* drill per day when the weather will permit, nor will any officer be excused from these drills unless it is unavoidable. For action, all the cannoneers not actually serving the guns will be provided with muskets, and will be stationed near the guns to which they belong, for service on the banquettes or elsewhere, in case of assaults.

14. Each company should be supplied with three copies of the *Tactics for Heavy Artillery*, and rigidly adhere to its directions. *Tables of Ranges* will be found in the work. One copy of *Instructions for Field Artillery* should be supplied to each company. All authorized books can be obtained on written application to the Chief of Artillery, who will obtain them from the Adjutant General of the Army. The books so drawn are the property of the United States for the use of the company, and will be accounted for on the Muster Rolls.

15. The Commanding Officer will make himself conversant with the approaches to his work, the distance to each prominent point commanded by his guns, the nature of the ground between them and his post, and the most probable points of attack upon it. He will also make it his duty to see that all of his officers, and, as far as possible, his non-commissioned officers, are thoroughly acquainted with these matters. The distances will be ascertained by actual measurement, and not left to conjecture. *Tables of Ranges* or *Distances* for each point, and the corresponding elevation, according to the nature of the projectile, with the proper length or time of the fuze, when shell or case-shot are used, will be made out for *each gun,* and furnished to the officer and non-commissioned officers serving it. These tables should be painted upon boards, and securely fastened in

[249]

a conspicuous place near the gun. As these tables differ for different kinds of gun, the same men should be permanently assigned to the same piece.

16. The projectiles should be used in their proper order. At a distance, *solid shot*; then, *shells* or *case-shot*, especially if firing at troops *in line*; *canister or grape is for use only at short ranges.* When columns are approaching so that they can be taken in direction of their *length*, or *very* obliquely, solid shot is generally the best projectile, because of its greater accuracy and penetrating power. If the column consists of cavalry, some shells or case-shot will be useful, from the disorder their bursting produces among the horses; but shells and case-shot should not be used against any troops when moving *rapidly*. The *absolute* distances at which the projectiles can be used with effect vary with the description and calibre of the gun, and can be ascertained only by consulting the Tables of Ranges. The prominent points on the approaches to the works should be designated, their distances noted, and directions drawn up for the different kinds of ammunition to be used at each gun for these different points. During the drills, the attention of the chiefs of pieces and gunners should be frequently drawn to this subject.

17. Commanding Officers will pay special attention to the police and preservation of the works. All filth will be promptly removed, and the drainage particularly attended to. No one should be allowed to walk on the parapets, or move or sit upon the gabions, barrels, or sand bags that may be placed upon them. When injuries occur to the earthworks, they should be repaired as quickly as possible by the garrison of the work. If of a serious nature, they should be at once reported to the *Engineer Officer* in charge of the work. *All injuries to the magazines or platforms of the guns will be promptly reported as soon as observed.* The *abattis* being a most important portion of the work, must be always well looked to and kept in perfect order.

18. Special written or printed instructions as to the supply of ammunition at the different posts, and the proportion for the different classes of guns, will be furnished by the Chief of Artillery to the Commanders of posts. Instructions will also be furnished as to the special objects of each work, on proper application for this purpose to the Chief Engineer or Chief of Artillery.

19. No persons not officially connected with the garrisons of the fieldworks will be allowed to enter them, except such as visit them on duty, or who have passes signed by competent authority; nor will any person

except commissioned officers, or those whose duty requires them to do so, be allowed to enter the magazine, or touch the guns their implements or equipments.

20. The garrison can greatly improve the work by sodding the slopes of the parapet, and those of the ramps and banquettes, or by sowing grass seed on the superior slope, first covering it with surface soil. The grass-covered or sodded portions of the parapets, traverses, magazines, &c., should be occasionally watered in dry weather, and the grass be kept closely cut. Early in the spring and late in the autumn they should be covered with manure.

21. As a great deal of powder is wasted in unnecessary salutes, attention is called to paragraph 268 of Army Regulations, edition of 1861-'3:
Paragraph 268.-A General Officer will be saluted but once in a year of each post, and only when notice of his intention to visit the post has been given.

22. The practice of building fires on the open parades, for cooking and other purposes, is prohibited, as it endangers the magazines.

23. The armament of a fort having been once established, will not be changed except by authority of the Commander of the District, Geographical Department, or Army Corps, and then only on consultation with the Chiefs of Engineers and Artillery.

24. The machinery of the Whitworth, or other breech-loading guns, will not be used except by special orders from the Commanding Officer of the post.

25. Experience having conclusively shown that rifled guns, of large calibre especially, must be subjected to most careful treatment and skillful management in order to secure their maximum efficiency, both in range and penetration, and especially their maximum endurance, the attention of all officers using rifled guns of large calibres is called to the following rules: Sponges well saturated with oil shall alone be used; and for this purpose the necessary supply of oil shall be provided for all batteries of position in which rifled guns form the part or whole of its armament. A little grease or slush upon the base of the projectile adds much to its certainty, and should be always used when possible. The bores of the guns should be washed, and the grooves cleaned of all residuum and dirt subse-

[251]

quent to the firing, after the gun has cooled. Great care must be taken to send the projectile home in loading, that no space may be left between the projectile and the cartridge.

Before using shells, unless already loaded and fuzed, they must be carefully inspected both on their exterior and interior; and scrapers should be used to clear the cavity of all moulding sand before charging the shell. Special attention should be given to the insertion of the fuzes, and the threads of the fuze hole should be carefully cleaned before screwing in the fuze. In all Parrott projectiles it should be carefully observed that the brass ring or cup is properly swedged, and that, in the case of the ring, the cavities between it and the projectile are not clogged with dirt or sand.

In loading shells care will be taken to fill them entirely with powder, leaving no vacant space after the fuze is screwed in.

For the 10, 20 and 30-pounder Parrott guns, powder of too large a grain should not be used. The best powder for the projecting charge of these guns is what is called "mortar powder."

26. Pole-straps and pole-pads of field limbers, not belonging to horsed batteries, are to be kept in the implement-room or in the trays of the limber chest. They should be occasionally washed and oiled, as prescribed for the care of harness in field artillery tactics.

27. The forts will be inspected daily by their Commanding Officers; and by the Brigade, Division, District, or Department Commanders, and by the Chief of Artillery, as frequently as possible. Particular attention will be paid, at all inspections, to the drill and discipline of the garrison and police of the work; to the condition of the armament, ammunition and magazines; and as to whether the proper supply of ammunition, implements, &c., is on hand at the Post.

INSTRUCTIONS FOR FIRING.

1. The firing in action should be deliberate—never more than will admit of accurate pointing. A few shots effectively thrown is better than a larger number badly directed. The object of killing is to inspire terror so as to deter or drive off the enemy, and precision of fire and consequent *certainty* of execution is infinitely more important in effecting this than a great noise, rapid firing, and less proportional execution.

2. To secure accuracy of fire, the ground in the neighborhood must be well examined, and the distance to the different prominent points within the field covered by *each* gun *measured* and *noted*.

[252]

The gunners and cannoneers should be informed of these distances, and in the drills the gun should be accurately pointed at the objects noted in succession, the gunner designating it, calling the distance in yards, and the corresponding elevation in *minutes* and *degrees*, until all the distances and corresponding elevations are familiar to the men. When hollow projectiles are used, the time of flight corresponding to the distance must be given to the man who goes for the projectile. He tells the ordnance sergeant, or the man who furnishes the ammunition, and the latter cuts the fuze to burn the required time.

3. The gunner is responsible for the aiming. He must therefore know the distance to each prominent object in the field covered by his gun, the elevation required to reach that point, and the time of flight of the shell or case-shot corresponding to each distance or elevation. He must have a table of these ranges, taken from the Heavy Artillery Tactics, pages 236 to 247, * (edition of 1862).

4. These tables will be promptly prepared under the direction of the Commanding Officer, and copies furnished for each gun, and used habitually in the drills. They will be examined and verified by the Chief of Artillery.

*NOTE.—(The last table on page 240 should read 8-inch sea-coast *howitzer* on barbette carriage, instead of 8-inch sea-coast *mortar.)*
For example: The cartridges for the 24-pounder guns all weigh six pounds, as issued in the Defences of Washington. The table (page 236) therefore applies as follows:

Twenty-four Pounder Gun on Siege or Barbette Carriage.

Cartridge.	Ball.	Elevation.		Range.	
Lbs.		°	′	Yards.	
6	Shot.	0	0	412	That is, the *bore* (not line of sight) being level, a range of 400 yards.
6	"	1	0	842	1 degree elevation, range about 850 yards.
6	"	1	30	953	1½ do. do. 950 do.
6	"	2	0	1,147	2 do. do. 1,150 do.
6	"	3	0	1,417	3 do. do. 1,400 do.
6	"	4	0	1,666	4 do. do. 1,660 do.
6	"	5	0	1,901	5 do. do. 1,900 do. The extreme range of 24-pounder round shot.

Thus, supposing the enemy at a point 1,000 yards distant, by looking at the table it will be observed that 950 yards require 1 ° 30 ′ elevation; 1,150 yards require 2 °; therefore, elevate a very little—5 ′ to 10 ′ over 1 ° 30 ′, or simply give 1 ° 30 ′ *full.*

5. The attention of all officers in charge of *artillery* in the works is directed to the articles in the Tactics on *"Pointing guns and howitzers," "Night firing,"* &c., pages 76 to 90.

6. Commanding Officers of the works will keep themselves accurately informed of the amount and kinds of ammunition in the magazines. The supply must always be kept up to the amount prescribed by the Chief of Artillery or other competent authority. When it is less than that amount, a special report of the fact will be made to the Chief of Artillery, with requisitions for the ammunition necessary to complete the supply. Commanding Officers will also see that the necessary equipments are always on hand for the service of all the guns, as prescribed in the Tactics or in General Orders.

7. Hand grenades are intended to be used against the enemy when he has reached such parts of the defenses (the bottom of the ditch for example) as are not covered by the guns, or by the muskets of the infantry posted on the banquettes.

8. After the enemy has passed the abattis and jumped into the ditch, hand grenades will be used; and then, if he mounts the parapet, he must be met there with muskets. A resolute defense against assault must also be made by posting men with muskets so as to fire over the tops of traverses, bomb-proofs, or magazines.

BY COMMAND OF MAJOR GENERAL HALLECK:

E. D. TOWNSEND.

Assistant Adjutant General.

OFFICIAL:

Assistant Adjutant General.

Notes

Notes to Chapter I

1. Charles P. Stone, "Washington on the Eve of the War," in Robert U. Johnson and Clarence C. Buel (eds.), *Battles and Leaders of the Civil War,* I, 24-25; Charles Elliott, *Winfield Scott: The Soldier and the Man,* 695-696; Allan Nevins, *The Emergence of Lincoln,* II, *Prologue to Civil War 1859-1861,* 457; Bruce Catton, *The Coming Fury,* 258-270.

2. Margaret Leech, *Reveille in Washington, 1860-1865,* 5-12; John Stepp. "Background to Conflict: An Introduction to the Civil War as Reported by the Star," Washington *Sunday Star Magazine,* 1 Jan 1961, 4-6.

3. Richmond *Examiner,* 25 Dec 60; Leach, *Reveille,* 23; Hunter-Lincoln, 18 Dec 60 in David C. Mearns (ed.), *The Lincoln Papers,* 346-347.

4. Mearns, *Lincoln Papers,* 346-435 passim; George Hochfield (ed.), *The Great Secession Winter of 1860-61,* 1-33.

5. Stone, "Washington on the Eve of the War," 7; Charles W. Davis-Gideon Welles, 11 Apr 61, 44, 27, 449, Gideon Welles papers LC.

6. Stone, "Washington on the Eve of the War," 11; Marcus Benjamin, "The Military Situation in Washington," in Benjamin (ed.), *Washington During War Time,* 15-26.

7. Washington *Star,* 7 Jan 1971; U.S. War Department, *The War of the Rebellion; A Compilation of the Official Records of the Union and Confederate Armies (OR),* Series I, Volume LI, 313.

8. Elliott, *Scott,* 691.

9. Benjamin, "Military Situation," 20-23.

10. The continued rumors are well represented by numerous letters in January folder, Winfield Scott papers, LC; Mearns, *Lincoln Papers,* and *OR,* I, LI, 436-438. Naval preparations may be found in U. S. Navy Department, *Official Records of the Union and Confederate Navies in the War of the Rebellion,* Series I, Volume IV, 410-413; and Congressional investigations appear in U. S. Congress, 36th, 2d sess., *The Congressional Globe,* 58; Benjamin P. Thomas and Harold M. Hyman, *Stanton: The Life and Times of Lincoln's Secretary of War,* 110-112; Burton J. Hendrick, *Lincoln's War Cabinet,* 253-257; John G. Nicolay and John Hay, *Abraham Lincoln: A History,* 136, 139-147.

11. Samuel P. Heintzelman Journal, 1861-1865, 30 Jan 61, Heintzelman papers, LC. Heintzelman concluded however, "I don't apprehend any danger. With the force now here I think we are secure, as Volunteers will come at a moments notice. The feeling that there will be a compromise is better."

12. *OR,* I, LI, 314.

13. Nicolay and Hay, *Abraham Lincoln,* 149-150.

14. Catton, *The Coming Fury,* 222-225.

[255]

Notes to Chapter 2

1. U.S. War Department, *War of the Rebellion: Official Records of the Union and Confederate Armies (OR),* Series I, Volume LI, Part 1, pages 320-321.

2. See for example Scott-Lincoln, 3 Apr 61 in David C. Mearns *(ed.), The Lincoln Papers,* 517; *OR,* I, LI, I, 319-320.

3. Scott-Lincoln, 5, 8 Apr 61, Mearns, *Ibid.,* 525-526, 530-531.

4. *Ibid.,* 534-542; Margaret Leech, *Reveille In Washington,* 53-54; *OR,* I, LI, 1 321-326.

5. Allan Nevins, *The War for the Union,* Volume I, *The Improvised War, 1861-1862,* 79, n.26; Frederick W. Seward, *Seward at Washington as Senator and Secretary of State,* 563.; and Dennett, *Lincoln and the Civil War,* chapter 1 is especially useful on the period 18 April-12 May 1861.

6. Clarence E. Macartney, *Little Mac: The Life of General George B. McClellan,* 74-75; Charles W. Davis-Gideon Welles, 11 Apr 61, Volume 44, Number 27, 449, Gideon Welles papers, LC.

7. Leach, *Reveille,* 58-64; Bruce Catton, *The Coming Fury,* 349. On Baltimore see *OR,* I, II, 12-21, 576-584; George William Brown, *Baltimore and the Nineteenth of April, 1861: A Study of the War,* chapter 4. On vigillantes see, David Dary, "Lincoln's Frontier Guard," *Civil War Times Illustrated,* XI, August 1972, 5, 12-14.

8. Elliott, *Scott,* 691; Willis R. Copeland, *The Logan Guards of Pottstown, Pennsylvania, Our First Defenders of 1861,* 15-21.

9. *Ibid.,* 21-23; Benjamin, "Military Situation," 20-23.

10. Copeland, *Logan Guards,* 23-24; Lewis G. Schmidt, "A Civil War History of the Forty-Seventh Pennsylvania Volunteer Regiment; 'The Wrong Place at the Wrong Time,'" typescript copy, Defending Washington collection, Fort Ward Museum and Historic Site, Alexandria, Virginia.

11. *OR,* I, II, passim; Emmons Clark, *History of the Seventh Regiment of New York, 1806-1889,* I, 479-498 and II, 1-4; Augustus Woodbury, *A Narrative of the Campaigns of the First Rhode Island in the Spring and Summer of 1861,* chapter 2. U.S. Navy Department, Naval History Division, *Civil War Naval Chronology* Part VI, 15.

12. Thomas N. Woodruff, "Early Days in the Nation's Capital" in Edward D. Neill, *Glimpses of the Nations Struggle,* 92-93; Washington *Evening Star,* 24 Apr 61; Benjamin P. Thomas and Harold Hyman, *Stanton: The Life and Times of Lincoln's Secretary of War,* 122.

13. Lincoln-Thomas Hicks and George W. Brown, 20 Apr 61; Lincoln-Baltimore Committee, 22 Apr 61, both in Roy P. Basler, (ed.), *Uncollected Letters of Abraham Lincoln,* 180.

14. Scott-Lincoln, 22 Apr 61, in Mearns, *Lincoln,* 583-584; Seward, *Seward,* 551.

15. Theodore Winthrop, "Yhe New York Seventh; Our March to Washington," *Atlantic Monthly,* June 1861.

16. U.S. Navy Department, Naval History Division, *Civil War Chronology, Part VI, Special Studies and Cumulative Index,* 15; U.S. Navy Department, *Official Records of Union and Confederate Navies in the War of the Rebellion, (ORN),* I, IV, 413-470, *supra.*

17. Seward, *Seward,* 559, 561; Leech, *Reveille,* 67-74; Lincoln-Scott, 27 Apr 61, in Basler, *Lincoln Papers,* 347. Copeland, *Logan Guards,* 28-32, 35.

18. Lincoln-Johnson, 24 Apr 61, in Basler, *Ibid.,* 342-343. On Butler and Baltimore, see Brown, *Baltimore,* chapter VI; also "Union Policy of Repression in Maryland" section, *OR,* II, I.

19. Scott-Lincoln, n.d.[30 Apr 61], 3, 4 May 61, in Mearns, *Op. cit.,* 593, 602-603; *OR,* I, II, 618-619; on Scott-McClellan, see *OR,* I, LI, 1, 338, 369-370.

20. Washington *Sunday Star Magazine,* 7 May 1961, 10-11; Leech, *Reveille,* 75-77 Chicago *Post,* 1 May 61.

21. Lee-George H. Terrett, 10, 15 May; Lee-Philip St. George Cocke, 15 May; Lee-Milledge L. Bonham, 22 May, all 1861, and all in Clifford Dowdy and Louis H. Manarin (eds.), *The Wartime Papers of R. E. Lee,* 24-25, 30, 33; *OR,* I, II, 23-27.

22. *OR,* Ibid., 37-42; Lincoln-Scott, 24 May 61, in Basler, *Lincoln Papers,* 385; Samuel P. Heintzelman Journal, 22, 23 May 61, LC.

23. *ORN,* I, 4, 476-482; Washington *Evening Star,* 25 May 61; Catton, *Coming Fury,* 390-392; Charles A. Ingraham, *Elmer Ellsworth and the Zouaves of '61,* chapter VII.

24. Washington *Evening Star,* 24 May 61; Heintzelman Journal, 24, 25, 26 May 61.

25. John G. Barnard, *Report on the Defenses of Washington,* 9.

26. Nevins, *Improvised War,* 145-146; *OR,* I, II, 653-654.

27. Gerald S. Henig (ed.), " 'Give My Love to All'; The Civil War Letters of George S. Rollins," *Civil War Times Illustrated,* XI, November 1972, 7, 18; Henry and James Hall, *Cayuga in the Field; A Record of the Nineteenth New York Volunteers . . .,* 38-42; Alfred S. Roe, *The Fifth Regiment Massachusetts Volunteer Infantry,* 38-63; Washington *Evening Star,* 9, 15 May 61. Albert W. Haarmann, (comp.), "The Blue and the Gray (and the Green and the Black and the Red, etc.), *"Military Images",* VI, May/June 1985, 16-23.

28. *OR,* I, II, 655. Copeland, *Logan Guards,* 35.

Notes to Chapter 3

1. Heintzelman Journal (L.C.), entries 25 May-20 Jul 61 indicated daily alarms and exchanges between pickets as well as fear of Confederate attack.

2. U.S. War Department, *War of the Rebellion: Official Records of the Union and Confederate Armies (OR)*, Series I, Volume II, pp. 55-59; U.S. Navy Department, *Official Records of the Union and Confederate Navies in the War of the Rebellion, (ORN)*, Series I, Volume IV, pp. 490-508; Joseph Mills Hanson, *Bull Run Remembers*, 42-44; Mary Alice Wills, "Death of Commander James H. Ward," 10-19. The best account of naval operations on the Potomac in this period is Mary Alice Wills, *The Confederate Blockade of Washington D.C. 1861-1862*, esp. chaps 4 and 5.

3. *OR*, I, II, 60-64.

4. *Ibid.*, 104-130.

5. *Ibid.*, LI, 1, 331-339; 369-370.

6. Kenneth P. Williams, *Lincoln Finds A General*, I, 68-74; R. H. Beatie, *Road to Manassas*, chapter 3.

7. *OR*, I, II, 695-696; Williams, *Lincoln Finds A General*, 72-73. Heintzelman Journal, 21 Jun 61.

8. *OR*, I, II, 719-721; Beatie, *Road*, 76-77.

9. *OR*, I, II, 484-485; 504-514; T. Harry Williams, *P.G.T. Beauregard: Napoleon in Gray*, 71-75; Hudson Strode, *Jefferson Davis: Confederate President*, 106-109. An example of a "spy" report may be found in D. L. Dalton-Jefferson Davis, 29 Jun 61, author files, copy, Defending Washington collection, Fort Ward.

10. Bruce Catton, *The Coming Fury*, 441-442, 446; Margaret Leech, *Reveille in Washington*, 90-93.

11. Washington *Sunday Star Magazine*, 9 Jul 1961; and Leech, *Reveille*, 88-89, on July 4 review; *OR*, 1, 2, 907 on Beauregard's proclamation.

12. K. P. Williams, *Lincoln*, 101-102; Leech, *Reveille*, 102-107; Catton, *Coming Fury*, 462-463.

13. Strode, *Davis*, 126.

14. Various interpretations of the Confederate inability to capture Washington after Bull Run include Williams, *Beauregard*, 96-98; Strode, *Davis*, 144-146, Catton, *Coming Fury*, 464-465; R. M. Johnston, *Bull Run; Its Strategy and Tactics*, 249-252; G. F. R. Henderson, *Stonewall Jackson and the American Civil War*, 117-118; Joseph E. Johnston, *Narrative of Military Operations*, 60-62; Nevins, *War for the Union, Volume I, The Improvised War, 1861-1862*, 220-221; Frank E. Vandiver, *Mighty Stonewall*, 166; J. J. Bowen, *The Strategy of Robert E. Lee*, chapter 2.

15. *Heintzelman Journal*, 6 Sept 61.

16. John G. Barnard, *A Report on the Defenses of Washington*, 10.

17. J. Harrison Mills, *Chronicles of the Twenty-First Regiment New York State Volunteers*, 94. On the planned Confederate invasion of southern Maryland, see Wills, *Confederate Blockade*, 58.

18. "Memoranda of Military Policy Suggested by the Bull Run Defeat," 23 Jul 61, as quoted in Roy P. Basler, ed., *The Collected Works of Abraham Lincoln,* 457.

19. George B. McClellan, *Report on the Organization and Campaigns of the Army of the Potomac,* 50, 51.

20. Carl Sandburg, *Abraham Lincoln; The War Years,* vol. I, 312; *OR,* I, LI part 1, 424-435; Leech, *Reveille,* 103-104 (Russell); *OR,* I, 2, 370-371, 755 (Sherman); Catton, *Coming Fury,* 466-467 (Whitman).

21. *OR,* I, 5, 679; McClellan, *Report,* 50.

22. *OR,* I, 5, 678, and 24 respectively.

23. William Todd, *The Seventy-Ninth Highlanders,* 72-73.

24. D. H. Mahan, *A Treatise on Field Fortification* (New York, 1862).

25. Barnard, *Report,* chapter 2; *OR,* I, 5, 678-685. William Dixon-wife 6 Sep 61; A.S. Brey-brother 30 Aug 61, both copies, Defending Washington collection, Fort Ward.

26. *Ibid.,* 14-15; 683.

27. McClellan, *Report,* 52.

28. *Ibid.,* 43; Warren G. Hassler, *General George B. McClellan, Shield of the Union,* 26-27. Stuart O. Lincoln—"Friend James," 17 Dec 61, copy, Defending Washington collection, Fort Ward.

29. McClellan, *McClellan's Own Story,* 84.

30. Williams, *Lincoln,* 401, 402 n. 13; Williams, *Beauregard,* 97-98; Govan and Livingood, *A Different Valour,* 72-74.

31. Williams, *Lincoln,* 123-124.

32. *Ibid.,* 127-131; Hassler, *McClellan,* 30-32.

33. Govan and Livingood, *Valour,* 75-76; Strode, *Davis,* 166-167; Williams, *Beauregard,* 100-101.

34. Reports of the actions mentioned may be found in *OR,* I, 5.

35. Hanson, *Bull Run Remembers,* 46-49; Heintzelman declared disgustedly in his journal on 15 Sept.: "I am expecting, everyday, to hear that the Potomac is closed. Aquia Creek should have been occupied by us more than two months ago & the railroad as far as the bridge across the Rappahannock at Fredericksburg. Now it will cost much more money and many men." See Wills, *Confederate Blockade,* chap. 3.

36. Quoted in Hanson, *Bull Run Remembers,* 49.

37. Williams, *Lincoln,* 134; Heintzelman Journal, 4 Nov and 28 Dec 61, also 9 Jan 62, Wills, *Confederate Blockade,* esp. 96-104.

38. New York *Tribune,* 12 Dec 61. J. E. Morgan-Miller H. Cook, 30 Nov 61, copy, Defending Washington collection, Fort Ward.

39. *The Congressional Globe,* 2d sess., 37th Cong., 13 Jan 62, 286.

SYMBOL, SWORD, AND SHIELD

Notes to Chapter 4

1. Henry and James Hall, *Cayuga in the Field: A Record of the Nineteenth New York Volunteers,* 99.

2. John L. Parker, *History of the Twenty-Second Massachusetts,* 46.

3. Fred C. Floyd, *History of the Fortieth Regiment New York Volunteers,* 64; J. Harrison Mills, *Chronicles of the Twenty-First Regiment New York State Volunteers,* 97.

4. George Wise, *History of the Seventeenth Virginia Infantry, C.S.A.,* 36-37.

5. See for example, W. J. Hardee, *Rifle and Light Infantry Tactics,* (1861); U.S. War Department, *U.S. Infantry Tactics,* (1861); U.S. War Department *Cavalry Tactics,* (1855); U.S. War Department, *Instruction for Field Artillery,* (1861); and U.S. War Department, *Revised Regulations for the Army of the United States,* 1861.

6. *History of the First Connecticut Artillery,* 13.

7. Alfred S. Roe, *The Tenth Regiment Massachusetts Volunteer Infantry,* 38, 39.

8. *Ibid.*

9. E. B. Bennett, (comp.), *First Connecticut Heavy Artillery; Historical Sketch,* 14; *Memorials of Col. J. Howard Kitching,* 26.

10. Daniel George Mcnamara, *The History of the Ninth Regiment Massachusetts Volunteer Infantry,* 49-50.

11. D.C. Civil War Centennial Commission, Program - Commemoration, Battle of Fort Stevens, 1964, n.p.

12. Edward A. Walker, *Our First Year of Army Life,* 56.

13. J. E. Morgan-Miller H. Cook, 30 Nov 61; Eben H. Gilley-mother, 10 Nov 61; both copies, Defending Washington collection, Fort Ward; also Judith Beck Helm, *Tenleytown, D.C.; Country Village into City Neighborhood,* 114.

14. Hall and Hall, *Cayuga in the Field,* 103.

15. Quoted in Parker, *Twenty-Second Massachusetts,* 55; also see Floyd, *Fortieth New York,* 101. Morgan-Cook, 30 Nov 61; Defending Washington Collection, Fort Ward.

16. Milton E. Flower, (ed.), *Dear Folks at Home,* 39.

17. Floyd, *Fortieth New York,* 105; Parker, *Twenty-Second Massachusetts,* 49.

18. Macnamara, *Ninth Massachusetts,* 46.

19. Samuel P. Heintzelman, Journal, 1861-65, LC, daily entries, Nov. 61-Mar. 62.

[260]

20. Flower, *Dear Folks,* 43-44; John D. Vautier, *History of the Eighty-Eighth Pennsylvania Volunteers,* 22. The best study of the Balls Bluff fiasco is Kim Bernard Holien, *Battle at Ball's Bluff.*

21. Mills, *Twenty-First New York,* 107.

22. Walker, *Army Life,* 55; also Hall and Hall, *Cayuga in the Field,* 99.

23. S. Millett Thompson, *Thirteenth Regiment of New Hampshire Volunteer Infantry,* 11; Vautier, *Eighty-Eighth Pennsylvania,* 19-20; and Peckham- "Dear Friend," 10 Oct 61, Defenses of Washington Collection, Fort Ward.

24. Newton M. Curtis, *From Bull Run to Chancellorsville,* 61-62; Heintzelman Journal, 21 Oct 61; "Colonel of the Bucktails; Civil War Letters of Charles Frederick Taylor," *Pennsylvania Magazine of History and Biography,* XCVII (July 1973), 333-363, esp. 346.

25. Curtis, *Bull Run,* 64-65.

26. Washington *Star,* 10 Oct 61.

27. Block, *Above the Civil War,* 68-69.

28. Nelson V. Hutchinson, *History of the Seventh Massachusetts Volunteer Infantry,* 20; Parker, *Twenty-Second Massachusetts,* 50.

29. Walker, *Army Life,* 62.

30. Floyd, *Fortieth New York,* 111; Flowers, *Dear Folks,* 64.

31. W. H. H. Davis, *History of One Hundred and Fourth Pennsylvania,* 32-33.
32. Flower, *Dear Folks,* 50; Floyd, *Fortieth New York,* 114; Davis, *One Hundred and Fourth Pennsylvania,* 38-39.

33. Mills, *Twenty-First New York,* 123. Gilley-mother, 14 Jan 62; copy, Defending Washington files, Fort Ward.

34. Walker, *First Year,* 56.

35. Quoted in Theodore B. Gates, *The "Ulster Guard" and the War of the Rebellion,* 163.

36. George B. McClellan, *Report on the Organization and Campaigns of the Army of the Potomac,* 98-99.

37. *OR,* I, 5, 671-672, 677-685, 699.

38. McClellan, *Report,* 99.

Notes to Chapter 5

1. Allan Nevins, *War for the Union,* v. 1, 303.

2. Roy Basler, (ed.), *Collected Works of Abraham Lincoln,* V, 34-35; Actually some notion of the Occoquon flanking movement had been talked of in policy-making circles even before Bull Run, as Samuel Heintzelman noted in his journal on 26 Jun 61: "I had another gentleman today tell me a plan he laid before Gen. Scott, to land near Occoquan, march 20 miles and cut the railroad to Richmond. A force of 8 or 10,000 men can do it, I would combine it with an advance on Fairfax C. House."

3. Barnard-Sherman, 6 Jan 62, v. 44, John Sherman papers, LC; also McDowell-Heintzelman exchange noted in Heintzelman Journal, 21 Feb 62; for a revisionistic survey of the opinions on McClellan, see Joseph L. Harsh, "On the McClellan-Go-Round," *Civil War History,* XIX (June 1973), 101-118.

4. U.S. War Department, *War of the Rebellion, Official Records of the Union and Confederate Armies,* Series I, Volume 5, page 41 ff.

5. Bruce Catton, *Terrible Swift Sword,* 198; also Warren Hassler, *General George B. McClellan, Sword of the Union,* chapter 3.

6. Heintzelman Journal, 8 Mar and 4 Mar 62, respectively.

7. Catton, *Terrible Swift Sword,* 198.

8. Basler, *Lincoln,* V, 149-151.

9. Joseph Johnston, *Narrative of Military Operations,* 98-106 passim; Joseph M. Hanson, *Bull Run Remembers,* 72-78.

10. Henry G. Pearson, *James Wadsworth,* 113; also S. F. M. Lambniece, 11 Mar 62, copy, Defending Washington Collection, Fort Ward; Frank Moore, (ed.), *The Rebellion Record,* IV, 280-282.

11. Hanson, *Bull Run Remembers,* 77.

12. Basler, *Lincoln,* V, 151.

13. Gideon Welles, *Diary,* I, 61-67, 473-474; Hassler, *McClellan,* 64-65; Hanson, *Bull Run Remembers,* 77-78, concerning Washington's vulnerability.

14. *OR,* I, 5, 55-56.

15. *Ibid.,* 627.

16. *Ibid.,* 672, 683, 699 "garrisons" were apparently interpreted as actual artillerists serving pieces or in relief. Barnard and Barry computed on the Torres Verdras base of two men per running yard of front covering line and one man per running yard of rear line, deducting spaces occupied by guns.

17. *OR,* I, 5, 56. J. E. Morgan-Miller H. Cook, 2 May 62; copy, Defending Washington collection, Fort Ward.

18. *Ibid,* 57; Hassler, *McClellan,* 71 discusses his view of the non-vulnerability of Washington at this time.

19. *OR,* I, 11, pt. 3, 61; also T. Harry Williams, "The Committee on the Conduct of the War," 151; Pearson, *Wadsworth,* 117-118.

20. *OR,* I, 11, pt. 3, 65-66; 19 pt. 2, 726; Colin R. Ballard, *Military Genius of Abraham Lincoln,* 74-75, critiques McClellan's figures; also useful on the controversies, Hassler, *McClellan,* 78-85 passim.

21. Basler, *Lincoln,* 638-639.

22. *OR,* I, 5, 62-63, 1095-1108; Douglas S. Freeman, *Lee's Lieutenants,* I, 142; McClellan's postwar comments appear in *McClellan's Own Story,* 237.

23. Freeman. *Lee's Lieutenants,* I, 149-151; Govan and Livingood, *A Different Valor,* 110-113.

24. Pearson, *Wadsworth,* 126-127; *OR,* I, 12, pt. 3, 29-30.

25. *OR,* I, 19, 126, 130.

26. *Ibid,* I, 12, pt. 3, 241.

27. Basler, *Lincoln,* V, 235, 236; also *OR,* I, 12, pt. 3, 308.

28. *Ibid.,* 239-308, inter alia.

29. Pearson, *Wadsworth,* 126-127; Washington *Sunday Star Magazine,* 6 May 1962. "Alexander"-sister, 29 May 62, copy Defending Washington files, Fort Ward.

30. Nevins, *War For The Union,* II, 125.

31. Heintzelman indicated that he thought so too, see Journal, 20 May 62.

32. William A. Croffut, *Fifty Years in Camp and Field,* 145-146; 443-444.

33. Lynn Case and Warren Spencer, *The United States and France: Cvil War Diplomacy,* 297-298.

34. *OR,* I, 12, pt. 3, 409, 435.

35. Hassler, *McClellan,* 80 citing Pope's testimony; Nevins, *War For The Union,* II, 158; Freeman, *Lee's Dispatches,* 28-29; Basler, *Lincoln,* V, 644-646.

36. *OR,* I, 12, pt. 2, 9; also Hassler, *McClellan,* 198-199.

37. *OR,* I, 12, pt. 2, 10.

38. Catton, *Terrible Swift Sword,* 392-393; Nevins, *War For The Union,* II, 167, 172; strength figures appear in *OR,* I, 12, pt. 3, 523; and regimental accounts of service in the defenses at this time are illustrated by William Spicer, *History of the Ninth and Tenth Rhode Island,* passim, and James Mowris, *History of the One Hundred and Seventeenth New York,* 50, 51.

39. Hassler, *McClellan,* 206-215 inter alia; Nevins, *War For The Union,* II, 172-180.

40. *OR,* I, 12, pt. 3, 708; *McClellan's Own Story,* 511-514; Nevins, *War For The Union,* II, 179; Heintzelman Journal, 22, 23 Aug 62 ; also Hassler, *McClellan,* 221; Dennett, *Lincoln and the Civil War,* 45-47.

41. *OR,* I, 12, pt. 3, 710-713.

42. Quoted in Hassler, *McClellan,* 215; see also *OR,* I, 12, pt. 3, 719-730 passim; *McClellan's Own Story,* 530-533.

43. *OR,* I, 12, pt. 2, 557-558; Cooling, "Civil War Deterrent," fn. 23, 24; Hassler, *McClellan,* 218-221. Eben Gilley-mother, 2 Sep 62; copy, Defending Washington collection, Fort Ward.

44. Robert Smith, "Battle of Ox Hill," 19, 26.

45. Hassler, *McClellan,* 223-224, 230; *McClellan's Own Story,* 535, 542-543; K. P. Williams, *Lincoln Finds A General,* I, 351-354; *OR,* 12, pt. 3, 802, 805, 807.

46. Welles, *Diary,* I, 105-106.

47. Heintzelman Journal, 31 Aug 62.

48. McClellan's Own Story, 536, 538; Welles refers to panic in *Diary,* I, 99.

49. Clifford Dowdey and Louis Manarin, *Wartime Papers of Robert E. Lee,* 293; Hassler, *McClellan,* 233-234.

50. McClellan, *Report on the Organization and Campaigns of the Army of the Potomac,* 347; Edward Stackpole, *Cedar Mountain To Antietam,* 284, 289; *OR,* I, 19, pt. 2, 169.

51. *Ibid.,* 192-193; 200-201; McClellan, *Report,* 349-352; Hassler, *McClellan,* 234, 236.

52. Banks reported 73,000 and 120 guns (40 of which were listed as "heavy"), on 11 September; 84,253 men and 127 guns on 20 September; and he repeated the September 11 figure on the last day of the month, *OR,* I, 19, pt. 2, 264, 337, 374; McClellan's comments appear on 211, 271.

53. *Ibid.,* 190, 202, 212, 297; Alanson Haines, *History of the Fifteenth New Jersey,* 15-17; other regimental accounts illustrating activity include Rowe, *One Hundred and Twenty-Sixth Pennsylvania;* Weygant, *One Hundred and Twenty-Fourth New York;* Bowen, *Thirty-Seventh Massachusetts;* Survivors Association, *One Hundred and Eighteenth Pennsylvania;* Thorpe Fifteenth Connecticut.

54. *OR,* I, 19, pt. 2, 283-284, 219-292, 302.

55. Wentworth-wife, 16 Sep 62, Wentworth papers; also Orlando Poe-wife, 10 Sep 62, Poe papers, both LC; strength figures, *OR,* I, 19, pt. 2, 264.

56. Case and Spencer, *United States and France*, 337.

57. Heintzelman Journal, 7-29 Sep 62; *OR* , I, 19, pt. 2, 299, 301, 309-310, 316-317, 331, 345, 347, 353, 374, 454. The Washington garrison never numbered less than 73,000 men in September and October; see Hassler, *McClellan*, chapter 11 for McClellan's activities after Antietam.

58. McClellan, *Report*, 405; *OR*, I, 19, pt. 2, 359, 360.

59. Heintzelman Journal, 13 Oct 62; *OR*, I, 19, pt. 2, 425-430, also 52-54.

60. *Ibid.*, I, 19, pt. 2, 443; Stackpole, *Fredericksburg*, 22-29; Williams, *Lincoln Finds A General*, 72-79; Heintzelman Journal, 28 Oct 62.

Notes to Chapter 6

1. Lambie-*"Dear Friends,"* 26 Oct 62; Lambie papers AMHI; Roe, *Ninth New York Heavy Artillery*, 26-28; Grant, *Journal . . . 12th Rhode Island*, 14-16.

2. Brooks, *Washington D.C. In Lincoln's Time*, 15-16.

3. U.S. War Department *War of the Rebellion; Official Records of the Union and Confederate Armies*, I, 21, 390-392.

4. The commission was established in Special Order 312, 25 Oct 62 and its members included, Brigadier Generals Joseph G. Totten, Chief of Engineers; W. F. Barry, Chief of Artillery; Montgomery C. Meigs, Quartermaster General; G. W. Cullum, Chief of Staff to the General-in-Chief; and Barnard.

5. *OR*, I, 21, 871-872.

6. *Ibid.*, 904; see whole report, 903-916.

7. *Ibid.*, 902-903.

8. McGrath, *History of the One Hundred and Twenty-Seventh New York*, 19-20, 30, 34; Robertson, *Civil War Letters . . . McAllister*, 221; Williams, *Life in Camp*, 35.

9. Grant, *Journal . . . 12th Rhode Island*, 26-34 inter alia; Benedict, *Army Life in Virginia*, 50, 85, 92-93; Lounsbury, "In The Defenses," 387; Williams, *Life in Camp*, 42, 54, 57, 59, 71, 99; Heintzelman Journal 22 Nov 62, LC.

10. *OR, I. 21,* 707, also 706-742 inter alia; Heintzelman Journal, 27-29 Dec 62; Benedict, *Army Life in Virginia,* 102-107; Williams, *Life in Camp,* 60-62; Rock, *Eleventh Rhode Island,* 76-78; Lounsbury, "In the Defenses," 392-394.

11. Jones, *Ranger Mosby*; Alexander, *Mosby's Men*; *OR,* I, 25, pt. 1., all inter alia.

12. *OR,* I, 25, pt. 2, 3; Heintzelman Journal, 26, 29 Jan 63.

13. *OR,* I, 25, pt. 2, 13, also 15, 29, 42, 60; Heintzelman Journal 26, 27 Jan 63; Livermore, *Story of the Civil War,* pt. III, 110; see also, Lincoln's memorandum on Hooker's Plan of Campaign against Richmond 6-10 Apr 63, Robert Todd Lincoln Papers, LC; and K. P. Williams, *Lincoln Finds a General,* II, 561, states that Hooker "did not wish to be bothered with the command of troops in the place."

14. *OR,* I, 25, pt. 2, 108-109, 136-137, 140-141, 150, 186-187, 568-569; Heintzelman Journal 28 Feb, 1 Mar 63.

15. *OR,* I, 25, pt. 2, 177-185.

16. *Ibid.,* 177-185, 215-216.

17. Headquarters letterbooks of the defenses are filled with urgent requests for laborers, pleas to superiors in the War Department to allow convalescents to work, and frustrated notes to troop commanders in the forts and adjacent camps concerning the need for work details. By early 1864 even Confederate deserters were pressed into service. With respect to laborers from New York city, see Alexander-Trowbridge, 14 Jan, 16 Mar, both 63 and Barnard-Opdyke, 16 Apr 63, Ltrbk. Ltrs Sent, 19 Aug 62-10 May 64; and on deserters Ingraham-Cokander; 12 Mar 64, Ltrbk. Ltrs. Rec., Aug 62-Jan 65, both RG 77, NA; as well as Childs-Calymre, 18 Mar 63, US Army Engineers, Frosts Ltrbk, AC 7609 III-19-C3 LC; also Townsend, *Washington, Outside and Inside,* 58; Ward, *History of Second Pennsylvania Heavy Artillery,* 19.

18. *OR,* I, 25, pt. 2, 513-514.

19. *Ibid.,* 473, 499-500, see also volume 51, pt. 1, 975.

20. *Ibid.,* 25, pt. 2, 499-500.

21. *Ibid.,* 504-506.

22. *Ibid.,* 515-516.

23. *Ibid.,* 305; volume 27, pt. 3, 881-882.

24. *Ibid.,* 886, 917, 924-925, 930-933; also volume 27, pt. 1, 75-77, 168-169; and K. P. Williams, *Lincoln Finds A General,* II, 667-668.

25. *OR,* I, 25, pt. 2, 543, 586; v. 27, pt. 3, 21-23, 29-31, 34-35, 74, 191.

26. *Ibid.,* I, 27, pt. 1, 54 and pt. 3, 269; Hooker-Lincoln, Halleck-Hooker, 5 Jun 63, v. 1, pp. 250, 258, Robert Todd Lincoln papers, LC; Coddington, *Gettysburg Campaign,* chapters II-V inter alia; Welles, *Diary,* I, chapter IX.

27. Quaife, ed., *From Cannon's Mouth,* 219: Nevins, *War for the Union,* III, 91-94 offers a succinct analysis; also Coddington, *Gettysburg Campaign, op. cit.,* and Welles, *Diary,* I, 333-335.

28. Heintzelman Journal, 16 Jun 63.

29. Coddington, *Gettysburg Campaign*, 97-99; Heintzelman Journal 20-30 Jun 63; Williams, *Life in Camp*, 126-127, 133-136; Rock, *Eleventh Rhode Island*, 123-124.

30. *OR*, I, 27, pt. 3, 323, 331-332, 345-346, 355-358; Heintzelman Journal, 26 Jun 63.

31. *OR*, I, 27, pt. 2, 692-697, 823, also part 3, 378-382; Tucker, *Lee and Longstreet*, chapter 13; Nye, *Here Come the Rebels*, 316-320; Moore, *Rebellion Record*, VII, 325-326; K. P. Williams, *Lincoln Finds A General*, II 659-660; Coddington, *Gettysburg Campagin*, 196-208; Welles, *Diary*, I, 349-352.

32. *OR*, I, 27, pt. 3, 378.

33. Heintzelman Journal, 30 Jun 63; Welles, *Diary*, I, 350-352; Leech, *Reveille in Washington*, 250-256; Moore, *Rebellion Record*, VII, 85; Mitchell, *Divided Town*, 122, *OR*, I, 27, pt. 3, 717.

34. *OR*, I, 27, pt. 3, 429-431; *Abbott's comments appear in Fenner, Battery H, First Rhode Island Artillery*, 22-23.

35. *OR*, I, 27, pt. 3, 491, 492, 506; Heintzelman Journal, 1-4, Jul 63.

36. *OR*, I, 27, pt. 3, 567; Welles *Diary*, I, 363-364; Case and Spencer, *The United States and France*, 423-424.

37. *OR*, I, 27, pt. 3, 596-597, 736.

38. Heintzelman Journal, esp. 3, 20 Aug 63; *OR*, I, 27, pt. 3, 755, 772, 786-787, 830-831, 837; Roe, *Ninth New York Heavy Artillery*, 58; and Barnard-Lincoln, 10 Aug 63, v. 120, Lincoln papers, LC.

39. Lincoln-Halleck, 19 Sep 63, Basler, (ed.), *Abraham Lincoln*, VI, 726; *OR*, I, 29, pt. 2, 363.

40. Lincoln-Thomas, 17 Oct 63, *Ibid;* *OR*, I, 29, pt. 1, 8-11, 406, 408; Welles *Diary*, I, 469-472.

41. *OR*, I, 29, pt. 1, 90; see also Jones, *Gray Ghosts and Rebel Raiders*, pt. 2, chapter 6; Benedict, *Army Life in Virginia*, 127-130.

42. *OR*, I, 29, pt. 2, 310-311; see also 111, 154, 226; Heintzelman Journal, 12 Oct 63; Barnard, *Defenses of Washington*, 33 fn, The British were not the only foreign officials to inspect the forts in late 1863. Lieutenant Colonel George E. Chamberlin of the Eleventh Vermont wrote to his wife in December: "We had a visit from the Russians [navy] about three weeks ago. This fort was selected from among all north of the river as being the one for them to see. We fired a salute of thirteen guns, had a band here, and quite a crowd to see the strangers." Lamb, *Letters of George E. Chamberlin*, 304.

43. *OR*, I, 29, pt. 2, 316-317.

44. *Ibid.*, 394-395, 443.

SYMBOL, SWORD, AND SHIELD

Notes to Chapter 7

1. Lounsbury, "In the Defenses," 408-409.

2. McCormick, *General Background, Forts Mahan, Chaplin, Dupont, Davis,* 66-79; Kirk, *Heavy Guns and Light,* 32-33; Blanding, *In the Defenses,* 25, 39-41; Cannon, *Company K,* 10; Misc. diary entries, Henry P. Fox, Fort Lyon, 5-21 Oct 62; S. B. Brace ltr. 27 Mar 63; Eben H. Gilley-mother 11 Jan, 2 and 17 Apr all 63, and 7 May 64, all copies, Defending Washington collection, Fort Ward.

3. *Ibid.;* General Order 45, War Department, 16 Feb 63.

4. Barnard-Kelton, 15 Jan 64, Ltrbk, Ltrs sent, 62-64, RG 77, NA; Chamberlin, *Letters,* 239, 253.

5. Commissary Book, Camp Woodbury 1861-1862, Defenses of Washington, RG 77, NA; Houghton, *Campaigns of Seventeenth Maine,* 8; Smith, *Nineteenth Maine,* 8-9; Chamberlin, *Letters,* 233, 246-247, 256; Lounsbury, "In the Defenses," 391-392.

6. House, *First Maine Heavy Artillery,* 99, also 103-107; Benedict, *Vermont in the Civil War,* 350; Lounsbury, "In the Defenses," 398-399; Ward, *Second Pennsylvania Heavy Artillery,* 26; Cannon, *Company K,* 12.

7. Kirk, *Heavy Guns and Light,* 32, 43; Ward, *Eighty-Eighth Pennsylvania,* 26; Chamberlin, *Letters,* 248; Webb, *Tenth New York Heavy Artillery,* 22; Smith, *Nineteenth Maine,* 36; Snyder, "A Teenage G. I.," 20, 35. Aldace F. Walker-father, 12 Oct, 28 Dec both 62; 7, 25 Jan, and 25 Nov all 63, typescript copy of Walker letters, Vermont Historical Society, Montpelier, Vermont, copies, Defending Washington collection, Fort Ward.

8. Walker-father, esp. 21 Sep, 1, 5, 12, 14, 26 Oct, all 62; 4, 9, 10, 11, 12, 21, 28 Jan, 4 Mar, 5 Apr, 10 May, 8 Jul, 16 Aug all 63; 13 May 64, all copies, Defending Washington collection, Fort Ward.

9. Chamberlin, *One Hundred and Fiftieth Pennsylvania,* 51; Lounsbury, "In the Defenses," 395; Thorpe, *Fifteenth Connecticut Volunteers,* 23-24.

10. Lounsbury, "In the Defenses," 409, also 393, 396; Rock, *Eleventh Rhode Island,* 41-42; Chamberlin, *Letters,* 244, 255; Dyer, *AG Report, Rhode Island, 1865,* 3, 1836; Kirk, *Heavy Guns and Light,* 28-30; Barnard, *Report on the Defenses of Washington,* 128.

11. Quoted in McCormick, *General Background,* 76.

12. Ropes, *Campaigns in Virginia, 1864,* 368; *OR,* I, 33, 383-384, 472; Barnard-Stanton, 14, 16 Jan, 19 Apr 64; Barnard-Totten, 14 Jan, 1, 25 Mar 64; Barnard-Ramsay, 30 Mar 64, all Ltrbk, HQ Def. of Wash., Ltrs. Sent 1862-64; and Rept. Maj. J. D. Mautz, 23 Jan 64, Ltrbk, Ltrs Recd. 1861-65, HQ Def. of Wash., all RG 77, NA.

13. *OR,* I, 33, 660-661, 673; A. G. Childs-B.S. Alexander, 9 Feb 64, US Army Engineers Ltrbk, LC; F. B. Munther-Barnard, 14 Apr 64, Misc. Records, HQ Def. of Wash., RG 77, NA.

14. *OR,* I, 33, 708-709, also 472, 1047; Ward, *Second Pennsylvania Heavy Artillery,* 38-39.

15. Quoted in Barnard, *Report,* 123-128; Beale, (ed.), *Bates Diary,* 360-361; Ropes *Grant's Campaign in 1864,* 370-374.

16. *OR,* I, 33, 888.

17. Barnard-J.C. Woodruff, 16 May 64, Barnard-Stanton, 21 May 64, both Ltrbk, Ltrs Sent 1864-66, RG 77, NA; *OR,* I, 37, pt. 1, 602-611-612- I, 36, pt. 3, 665-666; Miller, *Drum Taps in Dixie,* 79; Dudley, *Reminiscences,* 109.

18. *OR,* I, 37, pt. 3, 3-4, 697; Vandiver, *Jubal's Raid,* inter alia.

19. Dowdey and Manarin, *Wartime Papers of Lee,* 666-667, 699-701; Freeman, *Lee's Dispatches,* 159-160 fn. Early's operation is adequately covered in Vandiver, *Jubal's Raid.* Concerning faulty Union intelligence, see William B. Freis, "A Union Military Intelligence Failure: Jubal Early's Raid, June 12-July 14, 1864," *Civil War History,* XXXVI, Sep 90, 209-225.

20. Early, *War Memoirs,* 384-386; T. E. Morrow-father, 2 Aug 64, Tulane University Library.

21. Welles, *Diary,* 68; Beale, *Bates Diary,* 384; Croffut, *Fifty Years in Camp and Field,* 463-468; Dana, *Recollections,* 228-229; Doster, *Episodes,* 241, 245, 247-248.

22. Alvord, "Early's Attack," 8, 14, Dudley, *Reminiscences,* 119-121. Concerning Grant's actions, see correspondence in John Y. Simon, ed., *The Papers of Ulysses S. Grant,* volume 11, 19-199 inter alia.

23. Morrow-father, 2 Aug 64, Tulane Univ.; for detailed accounts of Monocacy, see, Worthington, *Fighting For Time*; Wallace, *Autobiography,* 698-811; Vandiver, *Jubal's Raid,* chapter 4. Colonel Abner Pickering, "Early Raid in 1864," 27, suggests that Wallace should have continued to harass Early all the way to Washington, failing to comprehend the rigidity of departmental responsibilities at the time.

24. Barnard, *Report,* 107; Augur's official returns dated 10 July noted 31, 231 effectives and 979 guns in the department, with 17, 365 effectives in position north of the Potomac, *OR,* I, 37, pt. 2, 171.

25. Quoted in Alvord, "Early's Attack," 18; Jones, *Ranger Mosby,* 188; *OR,* I, 37, pt. 2, 140-173.

26. Alvord, "Early's Attack," 17-18.

27. Early, *Autobiographical Sketch,* 389-391; Jones, *Ranger Mosby,* 189; Smith, "Rebels at Washington," 5 fn. 4.

28. Much has been written on the events before Washington in 1864 and material on the action at Fort Stevens and the northern defense line herein is based on official documents found in *OR,* I, 37, pts. 1 and 2.

29. See for example Wheaton's report, *Ibid.,* 275-276; Cox, "Defenses," 14-15.

30. Early, *Autobiographical Sketch,* 391-192.

31. *OR,* I, 37, pr. 2, 223; Brooks, *Washington,* 159; Nicolay and Hay, *Lincoln,* IX, 403.

32. Doster, *Episodes,* 252; Brooks, *Washington,* 159-160.

33. Welles, *Diary,* I, 73.

34. Brown, *Signal Corps,* 662.

35. Gordon, *Reminiscences,* 315; Early, *Autobiographical Sketch,* 394.

36. Alvord, "Early's Attack," 22-23; *OR,* I, 37, pt. 2, 222-223, 229-230.

37. Wilson, "Defenses," 21-22; Cramer, *Lincoln Under Fire,* 123; and the fullest discussion of the various legends of the Lincoln incident appears in Smith, "Rebels at Washington," 9-10. See also Denett, *Lincoln and the Civil War,* 208-209. John Henry Cramer, *Lincoln Under Enemy Fire,* discusses various accounts of Lincoln at Fort Stevens; see also, Walker-father, 13 Jul 64, copy, Defending Washington collection, Fort Ward.

38. *Ibid.,* 12-24; *OR,* I, 37, pt. 1, 275-277; Durkin, *Confederate Chaplain,* 93-95; Nichols, *Soldier's Story,* 173; Worsham, *Foot Cavalry,* 242; McDonald, *Make Me A Map,* 215.

39. *OR,* I, 37, pt. 1, 258-260. Rick Griffin, "A Darnestown Confederate Soldier," *The Maryland Line,* 10 Oct 89, 7; Walker-father 15 Jul 64, copy, Defending Washington collection, Fort Ward.

40. Beale, *Bates Diary,* 384; Badeau, *Grant,* II, 346; Nicolay and Hay, *Lincoln,* IX, 174-175; Dana, *Recollections,* 231-232; Welles, *Diary,* II, 75-77.

41. Morrow-father, 2 Aug 64, Tulane Univ.; Douglas, *I Rode with Stonewall,* 295-96; Vandiver, *Jubal's Raid,* 174; Bates, *Telegraph Office,* 255-256. "Story by Corporal Tanner," *Confederate Veteran,* 5, Feb. 99, 83.

Notes to Chapter 8

1. *OR,* I, 37, pt. 2, 599; Barnard-Augur, 19 Jul and Alexander-Delafield, 31 Jul, both 1864, Ltrbk, Ltrs Sent, RG 77, NA; Pond, *Shenandoah Valley,* chapter V; Jones, *Ranger Mosby,* 190-191.

2. Pond, *Shenandoah Valley,* chapter V; Wild, *Alexander's Battery,* 136-154; *OR,* I, 37, pt. 2, 314-315, 338-339, 543, 547; Nicolay and Hay, *Lincoln,* IX, 176-179; Ballard, *Military Genius,* 211.

3. Catton, *Stillness at Appomattox,* 257-258; Grant, *Personal Memoirs,* II, 315, 317.

4. *OR,* I, 37, pt. 2, 301, 328-329, 350, 361, 374.

5. *Ibid.*

6. *OR,* I, 37, pt. 2, 293-329 inter alia, 339-341; Kitching, *Memorial,* 181, Catton, *Stillness at Appomattox,* 289-290.

7. *OR,* I, 37, pt. 2, 384-385.

8. *Ibid.,* 400, 408, 413-414, 422, 426-427; Catton, *Stillness at Appomattox,* 268-270.

9. *OR,* I, 37, pt. 2, 433-434, 463.

NOTES TO CHAPTER 8

10. *Ibid.*, 509, 527, 558-559, 572.

11. *Ibid.*, 553, 582; Catton, *Stillness at Appomattox,* 271.

12. *Ibid.*, 272; Pond, *Shenandoah Valley,* 119-121.

13. Catton, *This Hallowed Ground,* 353-354; Jones, *Ranger Mosby,* chapters 16-18 inter alia; Pond, *Shenandoah Valley,* as well as Sheridan's report, *OR,* I, 46, pt. 1, for the overall campaign. Definitive studies of the Shenandoah Valley campaign of 1864 include; Jeffrey D. Wirt, *From Winchester to Cedar Creek,* and Thomas A. Lewis, *The Shenandoah in Flames; The Valley Campaign of 1864,* as well as the dated but still useful Edward J. Stackpole, *Sheridan in the Shenandoah; Jubal Early's Nemesis.*

14. *OR,* I, 43, pt. 2, 272-273; Pond, *Shenandoah Valley,* 244-245.

15. *Ibid.*, 245; *OR,* I, 43, pt. 2, 468-469, 487-488.

16. *Ibid.*, 846-847, and 46, pt. 2, 841; Pond, *Shenandoah Valley,* 248-254.

17. Jones, *Ranger Mosby,* 200-228 inter alia; *OR,* I, 43, pts. 1 and 2, inter alia, effectively illustrate the acute irritations of Mosby's rangers on Sheridan and other Union forces in northern Virginia.

18. Jones, *Ranger Mosby,* chapters 20, 21; Pond, *Shenandoah Valley,* 247-248; *OR,* I, 43, pt. 1, 55-56 and pt. 2, 247, 501, 648, 671-672, 679-680, 689, 715, 730, 749, 846.

19. *OR,* I, 46, pt. 2, 781.

20. *Ibid.*, 669, 704.

21. Kimball—J. B. Upham, 10 Aug 64, Kimball papers, AMHI, Richards, "Civil War Diary," 189.

22. For details on the engineer matters, see Barnard, *Report on the Defenses of Washington; OR,* I, 43, pt. 2, 280-288; and various letters in Ltrbk. Ltrs. Sent, 1864-66, RG 77, NA. G. J. Clark-Lena Shaw, 18 Nov 64, copy, Defending Washington collection, Fort Ward.

23. *OR,* I, 43, pt. 2, 287.

24. *Ibid.*, 287-288.

25. *OR,* I, 46, pt. 3, 962, 1038 and inter alia for assassination of Lincoln. Clark-Shaw, 23, 26 Apr 65; various requisitions and equipment returns, copies, Defending Washington collection, Fort Ward.

26. *Ibid.*, 1099.

27. *Ibid.*, 1130, 1286, 1293, 1298-1299; Delafield-Alexander, 26 May 65, Ltrs. Recd., HQ Def. of Wash., RG 77, NA.

28. Alexander-Delafield, 1 Jul, 18 Oct; Alexander-Taylor, 5 Jul, all 1865, all Ltrbk, Ltrs. Sent, HQ Def. of Wash., 1864-66, RG 77, NA.

29. Armes, *Army Officer*, 143-155 inter alia; "Dear Jim," unidentified ltr, 3 Jun 65, copy, Defending Washington Collection, Fort Ward. Andrew J. Boies, *Record of the Thirty-Third Massachusetts*, 131; J. M. Hartwell-Lena Shaw, 13 Feb 65, copy, Defending Washington collection, Fort Ward.

30. Washington *Sunday Star*, 16 Aug 1914, 10 Jul 1921; also Alexandria *Gazette*, 14 Jun 1870.

31. Alexander-Delafield, 27 Nov 65, Ltrbk, Ltrs Sent, 1864-66; RG 77, NA; McCormick, *General Background, Forts Mahan, Chaplin, Dupont, Davis,* 76-77; U.S. Q.M., *Outline Description*, 1904, 165.

32. For a useful discussion of coastal defense fortifications and concepts, see Lewis, *Seacoast Fortifications.*

33. Raymond, *Engineers Reports; Analytical and Topical Index,* 1488-1492; Nelson, *Fort Hunt;* Department of the East, *Roster, 1896,* 2, 19, 27, *1909,* 2, 5, 32.

34. AWC Cmte. 23, Report, Defense of Washington, 1926, 5, AWC archives, AMHI; Beane-Watson, 16 Jun 42, OPD 370.5, Change of Stations, Sect. IV (148-217, OPD files, 1942, NA; Washington *Post,* 30 Jul 72.

35. William O. Stoddard, *Inside the White House in War Times*, 82.

Bibliography

MANUSCRIPT SOURCES

National Archives (NA)
Record Group 77—Records of U.S. Army Corps of Engineers, Defenses of Washington
Record Group 319—Records of Army Staff, Plans and Operations Division

Library of Congress (LC)
Asa T. Abbott papers
Edgar Brown papers
William Coffee papers
Logan Fay papers
Mark Hanna papers
C. B. Hanno papers
George Harrison papers
Joseph Kirkley papers
Abraham Lincoln papers
Robert T. Lincoln papers
Joseph K. F. Mansfield papers
Montgomery C. Meigs papers
James B. Merwin papers
E. J. Moore papers
Orlando M. Poe papers
Winfield Scott papers
John Sherman papers
U.S. Army Engineers Letterbook, Defenses of Washington
Gideon Welles papers
Edwin O. Wentworth papers

U.S. Army Military History Institute, Carlisle Barracks, Pa. (AMHI)
George G. Kimball papers
Gavin A. Lambie papers
Joseph Laycox papers

Fort Ward Museum and Historic Site, Alexandria, Va.
Defending Washington Collection

Other collections
T. E. Morrow letter, Special Collections, Tulane University
Library, New Orleans, La.
William Seward papers, The Seward House, Auburn, NY
Abel T. Sweet diary (typescript), Mrs. Carrie Arnold, Morrison,
Col.
Aldace F. Walker letters (typescript), Vermont Historical
Society, Montpelier, Vt.

JOURNALS AND NEWSPAPERS

Chicago *Post*
New York *Herald*
New York *Times*
The Congressional Globe
The National Tribune
Washington *Post*
Washington *Star*

GOVERNMENT DOCUMENTS

Barnard, John Gross. *A Report on the Defenses of Washington, To the
Chief of Engineers, U.S. Army,* Professional Papers of the Corps of
Engineers, Number 20. Washington: Government Printing Office, 1871.

Raymond, C. W. *Analytical and Topical Index To The Reports of the Chief of Engineers and Officers of the Corps of Engineers, United States Army 1866-1900, Volume III.* Washington: Government Printing Office, 1903.

U.S. Congress, 37th, 3d sess., House of Representatives, Rep. Com. *Report of the Joint Committee on the Conduct of the War.* Washington: Government Printing Office, 1863.

_____, 46th, 2d sess., Senate, Ex. Doc. 206, June 10, 1880. *Letter, Secretary of Treasury in response to Senate Resolution of March 8, 1880. A Statement Showing the Expenditures of Government on Account of War of the Rebellion from July 1, 1861 to June 30, 1879 incl. and c. June 10, 1880.* Washington: Government Printing office, 1880.

_____, 57th, 1st sess., House Doc. 618, *A Letter From Secretary of War Tansmitting Results of Preliminary Surveys and Examinations of Sites For Military Posts.* Washington: Government Printing Office, 1902.

_____, 57th, 1st sess., Senate Doc. 433. *Letter From The President and other officers of the Fort Stevens-Lincoln National Military Park Association, With Appendices A, B, C, D.* Washington: Government Printing Office, 1902.

_____, 68th, 2d sess., House of Representatives, 1924-1925. *National Military Park To Commemorate Battle of Fort Stevens.* Washington: Government Printing Office, 1925.

_____, 70th, 1st sess., *National Military Park at Battlefield of Monocacy, Maryland, Hearings Before the Committee on Military Affairs . . . H. R. 11722.* Washington: Government Printing Office, 1928.

U.S. Navy Department. *Official Records of the Union and Confederate Navies in the War of the Rebellion.* Washington: Government Printing Office, 1894-1927.

U.S. War Department, Adjutant Generals Office. *Military Posts and Stations of the United States. . . .* Washington: Government Printing Office, 1874.

_____, Department of the East. *Roster of Troops*, 1869-1873, 1896, 1899, 1900, 1902, 1903, 1905, 1907-1910, 1913, 1914.

_____, Inspector Generals Department. *Outline Descriptions of the Posts and Stations of Troops in the Geographical Divisions and Departments of the United States.* Washington: Government Printing Office, 1872.

_____, Judge Advocate Generals Department, *Military Reservations, National Military Parks, and National Cemeteries.* Washington: Government Printing Office, 1898.

_____, Quartermaster General's Office, *Outline Description of U.S. Military Posts and Stations in the Year 1871.* Washington: Government Printing Office, 1872.

_____, *Outline Description of Military Posts and Reservations in the United States and Alaska and of National Cemeteries.* Washington: Government Printing Office, 1904.

_____, Surgeon General's Office. *A Report on Barracks and Hospitals with Descriptions of Military Posts.* Washington: Government Printing Office, 1870.

_____, *A Report on the Hygiene of the United States Army, Descriptions of Military Posts.* Washington: Government Printing Office, 1875.

_____, *War of the Rebellion: A Compilation of the Official Records of the Union and Confederate Armies.* Washington: Government Printing Office, 1880-1901.

GENERAL WORKS

Ballard, Colin R. *The Military Genius of Abraham Lincoln.* Cleveland and New York: World, 1952.

Barnard, John Gross. *The Peninsular Campaign and Its Antecedents.* New York: D. Van Nostrand, 1864.

Bates, David H. *Lincoln in the Telegraph Office.* New York: Century, 1907.

Benjamin, Marcus, editor. *Washington During War Time.* Washington: Byron S. Adams, 1902.

Bigelow, John. *The Principles of Strategy.* Philadelphia: Lippincott, 1894.

Bowen, J. J. *The Strategy of Robert E. Lee.* New York: Neale, 1914.

Brooks, Noah, Herbert Mitang, editor. *Washington, D.C. In Lincoln's Time.* Chicago: Quadrangle, 1971 edition.

Brown, George W. *Baltimore and the Nineteenth of April, 1861—A Study of the War.* Baltimore: N. Murray, Publication Agent, Johns Hopkins University, 1887.

Brown, J. Willard. *The Signal Corps, U.S.A. in the War of the Rebellion.* Boston: U.S. Veteran Signal Corps Association, 1896.

Brown, Lenard, *Forts De Russy, Stevens, and Totten; General Background.* Washington: U.S. Department of the Interior, 1968.

Case, Lynn M., and Warren E. Spencer. *The United States and France: Civil War Diplomacy.* Philadelphia: University of Pennsylvania Press, 1970.

Catton, Bruce. *Never Call Retreat.* [Centennial History of the Civil War, v. III] Garden City: Doubleday, 1965.

Coddington, Edwin B. *The Gettysburg Campaign: A Study in Command.* New York: Charles Scribners, 1968.

Cooling, B. Franklin. *Historical Highlights of Bull Run Regional Park.* Fairfax, Va.: Fairfax County Division of Planning and Northern Virginia Regional Park Authority, 1971.

Cooling, B. Franklin. *Jubal Early's Raid on Washington 1864.* Baltimore: Nautical and Aviation Publishing Company of America, 1989.

Cooling, B. Franklin and Walton H. Owen II. *Mr. Lincoln's Forts: A Guide to the Civil War Defenses of Washington.* Shippensburg, Pa.: White Mane Publishing Company, 1988.

Cramer, John H. *Lincoln Under Enemy Fire.* Baton Rouge: Louisiana State University Press, 1946.

Cuthbert, Norma B., editor. *Lincoln and the Baltimore Plot 1861; From Pinkerton Records and Related Papers.* San Marino, Calif.: Huntington Library, 1949.

de la Croix, Horst, *Military Considerations in City Planning: Fortifications.* New York: George Braziller, 1972.

Dennett, Tyler, *Lincoln and the Civil War in the Diaries and Letters of John Hay.* New York: Dodd, Mead, 1939.

Dickman, William J., *Battery Rodgers.* Manhattan, Ks.: MA/AH Publishers, 1980.

District of Columbia Civil War Centennial Commission. *The Symbol and The Sword: Washington, D.C.—1860-1865.* Washington: D.C. Civil War Centennial Commission, 1962.

Doster, William E. *Lincoln and Episodes of the Civil War.* New York: G. P. Putnams, 1915.

Engineering Platoon, Engineer Corps, D.C. National Guard. *Guide To The National Capital and Maps of Vicinity Including the Fortifications.* Washington: n.p., 1892.

Fairfax County Civil War Centennial Commission. *Fairfax County and the War Between The States.* Fairfax: Fairfax County Civil War Centennial Commission, 1961.

Fernald, Granville. *The Story of the First Defenders; District of Columbia, Pennsylvania, Massachusetts.* Washington: Clarence E. Davis, 1892.

Fort Myer, Va. (originally Fort Whipple), Historical Sketch. n.p., 1934.

Freeman, Douglas S., editor, *Lee's Dispatches: Unpublished Letters of General Robert E. Lee, C.S.A. to Jefferson Davis and the War Department of the Confederate States of America 1862-1865 from the Private Collection of Wymberley Dorres De Renne.* New York: G. P. Putnams, 1915.

Goode, Paul R. *The United States Soldier's Home; A History of Its First Hundred Years.* Richmond: William Byrd Press, 1957.

Gordon, George H. *History of the Campaign of the Army of Virginia* . . . Boston: Houghton, Osgood, and Company, 1880.

Hanson, Joseph Mills. *Bull Run Remembers . . . History, Traditions and Landmarks of the Manassas (Bull Run) Campaign Before Washington 1861-1862.* Manassas, Va. National Capital Publishers, 1953.

Hassler, Warren W., Jr. *General George B. McClellan, Shield of the Union.* Baton Rouge: Louisiana State University Press, 1957.

Helm, Judith Beck. *Tenleytown, D.C.; Country Village into City Neighborhood.* Washington: Tenley Press, 1981.

Henderson, G. F. R. *Stonewall Jackson and the American Civil War.* New York: Van Rees, 1955 edition.

Hendrick, Burton J. *Lincoln's War Cabinet.* Boston: Little, Brown, 1946.

Hibben, Henry B. *History of the Washington Navy Yard 1799-1889.* Washington: Government Printing Office, 1890.

Hoke, Jacob. *The Great Invasion of 1863; or General Lee in Pennsylvania.* New York: Yoseloff, 1959 reprint.

Holien, Kim Bernard. *Battle of Ball's Bluff.* Alexandria, Va.: By Author, 1985.

Irwin, Richard B. *History of the Nineteenth Corps*. New York: G. P. Putnams, 1893.

Johnson, Robert U. and Clarence C. Buel, editors. *Battles and Leaders of the Civil War*. New York: Century, 1887.

Johnston, R. M. *Bull Run: Its Strategy and Tactics*. Boston: Houghton Mifflin, 1913.

Klonis, N.I. *Guerrilla Warfare: Analysis and Projections*. New York: Robert Speller and Sons, 1972.

Lee, Richard M. *Mr. Lincoln's City: An Illustrated Guide to the Civil War Sites of Washington*. McClean, Va.: EPM Publications, 1981.

Leech, Margaret. *Reveille in Washington 1860-1865*. New York: Harper and Brothers, 1941.

Lewis, Emanuel Raymond. *Seacoast Fortifications of the United States: An Introductory History*. Washington: Smithsonian Institution Press, 1970.

Lewis, Thomas A., et al. *The Shenandoah in Flames; The Valley Campaign of 1864*. Alexandria, Va.: Time-Life Books, 1987.

Livermore, William R. *The Story of the Civil War: A Concise Account of the War in the United States of America between 1861 and 1865, in Continuation of the Story by John Codman Ropes. Part III: The Campaigns of 1863 to July 10th*. New York: G. P. Putnams, 1913.

Manual For Heavy Artillery, For the Use of Volunteers. New York: D. Van Nostrand, 1862.

McClure, Stanley. *Guide Leaflet to the Defenses of Washington*. Washington: U.S. Department of the Interior, 1956.

McCormick, Charles H. *General Background; Forts Mahan, Chaplin, Dupont, Davis*. Washington: U.S. Department of the Interior, 1967.

Military Historical Society of Massachusetts. *The Shenandoah Campaigns of 1862 and 1864 and the Appomattox Campaign 1865*. Boston: By the Society, 1907.

Miller, David V. *The Defenses of Washington During the Civil War*. Buffalo: Mr. Copy, Inc., 1976.

Milton, George Fort. *The Eve of Conflict; Stephen A. Douglas and the Needless War*. New York: Octagon, 1969 edition.

[279]

Mitchell, Mary. *Divided Town: A Study of Georgetown, D.C. During the Civil War.* Barre Publishers, 1968.

Moore, Frank, editor. *The Rebellion Record.* New York: G. P. Putnams, 1861-1868.

Murfin, James V. *The Gleam of Bayonets: The Battle of Antietam and the Maryland Campaign of 1862.* New York: Yoseloff, 1965.

Nelson, Robert T. *Fort Hunt, Virginia; An Historical Sketch.* Washington: U.S. Department of the Interior, 1962.

Nevins, Allan R. *The Emergence of Lincoln; v. II, Prologue to Civil War, 1859-1861.* New York: Charles Scribners, 1950.

_____. *The War For The Union; v. I, The Improvised War, 1861-1862.* New York: Charles Scribners, 1959.

_____. *The War For The Union; v. II, War Becomes Revolution, 1862-1863.* New York: Charles Scribners, 1960.

_____. *The War For The Union; v. III, The Organized War, 1863-1864.* New York: Charles Scribners Sons, 1971.

_____. *The War For The Union, v. IV, The Organized War To Victory, 1864-1865.* New York: Charles Scribners Sons, 1971.

Niven, John. *Gideon Welles, Lincoln's Secretary of the Navy.* New York: Oxford University Press, 1973.

Nye, Wilbur S. *Here Come The Rebels!* Baton Rouge: Louisiana State University Press, 1965.

Prucha, Francis Paul. *A Guide To The Military Posts of the United States.* Madison: State Historical Society of Wisconsin, 1964.

Ropes, John Codman. *The Story of the Civil War; Part I, To That Opening of the Campaigns of 1862.* New York: G. P. Putnams, 1907.

Sedgwick, Paul. *The Shield.* Washington: D.C. Civil War Centennial Commission, 1965.

Simon, John Y., editor. *The Papers of Ulysses S. Grant. Volume 11 (June 1-August 15, 1864).* Carbondale and Edwardsville: Southern Illinois University Press, 1984.

Smith, Eugenia B. *Centreville, Virginia: Its History and Architecture.* Fairfax, Va.: Fairfax County Office of Planning, 1973.

Townsend, George. *Washington, Outside and Inside.* Hartford and Chicago: J. Betts, 1874.

Tucker, Glenn. *Lee and Longstreet at Gettysburg.* Indianapolis: Bobbs-Merill, 1968.

U.S. Army, The Engineer School. *Engineer Operations in Past Wars; Part One.* Fort Humphreys, Va.: The Engineer School, 1926.

U.S. Navy Department, Naval History Division. *Civil War Naval Chronology.* Washington: Government Printing Office, 1961-1965.

Wert, Jeffrey D. *From Winchester to Cedar Creek: The Shenandoah Campaign of 1864.* New York: Simon and Schuster, 1987.

Wert, Jeffrey D. *Mosby's Rangers.* New York: Simon and Schuster, 1990.

Wilson, John M. *The Defenses of Washington, 1861-1865. War Papers 38.* Washington: D.C. Commandery, Military Order of the Loyal Legion, 1901.

Williams, Kenneth P. *Lincoln Finds A General.* New York: Macmillan, 1949-1959.

Wills, Mary Alice. *The Confederate Blockade of Washington D.C. 1861-1862.* Parsons, WVa.: McClain Publishing Company, 1975.

BIOGRAPHY AND PERSONAL REMINISCENCES

Ames, George A. *Ups and Downs . . . of An . . . Army Officer.* Washington: n.p., 1900.

Basler, Roy P., editor. *The Collected Works of Abraham Lincoln.* New Brunswick: Rutgers University Press, 1953.

Beale, Howard K., editor. *The Diary of Edward Bates 1859-1866.* New York: De Capo reprint, 1971.

Blanding, Stephen F. *In the Defenses of Washington or Sunshine in a Soldier's Life.* Providence: Freeman, 1889.

Block, Eugene B. *Above The Civil War: The Story of Thaddeus Lowe, Balloonist, Inventor, Railway Builder.* Berkeley: Howell-North, 1966.

Chamberlin, Caroline, editor. *Letters of George E. Chamberlin.* Springfield, Ill., Rokker, 1883.

Chambers, Lenoir. *Stonewall Jackson.* New York: William Morrow, 1959.

Croffut, W. A., editor. *Fifty Years in Camp and Field; Diary of Major General Ethan Allen Hitchcock.* New York: G. P. Putnams, 1909.

Dana, Charles A. *Recollections of the Civil War.* New York: D. Appleton, 1902.

Dowdey, Clifford and Louis H. Manarin, editors. *The Wartime Papers of R. E. Lee.* Boston: Little, Brown and Co., for Virginia Civil War Centennial Commission, 1961.

Durkin, Joseph T., editor. *Confederate Chaplain: A War Journal of Rev. James B. Sheeran c.ss.v., Fourteenth Louisiana C.S.A.* Milwaukee: Bruce, 1960.

Early, Jubal A. *War Memoirs.* Bloomington: Indiana University Press, 1960 reprint.

Eckenrode, H. J. and Byran Conrad. *George B. McClellan: The Man Who Saved The Union.* Chapel Hill: University of North Carolina Press, 1941.

Elliott, Charles Winslow. *Winfield Scott: The Soldier and the Man.* New York: Macmillan, 1937.

Flower, Milton E., editor. *Dear Folks at Home: The Civil War Letters of Leo W. and John I. Fuller with An Account of Andersonville.* Carlisle, Pa.: Cumberland County Historical Society and Hamilton Library Association, 1963.

Freeman, Douglas *S.R.E. Lee: A Biography.* New York: Charles Scribners, 1935.

Gordon, John B. *Reminiscences of the Civil War.* New York: Charles Scribners, 1904.

Govan, Gilbert E. and James W. Livingood. *A Different Valor: The Story of General Joseph E. Johnston, C.S.A.* Indianapolis: Bobbs-Merrill, 1956.

Hagemann, E. R., editor. *Fighting Rebels and Redskins; Experiences in the Army Life of Colonel George B. Sandford, 1861-1892.* Norman: University of Oklahoma Press, 1969.

Haupt, Herman. *Reminiscences of Herman Haupt.* Milwaukee: Wright and Joys, 1901.

Howard, Oliver Otis. *Autobiography.* New York: Baker and Taylor, 1907.

Hunt, H. Draper. *Hannibal Hamlin of Maine, Lincoln's First Vice President.* Syracuse: Syracuse University Press, 1969.

Ingraham, Charles A. *Elmer E. Ellsworth and the Zouaves of '61.* Chicago: University of Chicago Press, 1925.

Johnston, Joseph E. *Narrative of Military Operations.* New York: D. Appleton, 1874.

Kitching, J. Howard. *"More Than Conqueror"* or *Memorials of Col. J. Howard Kitching.* New York: Hurd and Houghton, 1873.

Levin, Alexandra Lee. *"This Awful Drama";* General Edwin Cray Lee, C.S.A., and His Family. New York: Vantage Press, 1987.

Longstreet, James. *From Manassas to Appomattox, Memoirs of the Civil War in America.* Bloomington: Indiana University Press, 1960 reprint.

Lothrop, Thorton K. *William Henry Seward.* Boston and New York: Houghton Mifflin, 1899.

Macartney, Clarence E. *Little Mac: The Life of General George B. McClellan.* Philadelphia: Dorrance, 1940.

Maurice, Frederick. *Robert E. Lee: The Soldier.* Boston: Houghton Mifflin, 1925.

McKim, Randolph H. *A Soldiers Recollections: Leaves from the Diary of a Young Confederate.* New York: Longmans, Green, 1911.

Mearns, David C., editor. *The Lincoln Papers.* Garden City: Doubleday, 1948.

Miller, Delavan S. *Drum Taps in Dixie; Memoirs of a Drummer Boy 1861-1865.* Watertown, N.Y.: Hungerford-Holbrook Co., 1905.

Nicolay, John G. and John Hay. *Abraham Lincoln: A History.* New York: Century, 1904.

Nicolay, John G. *A Short Life of Abraham Lincoln.* New York: Century, 1902.

Noll, Arthur H. *General Kirby-Smith.* Sewanee, Tenn: University of the South Press, 1907.

Pearson, Henry G. *James S. Wadsworth of Geneseo.* New York: Charles Scribners, 1913.

Quaife, Milo M., editor. *From The Cannon's Mouth; The Civil War Letters of General Alpheus S. Williams.* Detroit: Wayne State University Press and Detroit Historical Society, 1959.

Randall, Ruth Painter. *Colonel Elmer Ellsworth: A Biography of Lincoln's Friend and First Hero of the Civil War.* Boston: Little, Brown, and Company, 1960.

Rhodes, Robert Hunt, editor. *All for the Union: The Civil War Diary and Letters of Elisha Hunt Rhodes.* New York: Orion, 1991 edition.

Robertson, James I., editor. *The Civil War Letters of General Robert McAllister.* New Brunswick: Rutgers University Press, 1965.

[283]

Sandburg, Carl. *Abraham Lincoln: The War Years, v.I.* New York: Harcourt Brace, 1939.

Seward, Frederick. *Seward at Washington as Senator and Secretary of State.* New York: Derby and Miller, 1961.

Smith, Fred. *Samuel Duncan Oliphant: The Indomitable Campaigner.* New York: Exposition Press, 1967.

Stevens, George T. *Three Years in the Sixth Corps.* New York: D. Van Nostrand, 1870.

Stoddard, William O. *Inside the White House in War Times.* (New York: Charles L. Webster and Sons, 1890.)

Strode, Hudson. *Jefferson Davis: Confederate President.* New York: Harcourt, Brace, 1959.

_____. *Jefferson Davis: Tragic Hero; The Last Twenty-Five Years 1864-1889.* New York: Harcourt Brace and World, 1964.

Thomas, Benjamin P. and Harold Hyman. *Stanton: The Life and Times of Lincoln's Secretary of War.* New York: Knopf, 1962.

Tracey, Gilbert A., editor. *Uncollected Letters of Abraham Lincoln.* Boston and New York: Houghton, Mifflin, 1917.

Truxall, Aida C., editor. *"Respects to All"; Letters of Two Pennsylvania Boys in the War of the Rebellion.* Pittsburgh: University of Pittsburgh Press, 1962.

Vandiver, Frank E. *Mighty Stonewall.* New York: McGraw-Hill, 1957.

Wallace, Lew. *An Autobiography.* New York: Harper and Brothers, 1906.

Welles, Gideon. *Diary.* Boston: Houghton-Mifflin, 1911.

Wilkenson, Frank. *Recollections of A Private Soldier in the Army of the Potomac.* New York: Putnams, 1898.

Worsham, John H. *One of Jackson's Foot Cavalry.* . . . New York: Neale, 1912.

UNIT HISTORIES

Baker, Levi W. *History of the Ninth Massachusetts Battery.* South Framingham, Mass.: Lakeview Press, 1888.

Banes, Charles H. *History of the Philadelphia Brigade.* Philadelphia: J. B. Lippincott, 1876.

Barrett, O. S. *Reminiscences, Incidents, Battles, Marches and Camp Life of the Old Fourth Michigan Infantry in War of Rebellion, 1861 to 1864.* Detroit: W. S. Ostler, 1888.

Bartlett, A. W. *History of the Twelfth Regiment New Hampshire Volunteers in the War of the Rebellion.* Concord, N.H.: Ira C. Evans, 1897.

Beach, William H. *The First New York (Lincoln) Cavalry.* New York: Lincoln Cavalry Association, 1902.

Benedict, George G. *Army Life in Virginia; Letters From the Twelfth Vermont Regiment and Personal Experiences of Volunteer Service in the War for the Union, 1862-63.* Burlington: Free Press Association, 1895.

_____. *A Short History of the Fourteenth Vermont Regiment.* Bennington: C. A. Pierce, 1887.

Bennett, Edgar B., compiler. *First Connecticut Heavy Artillery: Historical Sketch and Present Addresses of Members.* East Berlin, Conn.: Star Printing Co., 1889.

Boies, Andrew J. *Record of the Thirty-Third Massachusetts Volunteer Infantry From August 1862 to August 1865.* Fitchburg: Sentinel Publishing Company, 1880.

Bowen, James L. *History of the Thirty-Seventh Regiment Massachusetts Volunteers in the Civil War 1861-1865.* Holyoke, Mass. and New York: Clark W. Bryan, 1884.

Cannon, James C. *Record of Co. K. One Hundred and Fiftieth Ohio Volunteer Infantry, 1864.* n.p., 1907.

Chamberlin, Thomas. *History of the One Hundred and Fiftieth Regiment Pennsylvania Volunteers. . . .* Philadelphia: F. McManus, 1905.

Clark, Emmons. *History of the Seventh Regiment New York 1806-1889.* New York: By Regimental Association, 1890.

Committee of the Regimental Association. *History of the Thirty-Fifth Regiment Massachusetts Volunteers.* Boston: Mills, Knight, 1884.

Connecticut Adjutant General's Office. *Record of Service of Connecticut Men in the Army and Navy of the United States During the War of the Rebellion.* Hartford: Case, Lockwood and Brainard, 1890.

Copeland, Willis R. *The Logan Guards of Pottstown Pennsylvania, Our First Defenders.* Lewistown: Mifflin County Historical Society, 1962.

Cudworth, Warren H. *History of the First Regiment Massachusetts Infantry.* Boston: Walker, Fuller and Company, 1866.

Curtis, Newton M. *From Bull Run to Chancellorsville: The Story of the Sixteenth New York Infantry Together with Personal Reminiscences.* New York: G. P. Putnams, 1906.

[285]

Davis, W. W. H. *History of the One Hundred and Fourth Pennsylvania Regiment.* Philadelphia: J. B. Rodgers, 1866.

Dearing, Gilbert H. *Chronological History of the Seventh Regiment of N.Y. Infantry Volunteers.* Sing Sing, N.Y.: Sunnyside Printing Company, 1894.

Dudley, H. A. and A. M. Whaley, compilers. *History of Company "K" of the Seventeenth Regiment, N.Y.V.* Warsaw, N.Y.,?.

Eddy, Richard. *History of the Sixtieth Regiment New York State Volunteers.* Philadelphia: By author, 1864.

Fairchild, Charles B., compiler. *History of the Twenty-Seventh Regiment N.Y. Vols.* Binghampton: Carl and Mathews, 1888.

Farrar, Samuel Clarke. *The Twenty-Second Pennsylvania Cavalry and the Ringgold Battalion 1861-1865.* Akron and Pittsburgh: The New Werner Company, 1911.

Fenner, Earl. *The History of Battery H First Regiment Rhode Island Light Artillery in the War to Preserve the Union 1861-1865.* Providence: Snow and Farnham, 1894.

Fish, Joel C. and William H. D. Blake. *A Condensed History of the Fifty-Sixth Regiment New York Veteran Volunteer Infantry.* Newburgh, N.Y.: Newburgh Journal Printing House and Book Binders, 1906.

Floyd, Fred C. *History of the Fortieth (Mozart) Regiment New York Volunteers.* Boston: F. H. Gilson, 1909.

Frederick, Gilbert. *The Story of a Regiment . . . the Fifty-Seventh New York. . . . ?:* Veteran Association, 1875.

Gates, Theodore B. *The "Ulster Guard" [Twentieth N.Y. State Militia] and the War of the Rebellion.* New York: Tyrrel, 1879.

Grant, J. W. *The Flying Regiment; Journal of the Campaign of the Twelfth Regt. Rhode Island Volunteers.* Providence: Sidney S. Rider and Bro., 1865.

Haines, Alanson A. *History of the Fifteenth Regiment New Jersey Volunteers.* New York: Jenkins and Thomas, 1883.

Hall, Henry and James. *Cayuga in the Field; A Record of the Nineteenth N.Y. Volunteers, All the Batteries of the Third New York Artillery and Seventy-Fifth New York Volunteers.* Auburn, NY.:?, 1873.

Hall, Isaac. *History of the Ninety-Seventh Regiment New York Volunteers.* . . . Utica, N.Y.: L. C. Childs and Son, 1890.

Hard, Abner. *History of the Eighth Cavalry Regiment Illinois Volunteers. During the Great Rebellion.* Aurora, Ill., n.p., 1868.

[286]

Hardin, M. D. *History of the Twelfth Regiment Pennsylvania Reserve Volunteer Corps*. New York: by author, 1890.

Haynes, E. M. *A History of the Tenth Regiment, Vt. Vols., . . .* Rutland: Tuttle, 1894.

Hutchinson, Gustavus B. *A Narrative of the Formation and Services of the Eleventh Massachusetts Volunteers. . . .* Boston: Alfred Mudge and Son, 1893.

Hutchinson, Nelson V. *History of the Seventh Massachusetts Volunteer Infantry*. Taunton: Regimental Association, 1890.

History of the Fifth Massachusetts Battery. Boston: Luther E. Cowles, 1902.

History of the First Connecticut Artillery and of the Siege Trains of the Armies Operating Against Richmond 1862-1865. Hartford: Case, Lockwood and Brainard, 1893.

History of the Fourth Maine Battery Light Artillery in the Civil War, 1861-1865. Augusta: Burleigh and Flynt, 1905.

History of the Twelfth Regiment Rhode Island Volunteers in the Civil War. Providence: By Committee of Survivors, 1901-1904.

Hougton, Edwin B. *The Campaigns of the Seventeenth Maine*. Portland: Short and Loring, 1866.

Imholte, John Q. *The First Volunteers; History of the First Minnesota Volunteer Regiment 1861-1865*. Minneapolis: Ross and Haines, 1963.

Judd, Daniel W. *The Story of the Thirty-Third N.Y.S. Vols: or Two Years Campaigning in Virginia and Maryland*. Rochester: Benton and Andrews, 1864.

Kiefer, W. R. *History of the One Hundred and Fifty-Third Regiment Pennsylvania Volunteer Infantry*. Easton: Chemical Publishing Co., 1909.

Kirk, Hyland C. *Heavy Guns and Light: A History of the Fourth New York Heavy Artillery*. New York: C. T. Dillingham, 1890.

Lewis, Osceola. *History of the One Hundred and Thirty-Eighth Regiment Pennsylvania Volunteer Infantry*. Norristown: Wills, Iredell and Jenkins, 1866.

Lincoln, William S. *Life With the Thirty-Fourth Massachusetts Infantry in the War of the Rebellion*. Worcester: Noyes, Snow, 1879.

McGrath, Franklin. *The History of the One Hundred and Twenty-Seventh New York Volunteers "Monitors,"* n.p., 1898?

Macnamara, Daniel G. *The History of the Ninth Regiment Massachusetts Volunteer Infantry.* Boston: E. B. Stillings, 1899.

Macnamara, M. H. *The Irish Ninth in Bivouac and Battle; or Virginia and Maryland Campaign.* Boston: Lee and Shepard, 1867.

Marbaker, Thomas D. *History of the Eleventh New Jersey.* Trenton: Mac-Crellish and Quigley, 1898.

Mills, J. Harrison. *Chronicles of the Twenty-First Regiment New York State Volunteers.* Buffalo: Veterans Association, 1887.

Mowris, J. A. *A History of the One Hundred and Seventeenth Regiment, N.Y. Volunteers.* Hartford: Case, Lockwood and Co., 1866.

Nash, Eugene A. *A History of the Forty-Fourth Regiment New York Volunteer Infantry in the Civil War, 1861-1865.* Chicago: R. R. Donnelly and Sons, 1911.

Newcomer, E. Armour. *Cole's Cavalry; or Three Years in the Saddle in the Shenandoah Valley.* Baltimore: Cushing and Co., 1895.

Newell, Joseph K., editor. *"Ours." Annals of Tenth Regiments; Massachusetts Volunteers in the Rebellion.* Springfield: C. A. Nichols and Co., 1875.

New York Infantry, 12th Regiment. *Report, Annual Reunion and Dinner of the Old Guard Association, Twelfth Regiment, N.G.S.N.Y.* New York: n.p., 1894.

Orwing, Joseph R. *History of the One Hundred and Thirty-First Pennsylvania Volunteers.* Williamsport: Sun Book and Job Printing House, 1902.

Parker, Francis J. *The Story of the Thirty-Second Regiment Massachusetts Infantry.* Boston: C. W. Calkins and Co., 1880.

Parker, John L., and Robert G. Carter. *History of the Twenty-Second Massachusetts Infantry, The Second Company Sharpshooters, and the Third Light Battery in the War of the Rebellion.* Boston: Regimental Association, 1887.

Prowell, George R. *History of the Eighty-Seventh Regiment, Pennsylvania Volunteers.* York: Press of the York Daily, 1901.

Rawling, C. J. *History of the First Regiment Virginia Infantry.* Philadelphia: J. B. Lippincott, 1887.

[288]

Reid, J. W. *History of the Fourth Regiment of S. C. Volunteers, From the Commencement of the War Until Lee's Surrender.* Greenville, S. C.: Shannon and Co., 1892.

Rock, R. W. [John C. Thompson]. *History of the Eleventh Regiment Rhode Island Volunteers in the War of the Rebellion.* Providence: Providence Press Co., 1881.

Roe, Alfred S. *The Fifth Regiment Massachusetts Volunteer Infantry. . . .* Boston: Fifth Regiment Veterans Association, 1911.

_____. *The Ninth New York Heavy Artillery.* Worcester, Mass.: By author, 1899.

_____. *The Tenth Regiment Massachusetts Volunteer Infantry 1861-1864.* Springfield: Tenth Regiment Association, 1909.

Rowe, David W. *A Sketch of the One Hundred and Twenty-Sixth Pennsylvania Volunteers.* Chambersburg, Pa.: Cook and Hays, 1869.

Shaw, Albert D. *A Full Report of the First Re-Union and Banquet of the Thirty-Fifth N.Y. Vols.,* Watertown, N.Y. Times Printing and Publishing House, 1888.

Shaw, Horace H. and Charles J. House. *The First Maine Heavy Artillery 1862-1865.* Portland: ?, 1903.

Sheldon, Winthrop D. *The "Twenty-Seventh: [Connecticut Infantry] Regimental History.* New Haven: Morris and Benham, 1866.

Small, Abner R. *The Sixteenth Maine Regiment in the War of the Rebellion.* Portland: B. Thurston and Co., 1886.

Smith, A. P. *History of the Seventy-Sixth Regiment New York Volunteers.* Cortland, N.Y.: ?, 1867.

Smith, James E. *A Famous Battery and Its Campaigns 1861-64.* Washington: W. H. Lowdermilk and Co., 1892.

Smith, John C. *The History of the Nineteenth Regiment of Maine Volunteer Infantry 1862-1865.* Minneapolis: The Great Western Printing Co., 1909.

Souvenir of First Regiment Massachusetts Volunteers Excursion to Battle Fields. . . . Historical Sketch of Regiment. n.p., 1907.

Spicer, William A. *History of the Ninth and Tenth Regiments Rhode Island Volunteers and the Tenth Rhode Island Battery. . . .* Providence: Snow and Farnham, 1892.

Stackpole, Edward T. *Sheridan in the Shenandoah; Jubal Early's Nemesis.* New York: Bonanza Books, 1961.

[289]

Sterling, Pound. *Camp Fires of the Twenty-Third: Sketches of the Camp Life, Marches, and Battles of the Twenty-Third Regiment, N.Y.V.* . . . New York: Davies and Kent, 1863.

Stone, James M. *The History of the Twenty-Seventh Regiment Maine Volunteer Infantry.* Portland: Thurston, 1895.

Sypher, J. R. *History of the Pennsylvania Reserve Corps.* Lancaster: Elias Barr, 1865.

Terrill, J. Newton. *Campaign of the Fourteenth Regiment New Jersey Volunteers.* New Brunswick: Daily Home News Press, 1884.

The Survivors Association. *History of the One Hundred and Eighteenth Pennsylvania Volunteers.* . . . Philadelphia: J. L. Smith, 1905.

Thompson, S. Millett. *Thirteenth Regiment of New Hampshire Volunteer Infantry.* . . . Boston: Houghton, Mifflin, 1888.

Thompson, William M. *Historical Sketch of the Sixteenth Regiment N.Y.S. Volunteer Infantry.* Albany: n.p., 1886.

Thorpe, Sheldon B. *The History of the Fifteenth Connecticut Volunteers in the War For The Defense of the Union 1861-1865.* New Haven: Price, Lee and Adkins, 1893.

Todd, William. *The Seventy-Ninth Highlanders: New York Volunteers in the War of the Rebellion, 1861-1865.* Albany: Bradlow, Barton and Co., 1886.

Vaill, Dudley L. *The County Regiment; A Sketch of the Second Regiment of Connecticut Volunteer Heavy Artillery, originally the Nineteenth Volunteer Infantry in the Civil War.* Litchfield County, Ct.: University Club, 1908.

Van Santvoord, C. *The One Hundred and Twentieth Regiment New York State Volunteers.* Rondout, N.Y.: Press of Kingston Freeman, 1894.

Vautier, John D. *History of the Eighty-Eighth Pennsylvania Volunteers in the War For The Union, 1861-1865.* Philadelphia: J. B. Lippincott, 1894.

Veterans Association of Fifth New York Heavy Artillery. *Roster and Report of Eleventh Annual Re-Union.* New York: n.p., 1889.

Walker, Edward A. *Our First Year of Army Life. An Anniversary Address Delivered to the First Regiment of Connecticut Volunteer Heavy Artillery.* . . . New Haven: Thomas J. Stafford, 1862.

Ward, George W. *History of the Second Pennsylvania Veteran Heavy Artillery.* . . . Philadelphia: George W. Ward Printer, 1904.

Waters, Elizur W. *A Journal of Incidents Connected With The Travels of the Twenty-Second Regiment Conn. Volunteers, For Nine Months. In Verse.* Hartford: Williams, Wiley and Waterman, 1863.

Webb, E. P. *History of the Tenth Regiment N.Y. Heavy Artillery.* . . . Watertown: Post Book and Job Printing Establishment, 1887.

Wild, Frederick W. *Memoirs and History of Capt. F. W. Alexander's Baltimore Battery of Light Artillery U.S.V.* Baltimore: Lock Raven Press of the Maryland School for Boys, 1912.

Williams, John C. *Life in Camp: A History of the Fourteenth Vermont Regiment.* . . . Claremont Manuf. Co., 1864.

Wise, George. *History of the Seventeenth Virginia Infantry, C.S.A.* Baltimore: Kelly, Piet and Co., 1870.

Woodbury, Augustus. *A Narrative of The Campaign of the First Rhode Island Regiment; in the Spring and Summer of 1861.* Providence: Sidney S. Rider, 1862.

ARTICLES AND ESSAYS

Allan, William. "Strategy of the Campaign of Sharpsburg or Antietam," in Theodore Dwight, editor, *Papers of Military Historical Society of Massachusetts, v. III, Campaigns in Virginia, Maryland, and Pennsylvania, 1862-1863.* Boston: Griffeth-Stillings Press, 1903.

Alvoord, Henry E., "Early's Attack upon Washington, July 1864," *War Papers 26, Military Order of the Loyal Legion, DC Commandery.* Washington: By Commandery, 1907.

Anderson, Latham. "McDowell's Explanation of the Failure of the First Corps to Join McClellan" in Theodore F. Allen et al., editors. *Sketches of War History, 1861-1865.* Cincinnati Monfort and Co., 1908.

Chrismer, Wayne. "Baltimore Riot Kept Maryland in Union?" *Civil War Times,* III (April, 1961), 1, 7-9.

Cooling, B. Franklin. "Civil War Deterrent: Defenses of Washington," *Military Affairs,* XXIX (Winter, 1965-66), 4, 164-178.

———. "Defending Washington during the Civil War," in Francis Coleman Rosenberger, editor. *Records of the Columbia Historical Society of Washington, D.C. 1971-1972,* Washington: By the Society, 1973, 314-337.

Cowen, Benjamin R., "The One Hundred Days Men of Ohio," in W. H. Chamberlin et al. editors. *Sketches of War History 1861-1865.* Ohio Commandery, Military Order of the Loyal Legion, v V. Cincinnati: Robert Clarke, 1903.

Cox, William V., "The Defenses of Washington. General Early's Advance on the Capital," *Records of the Columbia Historical Society,* IV (1901), 1-31.

Cullen, Joseph P., "The McClellan-Lincoln Controversy," *Civil War Times Illustrated,* V, (November, 1966), 7, 34-43.

Dary, David, "Lincoln's Frontier Guard," *Civil War Times Illustrated,* XI, (August, 1972), 5, 12-44.

Davis, George B. "The Antietam Campaign," in Theodore Dwight, editor, *Papers of Military Historical Society of Massachusetts, v. III, Campaigns in Virginia, Maryland, and Pennsylvania,* Boston: Griffith-Stillings Press, 1903.

Donn, John W., "With the Army of the Potomac from the Defenses of Washington to Harrison's Landing," *War Papers 22,* Military Order of the Loyal Legion, DC Commandery. Washington: By Commandery, 1895.

Donnelly, Ralph. "District of Columbia Confederates," *Military Affairs,* XXIII (Winter, 1959-60), 4, 207-208.

Dudley, Edgar S., "Reminiscence of Washington and Early's Attack in 1864," *Sketches of War History 1861-1865,* v. I, Ohio Commandery, Military Order of the Loyal Legion. Cincinnati: Robert Clarke, 1888.

Early, J. A., "The Advance on Washington in 1864," *Southern Historical Society Papers,* IX, (July, August, 1881), 7 and 8, 297-312.

Freis, William B. "A Union Military Intelligence Failure: Jubal Early's Raid, June 12-July 4, 1864," *Civil War History,* XXXVI (September 1990), 3, 209-225.

Gibbs, George A., "With a Mississippi Private in a Little Known Part of the Battle of First Bull Run and at Ball's Bluff," *Civil War Times Illustrated,* 4 (April, 1965), 42-49.

Griffin, Rick. "A Darnestown Confederate Soldier," *The Maryland Line* (Montgomery County Civil War Round Table), 10 (October 1989), 2, 7.

Haarmann, Albert W., compiler. "The Blue and the Gray (and the Green and the Black and the Red etc.)," *Military Images*, VI, (May/June 1985), 6, 16-23.

Hall, James O. "Marylanders in the Civil War: The Death of Walter Bowie," *The Maryland Line* (Montgomery County Civil War Round Table), 10 (October 1989), 2, 2-3.

Hardin, Martin D., "The Defence of Washington Against Early's Attack in July, 1864," *Military Essays and Recollections, v. II*, Illinois Commandery, Military Order of the Loyal Legion. Chicago: A. C. McClurg, 1894.

Harsh, Joseph L., "On the McClellan-Go-Round," *Civil War History*, XIX (June 1972), 2, 101-118.

Henig, Gerald S., editor, " 'Give My Love to All:' The Civil War Letters of George S. Rollins," *Civil War Times Illustrated*, XI (November 1972), 7, 17-28.

Hobson, Charles F. and Arnold Sankman, editors. "Colonel of the Bucktails: Civil War Letters of Charles Frederick Taylor," *Pennsylvania Magazine of History and Biography*, XCVII (July 1973), 3, 333-361.

Horton, Charles P., "The Campaign of General Pope in Virginia, Its Objects and General Plan, First Part to the Nineteenth of August 1862," in Theodore F. Dwight, editor., *Papers of the Military Historical Society of Massachusetts, v. II, The Virginia Campaign of 1862 Under General Pope*. Boston: Houghton Mifflin for the Society, 1895.

Long, E. B., "The Battle That Almost Was—Manassas Gap," *Civil War Times Illustrated*, XI (December 1972), 8, 21-28.

Lounsbury, Thomas R., "In The Defenses of Washington," *Yale Review*, II, (April, 1913), 3, 385-411.

Mitchell, Joseph B., "Debacle at Ball's Bluff," *Civil War Times*, III, (January, 1972), 9, 9-11.

Moore, Wilton B., "Union Army Provost Marshalls in the Eastern Theater," *Military Affairs*, XXVI, (Fall, 1962), 3, 120-126.

Myers, Henry R., "Does Washington Need an ABM?" *Washington Post*, July 30, 1972.

Naisawald, L. Van Loan. "The Battle of Dranesville," *Civil War Times Illustrated*, IV (May 1965), 4-10.

[293]

Nofi, Albert A., "The Gettysburg Campaign 1 June-26 July 1863" *Strategy and Tactics: The Magazine of Conflict Simulation*, 38 (May 1973), 21-38.

Noordberg, Henry C., editor, "A Young Texan Goes to War; A Collection of Personal Letters by Captain Thomas Jewett Goree, C.S.A., Aide-de-Camp to General James Longstreet," *Journal of the Confederate Historical Society of Great Britain*, v. VIII, (Summer-Winter 1970), 2-4, 30-42, 64-71, 106-115 and v. X (Summer, 1972), 2, 80-87.

"Oberlin and the Civil War," *Oberlin Today*, 22 (First Quarter, 1964), 1, 3-11.

Quincey, Samuel M., "The Character of General Halleck's Military Administration in the Summer of 1862," in Theodore F. Dwight, editor, *The Virginia Campaign of 1862 Under General Pope* (Boston: Houghton Mifflin for Military Historical Society of Massachusetts, 1895.)

Ropes, John C., "General McClellan's Plans For The Campaign of 1862 and the Alleged Interference of the Government with Them," in Theodore F. Dwight, editor, *Campaigns in Virginia 1861-1862*. Boston: Houghton-Mifflin for Military Historical Society of Massachusetts, 1895.

_____, "Grant's Campaign in Virginia in 1864," in Military Historical Society of Massachusetts. *The Wilderness Campaign May-June 1864*, v. IV. Boston: By the Society, 1905.

Salamanca, Lucy. "When Washington was Fort Girdled," *Washington Post*, January 25, 1931.

Smelser, Marshall, "Naval Considerations in the Location of the National Capital," *Maryland Historical Magazine*, 52 (March 1957), 1, 72-74.

Smith, Everard, "Rebels at Washington: Lincoln Under Enemy Fire and Wheaton's Attack," *The St. Albans* [School, Washington, D.C.] *Review*, (1967), 3-15.

Smith, William F., "The Military Situation in Northern Virginia From the 1st to the 14th of November 1862," in Theodore Dwight, editor, *Papers of Military Historical Society of Massachusetts, v. III, Campaigns in Virginia, Maryland, and Pennsylvania, 1862-1863*. Boston: Griffith-Stillings Press, 1903.

Stackpole, Edward J. "The Day the Rebels Could Have Marched Into the White House," *Civil War Times*, II (February 1961), 10, 5, 6, 19.

_____, "Story by Corporal Tanner," *The Confederate Veteran.* 5 (February, 1897), 83.

Stinson, Byron, "The Invalid Corps," *Civil War Times Illustrated*, X, (May 1971), 2, 20-27.

Waterman, Arba N., "Washington At The Time of the First Bull Run," in *Essays and Recollections* of Illinois Commandery, Military Order of the Loyal Legion, Chicago: A. C. McClurg, 1894.

Weld, Stephen M., "The Conduct of General McClellan During His Stay at Alexandria in August, 1862. . . ." in Theodore F. Dwight, editor, *The Virginia Campaign of 1862 Under General Pope.* Boston: Houghton Mifflin for Military Historical Society of Massachusetts, 1895.

Whittier, Charles A., "Comments on the Peninsular Campaign of General McClellan," in Theodore F. Dwight, editor, *The Virginia Campaign of 1862 Under General Pope.* Boston: Houghton-Mifflin for the Military Historical Society of Massachusetts, 1895.

Whyte, James H., "The Unquiet Potomac: Spies, Mail and Goods Flowed Between Maryland, Virginia," *Civil War Times*, II (December 1960), 8, 16.

Williams, T. Harry. "The Committee on the Conduct of the War," *Journal of the American Military Institute*, III (Fall, 1939), 3, 139-156.

Wills, Mary Alice. "Death of Commander James H. Ward," *Civil War Times Illustrated*, XIII (July 1974), 10-19.

Winthrop, Theodore, "Washington as a Camp," *Atlantic Monthly*, 8 (July 1861), 105-118.

Woodruff, Thomas M., "Early War Days in the Nation's Capital," in Edward D. Neill, *Glimpses of the Nation's Struggle.* New York: D. D. Merrill, 1893.

UNPUBLISHED STUDIES

Albright, F. H., "The Peninsular Campaign of 1862 To Include The Battle of Beaver Dam Creek," Unpublished Army War College Student Paper, 1914-15.

Committee Twenty-Three, "Defense of Washington," Command Course, U.S. Army War College, 1925-26.

Drozdowski, Eugene C., "Edwin M. Stanton, Lincoln's Secretary of War: Toward victory," Unpublished Ph.D. dissertation, Duke University, 1964.

Fenton, Charles Wendell, "Early's Raid on Washington," Unpublished Army War College Student Paper, 1916.

Hagerman, Edward H., "The Evolution of Trench Warfare in the American Civil War," Unpublished Ph.D. dissertation, Duke University, 1965.

Lee, Jeo-Hwa, "The Organization and Administration of the Army of the Potomac Under General George B. McClellan," Unpublished Ph.D. dissertation, University of Maryland, 1960.

Manarin, Louis H., "Lee in Command: Strategical and Tactical Policies," Unpublished Ph.D. dissertation. Duke University, 1956.

Mayhew, Lewis Baltzell, "George B. McClellan," Unpublished Ph.D. dissertation, Michigan State University, 1952.

Pence, W. P., "The Peninsula Campaign To Include the Battle of Mechanicsville," Unpublished Army War College Student Paper, 1910-11.

Pickering, Abner, "Early's Raid in 1864, Including The Battle of the Monocacy," Unpublished Army War College Student Paper, 1913-14.

Skirtbunt, Peter D., "Aquia Creek Landing, Virginia, A Study of its History and Use During the American Civil War," Unpublished student paper, Department of History, Ohio State University, 1972, copy in Defenses of Washington Collection, Fort Ward Park, Alexandria, Virginia.

Smith, Everard Hall III, "The General and the Valley: Union Leadership During the Threat to Washington in 1864," Unpublished Ph.D. dissertation, University of North Carolina at Chapel Hill, 1977.

Index

ISBN 0-942597-24-9
(formerly ISBN 0-208-01479-9)

During the hot, dusty July days of 1864 a bedraggled Confederate army besieged Washington, D.C., and for the only time in the nation's history an American president was actually under hostile fire while in office. But the drama and comedy of Jubal Early's celebrated raid is not the whole story of how the national capital was defended during the Civil War, and here, for the first time, the conflict over the city of Washington is seen in the overall context of the strategy and conduct of the war in the Eastern theater from 1861 to 1865.

Basic to the protection of Washington and the Lincoln administration was the Army of the Potomac. Its two-fold mission, which students of the war have so far misunderstood or neglected, was to capture the Confederate capital at Richmond and to defeat Lee's Army of Northern Virginia, while it also covered Washington as part of a "team" effort. The conflict of missions which plagued army leaders from Scott, McDowell, and McClellan, to Halleck and Grant, stemmed from these tasks, and the threatened Rebel capture of Washington spawned a series of crises which ranged from Lincoln's election in 1860 to Early's scare and Sheridan's final campaign in the Shenandoah Valley in 1864.

In the past, the formal system styled "The Defenses of Washington" has been treated more often from the engineer's point of view, and has rarely been recognized as a vital part of a strategic concept. The photographs, charts, and maps in this book will help historians to understand the immense system of defensive works guarding the city— where more field works, heavy ordnance, and manpower for fortress garrisons were concentrated than in any other place during the war.

But Washington's defenses, and the graphic story of the four-year struggle to protect the capital, is best understood here in other terms. It is the story of men and events, fixed defenses and a mobile field army, crisis management—and the tedium of garrison life that may have been more the norm than the exception for the men who fought the war between the states.